with regards

from Southern Africa

John.

t3
TRA
15146

# SOCIAL SYSTEM
# AND TRADITION IN
# SOUTHERN AFRICA

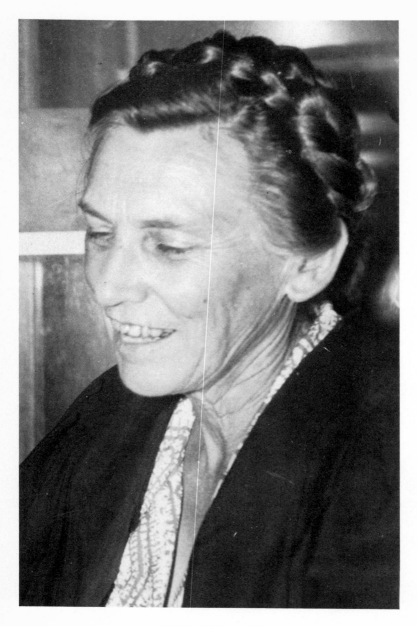

EILEEN JENSEN KRIGE

# SOCIAL SYSTEM AND TRADITION IN SOUTHERN AFRICA

*Essays in Honour of*
## EILEEN KRIGE

*Edited by*
## JOHN ARGYLE
## ELEANOR PRESTON-WHYTE

Cape Town
OXFORD UNIVERSITY PRESS
1978

*Oxford University Press*

OXFORD   LONDON   GLASGOW
NEW YORK   TORONTO   MELBOURNE   WELLINGTON
IBADAN   NAIROBI   DAR ES SALAAM   CAPE TOWN
KUALA LUMPUR   SINGAPORE   JAKARTA   HONG KONG   TOKYO
DELHI   BOMBAY   CALCUTTA   MADRAS   KARACHI

ISBN 0 19 570089 9

*The editors gratefully acknowledge a subsidy from the Natal University Development Foundation towards the publication costs of this volume in honour of one of the University's Emeritus Professors*

Set in 10 on 12 pt Times
Printed in South Africa by Citadel Press, Lansdowne, Cape
Published by Oxford University Press, Harrington House,
Barrack Street, Cape Town 8001, South Africa

# CONTRIBUTORS

W. JOHN ARGYLE: Professor of Social Anthropology, University of Natal, Durban.

JOHN BLACKING: Professor of Social Anthropology, The Queen's University of Belfast.

MANGOSUTHU G. BUTHELEZI: Chief Minister, Government of KwaZulu.

ANGELA P. CHEATER: Lecturer in Social Anthropology, University of Rhodesia, Salisbury.

A. TREVOR COPE: Professor of Bantu Languages, University of Natal, Durban.

W. DAVID HAMMOND-TOOKE: Professor of Social Anthropology, University of Witwatersrand, Johannesburg.

SABITHA JITHOO: Lecturer in Anthropology, University of Durban-Westville, Natal.

HILDA KUPER: Professor of Anthropology, University of California, Los Angeles.

MAX G. MARWICK: Reader in Humanities, Griffith University, Queensland.

DOUGLAS M. MZOLO: Senior Lecturer in Bantu Languages, University of Natal, Durban.

ELEANOR M. PRESTON-WHYTE: Senior Lecturer in Social Anthropology, University of Natal, Durban.

ISAAC SCHAPERA: Emeritus Professor of Anthropology, University of London.

ABSOLOM L. VILAKAZI: Professor of Anthropology and International Relations, American University, Washington.

MONICA WILSON: Emeritus Professor of Social Anthropology, University of Cape Town.

# CONTENTS

# EILEEN JENSEN KRIGE:

## HER CAREER AND ACHIEVEMENTS, TOGETHER WITH A BIBLIOGRAPHY

The title of this collection in honour of Professor Eileen Krige might initially suggest the now rather common assumption that Southern, and especially South, Africa has long been dominated by a single social system and tradition. Some of the contributors may indeed share that assumption, at least in the form given to it by (among others) Professor Gluckman, who re-emphasized 'the view of the field as a single social system' in one of his last publications (1975:22). The assumption is not necessarily belied by the contents of the individual contributions which reflect the fact that the 'single social system' is 'composed of groups of different culture' (Gluckman 1975:24). Even at this level of 'culture', rather than 'social system', the contributions are more unitary in range, if not in theme, than is usual with collections of this kind. For ten of the fourteen papers deal wholly or partly with one or more of the peoples conventionally included in the Nguni category, and five of those ten are devoted to aspects of Zulu culture or tradition.

This emphasis on Nguni, and especially Zulu, culture reflects, in varying degrees, the interests and experiences of contributors who, in several cases, have been Eileen's colleagues or students at the University of Natal, Durban, where she concluded her university career as Professor of Social Anthropology and Head of the Department of African Studies. During her time at the University, she initiated or supervised several research projects amongst the Zulu and one of her own early works, *The Social System of the Zulus* (originally published in 1936, still in print and deliberately alluded to in the title of this present collection), was a compilation of the then available Zulu ethnography. Moreover, she has herself added to that ethnography in some of her later publications (E. J. Krige 1968, 1969). The prominence of Zulu topics in the collection is therefore not inappropriate. Nevertheless, Eileen's own dominant and long-standing ethnographic concern has been not with the Zulu in Natal, but with the Lovedu in the Transvaal. To trace the origin, development and outcome of that concern is therefore to resume most of her anthropological career; it may also amplify and sometimes cor-

rect part of the still imperfectly recorded history of social anthropology in South Africa.

The beginnings of Eileen's interest in the Lovedu may be traced to
a childhood spent at Pietersburg in the north-eastern Transvaal before and during the First World War. At that time the settlement of
Pietersburg was scarcely more than twenty years old and 'for most
people in the Transvaal in the early years of the century [it] was the
last outpost of civilization' (Cartwright 1974:86). Beyond and below
it, eastwards of the Drakensberg range, lay that part of the isolated,
fever-ridden Lowveld area which was within the boundaries of the
Transvaal, but still had only tenuous links to the 'civilization' of
the Highveld. Such as they were, most of these links passed through
Pietersburg and along them would have travelled such 'curious
stories' about the Lovedu and their 'Rain Queen' as General Smuts
later testified had interested him for so long (Smuts 1941:vii). They
interested, too, a schoolgirl whose home was as close to the Lovedu
as 'civilization' had yet effectively reached and who heard at least one
vivid account of Lovedu country from a school friend who had
visited it.

However, a childhood interest could only mature into a scientific
one with an appropriate academic training. That training Eileen
eventually obtained during the 1920s at the newly founded University
of the Witwatersrand, which ran a joint scheme with the Johannesburg Training College designed to produce graduate teachers through
a four-year course that combined an undergraduate degree with a
teaching qualification. Since the scheme provided loan bursaries, it
attracted able students who could not otherwise have afforded a
University education. Eileen was one of them and entered the College
in 1922. She completed the degree requirements in three instead of
four years, so that she was able to add Honours (in Economics) to
them in her final year (1925). In the following year, while teaching
in Johannesburg, she completed a M.A. in Economics. Further
specialization in that subject might have been expected to follow
but Eileen's interests had always been wide and they were about to
take another turn.

During her undergraduate years, she had taken courses additional
to those required for her degree. Amongst them had been an initial
course in Social Anthropology that was first offered to full-time
degree students in Eileen's third year (1924). Since she had heard
from friends at the University of Cape Town (where Social Anthro-

pology was already being taught by its first Professor in South Africa, Radcliffe-Brown) that this novel subject was exciting, she decided to take it in addition to the final courses in her major subjects. The course was given by Winifred Hoernlé, who had been appointed Research Fellow and Lecturer at Wits* in 1923, and Eileen was therefore her first, successful university student (with Radcliffe-Brown as the external examiner). Mrs Hoernlé was later to be described by the Kriges, in their dedication of *The Realm of a Rain Queen* to her, as 'the mother of Social Anthropology in South Africa': it follows that Eileen was her eldest 'daughter' and, indeed, her eldest 'child'.

The advantages of such a parentage are perhaps less apparent now than they were then, for Mrs Hoernlé's achievements and influence have been overshadowed by those of Radcliffe-Brown to the extent that she is commonly characterized as his 'disciple' or 'follower' (for a recent example, see Kuper 1975:177). Even Professor Gluckman, who was another of her students, has written that Radcliffe-Brown 'had "taught" both Mrs A. W. Hoernlé and I. Schapera' (Gluckman 1963:2). The statement is potentially misleading, even though it is qualified by quotation marks. For Mrs Hoernlé (*née* Tucker) had been taught (in the usual sense) by Haddon, Rivers and Myers at Cambridge where she went in 1908 after an exceptionally successful undergraduate career (specializing in philosophy) at the old South African College. While at Cambridge, she seems to have concentrated on physical anthropology, to judge by two articles (one with Myers) that she published in 1911. But, on leaving Cambridge in that year, she went to Leipzig where she spent some time with Wundt (amongst others), from there to Bonn and finally to Paris where she seems to have heard, if not met, Durkheim. Certainly, 'it was Durkheim's approach that had the greatest influence on her anthropological thought' (E. J. Krige 1960:139). She had therefore bathed in the 'sociological stream' (as Gluckman, 1963:2, calls it) well before Radcliffe-Brown came to South Africa and, indeed, her immersion in it must have been almost as early as his own and was quite probably longer and deeper. Furthermore, after her marriage to Alfred Hoernlé she accompanied him to Harvard where he taught philoso-

* The usual, convenient abbreviation for the full 'University of the Witwatersrand'.

phy for several years. While there, she had contacts with American anthropology and contributed a paper to the *Harvard African Studies* series.

By the time Mrs Hoernlé returned to South Africa in 1920, her direct experience of the different prevailing schools in anthropology was therefore wider than Radcliffe-Brown's. So, too, was her command of South African ethnography. Her fieldwork amongst the Khoi in 1912 and again in 1923 was probably not inferior in quality to that which he had done amongst the Australian Aborigines and her extensive knowledge of the literature on the Bantu-speaking people was displayed in several papers, culminating eventually in those which she contributed to the original edition of *The Bantu-speaking Tribes of South Africa*. Therefore, although she was undoubtedly influenced by Radcliffe-Brown, the nature of the relationship between them is most aptly conveyed by his own acknowledgment that they were 'collaborating' in a projected (though never fully achieved) series of papers on 'some of the most difficult problems of African sociology and religion' (quoted in E. J. Krige 1960:142). Mrs Hoernlé's unusual combination of qualifications and experience clearly owed less than has commonly been supposed to Radcliffe-Brown (whose time in South Africa may well have been rather more significant for the development of his own career than for that of South African anthropology).

It is therefore not surprising that Eileen should have been attracted to return to Mrs Hoernlé as a part-time student, completing the second, major course in Social Anthropology in 1927 and starting the first year of the Honours course in 1928. By then Eileen's commitment to anthropology and her ability in it were evident enough for Mrs Hoernlé to offer her the chance of doing some fieldwork in the vacation. She was glad to take it and knew exactly where she wanted to go: to the Lovedu. For the early interest in that people had been rekindled by a brief, private visit to them in 1926 which Eileen had made in the company of General Smuts' daughter, Cato, who had been a fellow pupil at the Pretoria High School for Girls and was then a fellow student at the University. The visit had included a meeting with the reigning Queen Mujaji and General Smuts stressed this meeting, in the foreword he later wrote (1941:vii) to *The Realm of a Rain-Queen*, as the origin of a relationship between his family and the Queen. Rather oddly, he did not mention that the 'company of friends' who accompanied his daughter had included Eileen for whom the visit was the first of a long series that has continued until now.

In going to the Lovedu a second time, Eileen was initiated into fieldwork while still an Honours student, for she completed the degree in 1929 under the supervision of Isaac Schapera, who was acting for Mrs Hoernlé during her absence that year. It is therefore misleading to state, as Kuper does (1975:91, also 177), that 'in 1930' (it should be 1929) Schapera's 'first class included Max Gluckman, Ellen Hellman, Eileen (Jensen) Krige and Hilda (Beemer) Kuper', since the other three were still undergraduates. It is nevertheless remarkable enough that social anthropology should have attracted such a group of able students from a quite small student body within a short space of time.

Apart from the novelty of the subject and the way it was taught by Mrs Hoernlé, the appeal of social anthropology was doubtless enhanced by the fact that its emergence as an academic subject was part of a much wider development in the study and application of subjects with an African content during the decade, 1920–1930. At the University of the Witwatersrand alone, new and important contributions were being made by such scholars as Doke in linguistics, Dart in physical anthropology, McMillan in history and Kirby in music. Outside the University, but often having informal relations with it, such organizations as the Joint Councils of Europeans and Africans and the Institute of Race Relations were founded during this period. Some of Mrs Hoernlé's classes attracted persons active in these organizations, of whom perhaps the most conspicuous was Rheinhallt Jones.

Another recruit, whose attendance at the classes was partially inspired by his experiences as a barrister defending Africans on criminal charges in Johannesburg courts, was J. ('Jack') D. Krige. He had been one product of that combination of the Afrikaner admiration and appetite for learning with an essentially British system of higher education that had achieved some remarkable individual successes in the Cape during the early twentieth century. After graduating in science at Victoria College, Stellenbosch, Jack had gone on a Rhodes scholarship to Oxford where he read law. While there he was active in the League of Nations Union and, after leaving Oxford, he worked briefly for the International Labour Office in Geneva. He therefore came back to Johannesburg with unusually catholic interests and sympathies which he sought to broaden still further by regular attendance at Mrs Hoernlé's classes from 1928. By then, Eileen, whom Jack already knew, had started her Honours course so that, after their marriage in November 1928, her more advanced interest in anthropology helped to encourage his own. When Eileen made a second vacation trip to the Lovedu in 1930, Jack accompanied her and they had thus begun their academic partnership in what was to be an extended study of that people.

However, such a study could only be made with the necessary support and it is perhaps difficult to appreciate now what a formidable obstacle the search for support presented to prospective South African fieldworkers during the early 1930s, in the depth of the economic depression. It is true that the state had in 1926 begun encouraging research by the universities and other bodies into 'Native Life and Languages', through an annual grant of £1 400 (which may well have been the source of some or all of the money that Wits had given to finance Eileen's vacation field trips). But this grant came to an abrupt end in 1930 when 'subsidized research had to be abandoned' (Schapera 1934:228). Moreover, there were no prospects of new university teaching posts from which it would have been possible to conduct research during the vacations. For the newly-married Kriges, the nearest thing to such posts lay with an organization in Pretoria called the University Correspondence Courses, one of several such private bodies which offered tuition by correspondence for, amongst others, students taking the external examinations of the University of South Africa which did not then provide tuition, as it does today (Boucher 1973:196). Jack Krige, whose attachment to law had diminished as that to anthropology grew, accepted in 1931 the post of Principal and Manager of the Courses which at least allowed him to give special attention to those with an African content. Eileen also worked there, preparing and supervising all the courses in Social Anthropology and Ethnic History.

This rather unremitting form of teaching did not allow much opportunity for research, but Eileen was at least able to manage a third vacation trip to the Lovedu in 1932. During the same year, she also began, with some assistance from Jack, one of the first pieces of anthropological research amongst Africans in urban areas (E. J. Krige 1934b, 1936b). She also completed the conversion of what had originally been her Honours thesis into the book that appeared in 1936 as *The Social System of the Zulus*. It was an interpretation and synthesis of the previous literature on the Zulu, supplemented occasionally by material obtained from students taking the correspondence courses who happened to be Zulu (see Mahlobo & Krige 1934). After 40 years it is still in print which is sufficient indication of its success in accomplishing what it set out to do.

Such further achievements might have been expected to improve the prospects of obtaining support for extended fieldwork. But in the virtual absence of local sources, almost the only available alternative had become the recently founded International African Institute which supported at least three fieldworkers in South Africa during the early 1930s. Both the composition of the Institute and its location in London inevitably meant that its distribution of grants for field-work depended substantially on assessments made by senior British anthropologists, particularly those in London where Malinowski was by then pre-eminent. In those circumstances, it would be almost indispensable for an aspirant anthropologist from South Africa (or most other parts of the Empire) to acquire some metropolitan postgraduate training. Moreover, the path to the London School of Economics had already been followed by Isaac Schapera in the mid-1920s and, after Malinowski had himself been to South Africa in 1934, other South African students, such as Ellen Hellman, were drawn to visit the School.

By 1935, therefore, Jack and Eileen were keen to go to London, too, and had saved enough to make the trip which turned out to be decisive for their future as anthropologists. They were able to attend Malinowski's seminars and lectures during the first half of 1935 and Eileen read a paper at one of the seminars. It is therefore again mis-leading for Kuper (1975:92) to state that 'with the exception of Eileen Krige, all went on to study with Malinowski'. Indeed, of those other former Wits students he names – Gluckman, Hellman and Beemer – only the last was formally a student of Malinowski's. The other two simply participated in his classes at the School, as did a good many others at that time.

Such participation could be rewarding not only for the intellectual stimulus to be gained from it, but also as a mark of an appropriate training for fieldwork by the acknowledged master of it. There were also, of course, ample opportunities for participation in other activities at the School and outside it. Jack, for example, contributed an article to *Politica*, a journal of the School, and gave lectures at the Royal Institute of International Affairs. With all these extra demonstrations of their capacity and commitment added to what they had already achieved in South Africa, Eileen and Jack succeeded in obtaining a joint Research Fellowship from the International African Institute that would enable them to complete the work they had begun amongst the Lovedu. They therefore returned to South Africa early in 1936 and went to the field as soon as they could.

The circumstances of the fieldwork were in some ways unusual, at least by local standards which had usually been satisfied with shorter periods of fieldwork than they eventually achieved. Moreover a husband and wife team was novel in South Africa and not at all common elsewhere. Such teamwork had obvious advantages for the division of labour in the field, such as that described in the preface to *The Realm of a Rain-Queen*, and for the mutual supplementation and verification of the data collected by each. It also made for an unusual comprehensiveness that was perhaps aided by the concentration of the Lovedu within a relatively small area that was still quite isolated in the late 1930s, even if it was no longer as far beyond the reach of 'civilization' as it had been. The prominence of certain distinctive Lovedu institutions, such as the queenship, the linking of brother and sister through bridewealth transactions and the associated cross-cousin marriage, also gave to the work a more concentrated focus than was usual in the South African ethnography of that time.

The cumulative effect of all these circumstances rather reduces, for the Kriges' fieldwork at least, the force of the contrast drawn by Kuper between the earlier fieldwork done in Oceania and that done later in Africa where the

> fieldworkers were confronted not with tiny, bounded island populations, but with comparatively huge, extended, dispersed tribes and nations. It was quickly apparent that the sorts of social controls writers on Oceania had identified – reciprocal obligations, exchanges, magical controls – formed only a small part of the governmental mechanisms of these societies (Kuper 1975:107–8).

Certainly, the Lovedu population (about 33 000) was not 'huge', nor was it dispersed, but rather confined within an area of some 384 km$^2$. Moreover, as the fieldwork showed, 'reciprocal obligations, exchanges, magical controls' were major aspects of Lovedu political and social structure. It might even be argued that the Lovedu emphasis on the brother-sister link and the consequential cross-cousin marriage were more typically 'Oceanian' than 'African'.

Of course, the Oceanian analogy must not be pressed very far. The

Lovedu were not a 'bounded', let alone an 'island population'; besides being part of the 'single social field' comprehending South Africa and beyond, they were more immediately part of an ethnologically complex cluster of at least 26 distinguishable 'tribes'. Part of the fieldwork and some of the early publications resulting from it were devoted to unravelling some of this complexity (J. D. Krige 1937; E. J. Krige 1938). Although the results tended to emphasize the Sotho affiliations of the Lovedu, they also confirmed the strong Venda influence and noted the more recent Shangane elements. These multiple influences, combined and developed in an unique way by the Lovedu, contributed to their exceptional ethnographic interest which had earlier been partly displayed in the distorted versions of the popular and literary images of the Lovedu and their Queen.

The true dimensions of that interest were at last comprehensively exposed by the Kriges in their main report on their fieldwork, *The Realm of a Rain-Queen*. The book was completed within about a year of the end of the fieldwork, though publication was delayed by the war until 1943. The preface states that the book was designed to interest general readers as well as academics. This design may partly explain why the book gave a general account of Lovedu society and culture, rather than a detailed analysis of any one aspect. In doing so, it resembled the immediately preceding South African ethnographies by Stayt on the Venda and by Hunter on the Pondo, rather than the more specialized monographs for which Malinowski had set an example that was increasingly followed by others. It seems, though, that Malinowski would not have disapproved of the Kriges' procedure, since he had exhorted Raymond Firth to write first a general account of the Tikopia and had claimed that he himself would have given such an account of the Trobrianders, if he could have done the work again (Firth 1957:10). In that sense, *The Realm of a Rain-Queen* might be considered a Malinowskian work by precept, if not by example.

In any case, there were other, more direct senses in which the work displayed Malinowskian influences, as well as those deriving from Mrs Hoernlé, which together contributed to the quality that distinguished it from the earlier ethnographies it ostensibly resembled. It was markedly more interpretative of the 'institutions' and 'customs' it described and much of the interpretation was governed by the assumption that 'in the total complex of the culture all things are interconnected' (1943:241). The advantages of such an assumption

are perhaps most clearly seen in the two chapters (9 and 10) dealing
with marriage and the political system, but they are evident elsewhere, particularly in the degree to which the assumption encourages
the synthetic treatment of data and the subordination of them to
interpretation. In these respects, *The Realm of a Rain-Queen* marked
a distinct advance in South African ethnography: it does not read
like an inventory of facts (as Stayt's book tends to do) nor does it
overwhelm the reader with details (as Hunter's book quite often
does). Instead, as General Smuts observed in his Foreword (and his
own philosophical concern with 'holism' gave him some authority
for the observation), 'it paints the picture of a . . . society in which the
pattern or plan of the whole determines the character of all the main
lines of detail' (p. viii). The picture was nevertheless not offered by
its makers as a complete representation of Lovedu society and culture. Their preface announced an intention to provide further monographs on special topics which, as it turned out, circumstances did not
allow them to complete, so that *The Realm of a Rain-Queen* stands
now as the main monument to Jack and Eileen's joint work on the
Lovedu.

Amongst the intervening circumstances was their resumption of
teaching in settings which were especially demanding of time and energy. In 1940, shortly after the book was completed, Jack was appointed Senior Lecturer in Social Anthropology and Head of the new
Department of Bantu Studies at Rhodes University College, where he
taught all the anthropology and some Native Law, as well as doing
most of the administration himself, a combined load which he assumed with characteristic vigour and enthusiasm. A scarcely less onerous
one was carried by Eileen between 1942 and 1944 when she held the
lectureship in Sociology that was instituted at Rhodes as part of a
School of Social Sciences for which she also had the general responsibility of co-ordinating the disciplines represented in it.

After the war, the University of Natal also opened a Department
of Bantu (later African) Studies on its Durban campus and in 1946
Jack was appointed Professor of Social Anthropology and Head of
the Department which eventually comprehended, besides anthropology, the two other major subjects of Bantu Languages (i.e. Zulu)
and Native Administration, as well as a course (taught by Jack) in
Bantu Law. The complexities of such a department were compounded
by the provision of separate classes for European and non-European
students who were further divided into full-time and part-time cate-

gories, a system which sometimes entailed delivering the same lectures four times in a teaching week that had to be extended to Saturdays and even to Sunday mornings! It also entailed much extra administrative work to be done by a small number of senior academics with very little clerical assistance. It is hardly surprising that Jack Krige's particular combination of abilities, qualifications and experience soon led him to be included in that number and, indeed, he eventually served as Acting Principal of the University on more than one occasion. In meeting the increasing demands of these multiple roles, Jack had Eileen's direct support from 1948 when she was appointed Lecturer in Social Anthropology in the Department and subsequently (from 1953) Senior Lecturer. Together they formed a particularly effective teaching team of which a notable achievement, especially for that time and place, was the encouragement of an interest in anthropology amongst African students of whom several went on to do fieldwork in Natal with the aid of grants which Jack secured from the Nuffield Foundation for that specific purpose.

Although teaching and administration (to which were added, for Eileen, the responsibilities of a mother of two young children) commanded most of their attention for more than a decade after they came to Durban, they both published several articles including a joint contribution on Lovedu cosmology for the major symposium on *African Worlds* (Forde 1954). Their combined dedication to their subject would doubtless have brought more such additions to ethnography and to general anthropology, if Jack's health had not been deteriorating for several years, perhaps partly as a result of his earlier exertions. His death in 1959 ended a partnership of thirty years during which a most remarkable sharing of interests and opportunities had substantially advanced the development of anthropology in South Africa.

It did not, however, end the study of the Lovedu which Eileen actively resumed during the decade 1960–70 when she occupied until her retirement the Chair of Social Anthropology in Durban. From 1962, she made repeated field trips to the Lovedu, including one of six months in 1964. A very detailed report (1975d) on all this further work has been presented to the Human Sciences Research Council which provided some of the necessary funds and Eileen has also published a series of articles which have updated and extended the earlier work. Those dealing particularly with marriage (1964a, 1974, 1975c) do much more than amplify what is already available on the

Lovedu: they make original contributions to the comparative study of cross-cousin and woman-to-woman marriage which has often depended previously on sources that cannot match the depth and richness of what Eileen is now providing. Such originality is rare enough at any time or place; it is rarer still in the later stages of academic careers pursued far from the major centres of learning. But those who have known Eileen and her work, amongst whom we and the other contributors to this volume are privileged to be numbered, will not be astonished by her recent accomplishments and will be glad to join us in celebrating them along with all those past and those still to come.

JOHN ARGYLE
ELEANOR PRESTON-WHYTE

## REFERENCES

BOUCHER, M. 1973 – *Spes in Arduis*. Pretoria: Univ. of South Africa.

CARTWRIGHT, A. P. 1974 – *By the Waters of the Letaba*. Cape Town: Purnell.

FIRTH, R. (ed.) 1967 – *Man and Culture*. London: Routledge and Kegan Paul.

GLUCKMAN, M. 1963 – *Order and Rebellion in Tribal Africa*. London: Cohen & West.

———— 1975 – Anthropology and apartheid: the work of South African anthropologists. In *Studies in African Social Anthropology* (eds.) M. Fortes and S. Patterson. London: Academic Press.

KRIGE, J. D. 1937 – Traditional origins and tribal relationships of the Sotho of the northern Transvaal. *Bantu Stud.* **11**, 321–56.

KUPER, A. 1975 – *Anthropologists and Anthropology*. Harmondsworth: Penguin.

SCHAPERA, I. (ed.) 1934 – The present state and future development of ethnographical research in South Africa. *Bantu Stud.* **8**, 219–342.

SMUTS, J. C. 1941 – Foreword. *The Realm of a Rain-Queen*. E. J. Krige and J. D. Krige. London: Oxford Univ. Press.

## BIBLIOGRAPHY OF E. J. KRIGE

(*works written with J. D. Krige are indicated by asterisks preceding the entries*)

1931   – Agricultural ceremonies and practices of the baLobedu. *Bantu Studies* **5**, 207–39

1932   – The social significance of beer among the baLobedu. *Bantu Studies* **6**, 343–57.

1934a – (with G. W. K. Mahlobo) – Transition from childhood to adulthood among the Zulus. *Bantu Studies* **8**, 157–91.

1934b – Some social and economic facts revealed in Native family budgets. *Race Relations* (South African Inst. Race Relations) **1**, 94–108.

1936a – *The Social System of the Zulus*. London: Longmans, Green. (Second edition, 1950 – Pietermaritzburg: Shuter and Shooter).

1936b – Changing conditions in marital relations and parental duties among urbanized Natives. *Africa* **9**, 1–23.

1937a – Individual development. In *The Bantu-speaking Tribes of South Africa* (ed.) I. Schapera. London: Routledge and Kegan Paul.

1937b – Note on the Phalaborwa and their morula complex. *Bantu Studies* **11**, 357–67.

1938 – The place of the north-eastern Transvaal Sotho in the South Bantu complex. *Africa* **11**, 265–93.

1941 – Economics of exchange in a primitive society. *South African Journal of Economics* **9**, 1–21.

*1943 – *The Realm of a Rain-Queen*. London: Oxford Univ. Press.

1952 – The social background of malnutrition and gastro-enteritis cases at King Edward VIII hospital, Durban. *South African Journal of Science* **48**, 221–25.

1953 – Some aspects of the educational pattern of the Bantu. *Theoria* (Univ. of Natal) **5**, 29–36.

*1954 – The Lovedu of the Transvaal. In *African Worlds* (ed.) D. Forde. London: Oxford Univ. Press.

*1956 – Implications of the Tomlinson report for the Lovedu, a typical tribe of the north-eastern Transvaal. *Race Relations Journal* (South African Institute of Race Relations) **23**, 4, 12–25.

1960 – Agnes Winifred Hoernlé: an appreciation. *African Studies* **19**, 138–144.

1964 – Property, cross-cousin marriage, and the family cycle among the Lovedu. In *The Family Estate in Africa* (eds.) R. F. Gray & P. H. Gulliver. London: Routledge and Kegan Paul.

1968 – Girls' puberty songs and their relation to fertility, health, morality and religion among the Zulu. *Africa* **38**, 173–98.

1969 – Some Zulu concepts important for an understanding of fertility and other rituals. In *Ethnological and Linguistic Studies in Honour of N. J. van Warmelo* (ed.) The Ethnological Section. Pretoria: Dept. of Bantu Admin. and Development, Ethnological Publications No. 52.

1974a – Woman-marriage, with special reference to the Lovedu – its significance for the definition of marriage. *Africa* **44**, 11–37.

1974b – A Lovedu prayer – the light it throws on the ancestor cult. *African Studies* **33**, 91–7.

1975a – Traditional and Christian family structures. In *Religion and Social Change in Southern Africa* (eds.) M. Whisson & M. West. Cape Town: D. Philip.

1975b – Divine kingship, change and development. In *Studies in African Social Anthropology* (eds.) M. Fortes & S. Patterson. London: Academic Press.

1975c – Asymmetrical matrilateral cross-cousin marriage – the Lovedu case. *African Studies* **34**, 231–57.

1975d – *The Social and Political Structure of the Lovedu in the Setting of Social Change*. Unpublished report to the Human Sciences Research Council, Pretoria.

# DINGISWAYO DISCOVERED: AN INTERPRETATION OF HIS LEGENDARY ORIGINS

## John Argyle

The first chapter of Professor Eileen Krige's useful compilation, *The Social System of the Zulus*, is a summary of what was then known of Zulu history. It includes the remark that much of the traditional account of Dingiswayo's early career 'is undisguised fiction' (Krige 1936:7). This assessment was appropriately realistic and subsequent scholars in the field of Zulu history have not dissented from it. Professor Krige's scepticism was not, however, total for she went on to accept as

> certain . . . that Godongwane [as Dingiswayo was originally called], on quarrelling violently with his father, Jobe, escaped and, after leading the life of a refugee for many years among distant peoples, returned, riding upon a horse; and having killed his brother who was reigning, took possession of the Mthethwa throne (1936:7-8).

This view has also been shared by later writers (even if some of them may not subscribe fully to the epithet 'certain'); the common acceptance of these elements of the traditional story is hardly surprising, for they are not immediately improbable, as are many of its other elements.

Nevertheless, I contend in this paper that the elements quite reasonably accepted by Professor Krige as 'certain' were, except for the seizure of power by Dingiswayo, also 'fiction', though of a 'disguised', rather than an 'undisguised', nature. Indeed, I maintain that the whole purpose of the story of Dingiswayo's origins and later wanderings was to disguise the fact that he was not who he was made out to be. If I am correct, then this belated unmasking of the disguise raises the whole question of his original identity. My answers to that question entail some reassessment of a recent tendency amongst historians to treat the early development of the Zulu kingdom in isolation from what was happening elsewhere in South Africa.

To begin stripping away Dingiswayo's disguise, I use a comparative method more favoured by some anthropologists than by historians, who might therefore suspect that I am 'looking at historical evidence

1

"for the sake of extracting static conclusions from moving elements"'
(Marks 1970*a*: 441). But that is not an inevitable consequence of the
method; instead, it can mean looking at apparently unique historical
events as examples of widely recurrent processes, the elucidation of
which reveals that the events are not always what they seem to be.
This revelation means that there is little point in attempting to determine the precise form in which the illusory events involving Dingiswayo were originally presented to his Zulu[1] contemporaries. Such
an attempt would, in any case, be frustrated by the nature of the
sources. The earliest of them were provided by Fynn who claimed to
have received his information from Shaka himself, 'corroborated
from other sources' (Fynn 1888, 60; 1950, 1), but the versions Fynn
left were composed years after he first heard the traditions and they
can only be free paraphrases of what he had been told earlier.
Later sources, such as those provided by Shepstone and Bryant,
derived from (usually unidentified) informants at least one generation
removed from the events, and the printed versions are no better than
those of Fynn at stating what the informants actually said[2].

I therefore start with a summary of the supposed events, drawn
mostly from Fynn, which will nevertheless be sufficient to show, by
comparison, what the underlying processes are.

> Godongwana [Dingiswayo] was the son of one wife of Jobe, a
> chief of the Mthethwa tribe. Jobe was induced by the adherents
> of Mawewe, another son by a different wife, to believe that
> Godongwana was plotting to kill his father. Jobe therefore
> ordered that Godongwana should himself be killed. However,
> Godongwana escaped from Jobe's warriors after receiving a
> spear wound in his side, though Jobe was informed that he
> had been killed. Godongwana found refuge among a succession
> of Zulu tribes, leading him gradually to the north-west, where
> he arrived finally amongst that section of the Hlubi tribe under
> chief Bhungane. While with Bhungane, he displayed outstanding
> qualities by killing a lioness single-handed, for which he was
> rewarded with a subchiefship by Bhungane. Subsequently,
> Godongwana entered the service of that famous, though
> mysterious, *umlungu* [usually translated 'White man' or
> 'European', but see my discussion of the term below] who
> appeared amongst the Hlubi from the west, riding a horse and
> carrying a gun. Godongwana accompanied this *umlungu* nearly
> to the coast, where Phakathwayo, chief of the Qwabe, had the

*umlungu* killed. However, sufficient of the *umlungu's* prestige, particularly that deriving from his possession of the horse and gun, became attached to Godongwana to win the support of some of the Mthethwa. With their help Godongwana overcame the wariors of his half-brother, Mawewe, the successor of their father, Jobe, who had himself died during Godongwana's exile. Godongwana himself then became chief of the Mthethwa, under the name of Dingiswayo, by which he was thereafter known.

For purposes of comparison, this summary may, by abstraction, be reduced even further to the following set of elements:

a. The child of a ruler is suspected of being a threat to his father who orders him to be killed.
b. The child escapes death.
c. He goes into exile, where he manifests heroic qualities which attract the favourable attention of a patron who eventually bestows subordinate office on him.
d. In his original home, his father dies and is succeeded by a recognized heir.
e. Shortly afterwards, the exile returns to his former home, equipped with some source of prestige or power.
f. This prestige or power wins him a following amongst a section of the people in his former home, who recognize him as the child driven into exile.
g. They therefore support him in removing the incumbent heir whom he replaces as ruler, thus finally achieving the position to which he has a genealogical claim.

Once this reduction is made, the legendary form of the tradition should be readily apparent. It resembles quite closely some parts of the form which Lord Raglan abstracted from his analysis of the legends about such well-known 'heroes' as Oedipus, Romulus and Moses. He expressed that form in terms of 22 'typical incidents' of which all, or only some, may be found in any particular 'heroic' legend (Raglan 1949:178-89). Allowing for some differences of detail, seven of these incidents correspond to those I have traced in the Dingiswayo legend and at least another three correspondences may be recognized if the events leading to and following Dingiswayo's death are included. This comparison does, of course, associate in a rather crude way traditions from apparently disparate cultures, but it serves as a first step in the discovery of the processes beneath the supposed events.

A further step may be taken by a comparison with other legends that lie much closer to hand; as close, indeed, as some of the Zulu folk-tales collected and published by Callaway in the last century. The incidents in at least one of these tales, involving an imaginary hero (Callaway 1868:41-7), are formally similar both to those I have abstracted from the Dingiswayo story and to some of those in the classical legends (with which Callaway himself compares the tale). Elsewhere in the collection, there are further variations on the same general theme (ibid.: 60-9, 207-10, 237-53, 267-80), and yet others occur in an independently collected tale recorded about 1869 (Carbutt 1879). I assume therefore that the Zulu, like many other peoples, lived in a world where the idea of an exile returning to claim his rightful inheritance was sufficiently familiar to make its application to the figure of Dingiswayo quite plausible.

Perhaps because that world is one which they have lost and have tried to re-enter directly, European commentators have also accepted the story of Dingiswayo's exile and return, even though they have rejected many of the attendant details as fanciful. But if, instead, one goes back to that world by the indirect route of a comparative method, one sees such stories in a different perspective that alters their significance when they are attached to historical figures. It is doubtless the advantage of this perspective which has enabled one recent historian to see that what he calls 'the Moses-in-the-bulrushes theme' is 'an almost certain indication of a dynastic change', especially when it occurs some way down a kinglist or genealogy (Henige 1974:8-9, 66-7). He is, however, principally concerned with the chronological implications of such a 'dynastic change' and does not show what kind of evidence would make it 'certain' that one had occurred. In the case of Dingiswayo, there is no directly available evidence of any kind for its certainty (if there were, the story would not have been accepted until now) and my comparisons have so far shown only that the story has a legendary form which implies, but does not establish, that it was fabricated. Further comparison is therefore needed to show that stories of this kind have undoubtedly been used elsewhere in Africa to justify the assumption of political office by those with no hereditary claims to it. Such a comparison strengthens the probability that the story of Dingiswayo was used for the same purpose and also exposes the significance of elements in the story which otherwise pass unremarked.

For this further comparison I use material that I collected myself amongst the Soli people of Zambia³, long before I had even heard of Dingiswayo. The comparison is therefore literally adventitious, but without it I could not have arrived at my interpretation of the Dingis-wayo story. The Soli gave me a relatively large number of stories about some of their former chiefs that all have essentially the same theme, depending on the fact that, like many other Central African peoples, the Soli follow a matrilineal mode of succession. Typically, the theme is that a female member of a Soli chief's matrilineage was captured by some other tribe during a raid. In some versions, she already had a baby which was taken with her; in other versions, she bore a child later, at the home of her captors. Years afterwards, when the child had grown up, it was either set free by its masters or escaped from them, and returned to Soli country, about which it had supposedly heard from its mother. The child arrived back, just at the time when the local chief had died and the people were con-sidering the succession. The child was able to establish its identity by naming its mother and by describing the circumstances in which she had been abducted. It also had (or claimed to have) some source of power or prestige. The local Soli found the story and its teller acceptable and appointed him or her as their new chief, even though he or she might not even be able to speak their language.

Faced with stories of this kind about at least five different in-dividuals from four separate chiefdoms, I did not reject the notion that individual Soli were frequently carried off in raids, nor did it seem unlikely that some of them or their descendants eventually returned to their Soli homes. But I did become very sceptical about the possibility that *five* such persons were missing rightful heirs to chiefship. I eventually found that my scepticism was shared by at least some Soli over the most recent of the five cases.

In about 1912, after one of the Soli chiefs had died, and there had been an interregnum of about a year, an Ngoni man from Fort Jameson who was passing through Soli country on his way to the line of rail, succeeded in becoming the new chief on the grounds of a story of the kind I have related. He maintained his claim in the face of resistance from some members of the Soli chiefly matrilineage who were contending amongst themselves for the position, and he managed to convince the White officials of the British South Africa company that his story was true, so that they, too, recognized him as the rightful heir. However, when I persisted in questioning some of my most knowledgeable informants who had first given me the story as it stood, they revealed their own opinions that the story was untrue.

They told me how the Ngoni man had fallen in with a group of important Soli headmen, when he first arrived in the area. He learned of the death of the chief from them and told them that back in Fort Jameson he had a number of stores which brought him much wealth and that he was also the owner of large herds of cattle. He promised that if the headmen would support him as a candidate for the chief-ship, and he succeeded, he would transfer all his wealth and cattle to Soli country and use some of it to reward those who had helped him. The headmen accepted this proposition and supplied him with necessary circumstantial detail about a woman who had dis-appeared long ago and whose returned child he could claim to be. The scheme worked and he did become chief, though the riches he described so graphically never materialized, and his supporters got nothing for their pains.

There are certain features, that I cannot relate here, about the other Soli cases of this kind which strongly support the inference that essentially the same imposture must have happened in each case. If so, then the repeated use of the story amongst the Soli to justify a 'dynastic change' reinforces the supposition that the story of Dingiswayo had the same purpose. Besides this general reinforce-ment, the comparison yields more specific indications of features in the story itself which point to its real purpose. One of these is the occurrence of challenges to the supposed exile's claim at the time it was made. Such challenges are clearly recorded in the Soli stories and are contained in some versions of the Dingiswayo story, though their significance has apparently not been realized. In Bryant's version, we are told that Dingiswayo on his arrival in Mthethwa country went first to the homestead of a man called Mbangambi, who was supposedly a kinsman and a boyhood com-panion of Dingiswayo. As Bryant puts it:

> Mbangambi at once passed on the wondrous news to his local headman, Nqola. This [headman], however, proved a man of conservative politics, who did not approve of pretenders and revolutions; and Mbangambi was directed to acquaint the stranger with the fact (1929:90).

Instead of which, Mbangambi helped Dingiswayo raise a body of warriors who promptly put Nqola to death for his scepticism. Bryant's version is similar to that of Stuart (1924:20-22) and both of them record the further important fact that the 'conservative' Nqola was a son of the same father as the previous ruler, Jobe, and so a prominent representative of the chiefly lineage. He therefore reacted to Dingiswayo's claim in the same way as his Soli counterparts did in the case of the Ngoni impostor. Nqola was no more successful than they were, but unlike them he lacked the protection of colonial authority and so paid the supreme penalty for his scepticism.

The importance of force in determining the final outcome of a pretender's claim may be emphasized by another comparison with the especially apposite case of Sitimela who, in 1881, tried to follow Dingiswayo's example by claiming to be his grandson and therefore entitled to be chief of the Mthethwa. Indeed, at least one detail of the Sitimela episode resembles very closely that of Dingiswayo since, according to Bryant (1929:475), Sitimela first appeared in Mthethwa country 'mounted on a horse in true Dingiswayan style'. However, this time the representative of the chiefly lineage (a brother's son's son of Nqola in Bryant's genealogy), after an initial reverse, appealed to the superior power of John Dunn and his African followers who defeated and drove away Sitimela (Bryant 1929:476). As one result, Sitimela's claim is recorded merely as an unsuccessful imposture, whereas that of Dingiswayo has survived apparently unchallenged since the defeat and death of Nqola. There, as elsewhere, nothing succeeds like success.

To challenge that success now, as I do from the comparative safety of twentieth-century Durban, is not to diminish the historical significance of Dingiswayo. On the contrary, it grows by raising the question, if he was not who he claimed to be, who *was* he? Obviously, there cannot be any definitive answers to this question, since all the surviving evidence is predicated on the assumption that he was indeed the son of his father. But if one follows a procedure based on the contrary assumption, then different versions of the legend can be made to yield varying suggestions about his actual origins. That procedure is to assume that one of the places to which the legend claims Dingiswayo went during his supposed exile was, in fact, his place of origin.

The first version of the legend to which (after some preliminary evaluation) I apply the procedure, is best known from the famous, or notorious, statement of Theophilus Shepstone that Dingiswayo

in his travels . . . had reached the Cape Colony and must have
lived with or entered the service of some colonist . . . It was
during his stay in the Cape Colony that he acquired the information, or made the observations, which were to effect the
great change in his native land and the surrounding countries
(Shepstone 1888:163).

This statement has, it is true, frequently been dismissed by
historians of otherwise differing persuasions, as an uncomprehending
or prejudiced distortion of the Dingiswayo legend (e.g. Bryant
1929:95; Hattersley 1959:9; Omer-Cooper 1966:169; Wilson &
Thompson 1969:339; Marks 1967a: 89). On the other hand, Professor
Brookes (1965:9) has remarked that 'it is still hard to think that
Shepstone can have merely guessed it, and that there was no Zulu
legend behind it' and I happen to share this view, partly because I
have been able to identify at least one possible Zulu source from
which Shepstone's statement may have derived. In the course of a
conversation about Dingiswayo that I had in 1974 with Mr Harry
Lugg, himself a nonagenarian survivor of the earlier days of Natal
'Native administration' and a repository of one kind of oral history,
he dismissed Shepstone's statement (as most historians have done)
as a 'myth'. When I asked where, in that case, the myth came from,
Mr Lugg replied that its source could have been a Zulu who he said
was called Timuni and who lived in the Mapumulo area, though he
did not identify him more particularly. I presume that this man was
the 'Timoni' mentioned in Shepstone's own unpublished papers
(Folder 22630, Item 2[4], sheet B), as a member of 'the Zulu royal
family' who fled to Natal in 1838, after quarrelling with Dingane.
I further presume that it was he (or a descendant bearing his name
as an hereditary title) who was listed as 'Matymane' or 'Matyimane',
chief of the Amapumulo tribe, in 1852-3 (Proceedings:32, 35) and,
more correctly, as 'Utimuni', chief of the Amazulu of the Lower
Tugela district, in 1882 (Report:42). My final presumption is that
he was the father of Ndlovu ka Timuni,[5] who was one of the later
chiefs of the Mapumulo area caught up in the Bambata affair (Marks
1970b: 225, 227) and who was said by Samuelson (1929:257) to be
a grandson of Senzangakhona's brother, of whom Timuni himself
must, therefore, have been the son.

The possibility that there was such a source in the Mapumulo
area, from which Shepstone's 'myth' could have come, is strength-
ened by the existence of a second version of it which was definitely

collected from another chief in the Mapumulo area. This version was printed by James Stuart in his *uBaxolele* (1924), but none of the published criticisms of Shepstone seems to have taken any account of it, presumably because the critics (except for Bryant) could not read Zulu. I could not myself have made confident use of Stuart's text without access to an unpublished English translation which my colleague, Professor Trevor Cope, has kindly allowed me to see. At the beginning of the section in *uBaxolele* on Dingiswayo, Stuart states (1924:14) that the information it contains was collected in 1903 from Matshwili Mngoye, who was actually a grandson of Dingiswayo ('ka Mngoye ka Dingiswayo'), and was 'very well informed on the history of his tribe the Mtetwa'. Other sources show that he was also a contemporary of Ndlovu ka Timuni (who was another of Stuart's informants) and that their chiefdoms were next to one another in the Mapumulo area, where Matshwili was eventually killed during the Bambata episode (Stuart 1913:390; Marks 1970*b*:232, 407).

Matshwili's version of Dingiswayo's 'exile' states, *inter alia*, that he

> eventually reached Grahamstown [*eRini*].[6] He met a white man [*mLungu*] there who adopted him [*wamtola*] and gave him work with horses. He stayed there for a long time. Many years passed while he was in Grahamstown. After much time had elapsed and he had grown tired of work, he was stricken by a fever. He dreamt many dreams. He dreamt of his father [Jobe], of Nodunga [Jobe's *induna*] and of Xaba [Jobe's father's father?]. His body would not allow him to work any more. He bade his employer [*mLungu*] farewell and set out for home . . . his employer said to him, 'What would you like me to give you as wages?' He said, 'I would like a gun and a horse'. He gave him everything connected with a gun and a horse. He went. (Translation by E. R. Dahle of Stuart 1924:18-20; my parentheses.)[7]

The existence of this version is not, of course, conclusive evidence for either the provenance or the authenticity of Shepstone's earlier statement. It does, however, strongly suggest that he was summarizing traditions current amongst prominent Zulu, connected with both the Zulu and the Mthethwa ruling lineages, and living in an area that came under Shepstone's jurisdiction as Secretary for Native Affairs. Thus, although I would not attach much significance to the particular

details of either Shepstone's or Stuart's version, I do claim that
together they provide sufficient grounds for applying my suggested
procedure to their general assertion that Dingiswayo's exile included
a period in the Cape. I thus derive the proposition that the Cape was
not where Dingiswayo went, but whence he came.

To entertain this proposition means that I can then ask the supplementary question: if he came from the Cape, what kind of
person is he likely to have been? My general answer is that he would
have been a refugee from the Cape colonial society. Even Whites in
that society began trying to escape from it as soon as it was founded,
and some of those who were recaptured in the second half of the
seventeenth century claimed to have been heading towards 'the
Portuguese' in Mozambique (Moodie 1960:15, 367-8, 382-4). By
the second half of the eighteenth century, there were plenty of
Blacks in the Cape who had even stronger reasons to get as far away
from it as they could. They included escaped African slaves who, as
Professor Wilson remarks (Wilson & Thompson 1969:234), were
amongst those 'absorbed into Nguni chiefdoms'. It is true that
'Nguni' in this context means those often called 'Xhosa', but it is
not inconceivable that an escaped slave could have passed right
through those chiefdoms and have reached the Mthethwa. Professor
Wilson herself would be unlikely to disallow the possibility, since
she elsewhere comments (ibid.: 115) that the recorded presence
west of the Keiskamma, between 1802 and 1806, of two African men
from near Delagoa Bay 'makes nonsense of the argument that
Dingiswayo *could not* have visited the Cape as Shepstone thought
he had'. Her argument for the possibility of travelling such a distance
still holds, even after I have reversed the direction of Dingiswayo's
supposed journey. It may be reinforced by the consideration that
some twenty years later Fynn met two men in Mpondo country who
admitted that they had long ago escaped from slavery in the Cape
and gave him the names of their former owners (Fynn 1950:113).
Still, I do concede that Dingiswayo would have had to be exceptionally determined and lucky to reach the Mthethwa, particularly if he
were alone. So although the possibility that he was a former African
slave may not be excluded, there are more plausible Cape antecedents
for him.

One is that he was not an 'African', but a 'Khoikhoi' (or a
'Coloured'), refugee. That is, he could have been one of that 'considerable number of Khoikhoi [who] withdrew from the struggle

altogether [with the colonists] by going off north to the Orange River, carrying with them the key to white superiority – horses and guns' (Marks 1970a: 445). Such an identification of Dingiswayo accounts quite well for his horse and gun and it also reduces the distance he would have to travel through unfamiliar country. He might, that is, have become detached from one of those parties of what Dr Marks aptly calls 'VoorVoortrekkers', who had already penetrated well into the interior by the end of the eighteenth century, even as far as the Limpopo.

This identification would also account for the tendency in some versions of the Dingiswayo legend to fuse, or perhaps confuse, him with that mysterious *umlungu* who has been the subject of much fruitless speculation (as, for example, that he must have been Dr Cowan – see Bryant 1929:92-3). For Fynn states (1950:129) quite plainly that 'all persons wearing clothes (as our Hottentots did) were deemed by the Zulus to be Europeans' and, again, that the Zulu warriors who attacked and killed some 'Hottentots' near the Umzimkhulu told the Pondo there that 'they had met with and killed a party of "white men" – as they termed the Hottentots from their European dress, and comparatively light complexion'. In other words, at that time the term *umlungu* was used in Zulu for a category that was as much cultural as it was racial. It is, then, quite possible and indeed probable that the *umlungu* in some versions of Dingiswayo's return, who often, indeed, seems to be Dingiswayo himself, was a Khoikhoi or Coloured.

There are, of course, objections to the attribution of this ethnic identity to Dingiswayo himself: one is that the Mthethwa would not have accepted him so readily as their chief; a second is that if they *did* accept him, some clearer indication of his cultural and, especially, his racial distinctiveness would have survived in the oral tradition. Against the first objection, I would adduce the plentiful evidence of a long-standing assimilation of Khoisan peoples by Bantu peoples and conclude from it that many Mthethwa would not necessarily have objected to a Khoisan as chief; any that did object might well have been silenced, as Nqola was. We know, after all, that many Africans later accepted Whites like Fynn, John Dunn and even Shepstone as, in effect, their chiefs, so why should they have rejected a Brown one? Against the second objection, I suggest that by the time Dingiswayo reached the Mthethwa he could have acquired at least some Zulu (or Nguni) traits, such as a knowledge of the language; he may, in addition, have been a particularly dark Brown man. If so, his original ethnic identity might not have been conspicuous enough to survive in the oral traditions about him, especially since, on my interpretation of them, their main point was precisely to conceal that identity. There is, in any case, one piece of indirect evidence that the concealment may not have been completely successful. I refer to the remarkable (but previously unremarked) statement made by some of Faku's Pondo when they were interrogating Fynn, that 'Shaka was . . . of white extraction' and that Fynn 'was probably one of his relations' (Fynn 1950:113). As far as I know, the literature produced by those Whites who actually met Shaka contains no other suggestion that he was anything but an African. The Pondo attribution to him of White extraction is therefore inexplicable as it stands. Fynn himself presumably thought it was not worth trying to explain, since he makes no comment on it. I, however, find it at least worth the speculation that the Pondo, lacking any direct acquaintance with Shaka, may have accorded him an origin which was really that of Dingiswayo, with whom Shaka had been so closely associated during his own early career, and with whom it would have been easy to confuse him at such a distance.

This speculation does, though, take me to the limits of what is permissible and perhaps beyond them. I must therefore return to surer ground and consider a third possible ethnic identity for Dingiswayo, that I judge to be most consistent with *all* the available versions of his 'exile'. This possibility is that he was an Nguni-ized, former Sotho client of one or more of the Khoikhoi or Coloured 'Voor-Voortrekkers'. Service with them would explain his possession of the horse and gun (some versions actually state that he got them from the *umlungu* with whom he travelled), and specific justification for the Sotho identity is to be found in Bryant's material. After repeating the story of a White traveller, Bryant adds that the 'White man' arrived in the country of the Hlubi tribe 'accompanied by a party of Chwana-Sutu carriers or hunters' (1929:88) and that he there recruited Dingiswayo as a guide for the party on its way to the coast, which Dingiswayo supposedly knew as his original home. Bryant further identifies (1929:89) this 'Chwana-Sutu' party with a group of 'foreigners' (i.e. not Nguni), some of whose descendants (known collectively as *eziBisini*) he seems to have interviewed (1929:91). From them he presumably obtained their earlier 'clan-name' (*aba-Kwa-Mahlase*) which he suggests might have derived from the similar name (*Mahlatsi*) of a Sotho group which was 'about that time located in the Bethlehem district of the Free State' (1929:89).

Applying my procedure to this information, I reject the assertion that Dingiswayo had come *from* the coast and that he *returned* to it with this Sotho party; instead I propose that he was either already a member of the party when it reached Hlubi country or that he was himself a Hlubi who joined it there. The second alternative does not entirely deprive Dingiswayo of a 'Sotho' identity. Bryant alleges (1929:147, 181) that the Hlubi then dressed both themselves and their hair in a fashion that was more typical of the Sotho than of the Nguni; certainly, ethnic identities of this kind are not sharply discontinuous and the geographical location of the Hlubi at that time makes it likely that they were as much 'Sotho' as 'Nguni'.

My conclusion from this survey of the possible identities for Dingiswayo is, then, that if he was not a 'VoorVoortrekker', he was a Sotho of some kind with experience of 'VoorVoortrekker' culture. Although the material does not allow me to make any more precise identification of the man behind the legendary disguise, it has yielded positive indications that his antecedents were other than Nguni. These indications therefore have implications for some recent discussions of the rise of the Zulu kingdom with which the developments in the Mthethwa chiefdom were closely connected. These discussions have tended to emphasize factors described as 'internal' to Zulu (or, more broadly, Nguni) society and to depreciate 'external' factors. This tendency has been fostered by the adoption of a 'new approach to African history' which, among other things, insists that 'there is an African past prior to the coming of the white man [and] an African history apart from the interaction between the [European and African] groups' (Marks 1967b: 83, 87; see also Omer-Cooper 1966:168).

In its specific application to the problem of the rise of the Zulu kingdom, this 'new approach' has often favoured what is in fact a rather old 'internal' explanation originally offered by an anthropologist, Professor Gluckman, who first sketched this explanation nearly forty years ago (1940:149-51) and reiterated it in at least two subsequent publications (1960:161, 166; 1974:137-8). The gist of his argument was that by the late eighteenth century the population of Zululand had increased to the point where there was no longer sufficient land, under the Zulu farming system, to allow for the continuing proliferation of the independent, small chiefdoms which had until then been the prevailing political form. Consequently, the political units became larger and fewer, culminating in the great, single unit of Shaka's kingdom. The argument seems initially persuasive and, since it also emphasizes forces developing within Zulu society rather than impinging on it from without, it was likely to appeal to advocates of the 'new approach' (see e.g., Marks 1967*a*: 86-7; Omer-Cooper 1966:2-3, 1969:212, 1976:321). For one of them, indeed, it was so compelling that he treated as a fact 'the emergence of a pocket of high population pressure in Zululand' which was one of the 'developments entirely internal to Bantu society' leading to the appearance of new political forms there (Omer-Cooper 1966:170).

Yet there are cogent reasons for supposing that, in this case of 'historian[s] using the insights of anthropology . . . to answer the historical questions of happening, change and the particular' (Marks 1970*a*: 441), they have chosen the wrong anthropological insight. The first reason is that neither Professor Gluckman nor the historians could produce appropriate numerical evidence to show what the size and density of the Zulu population in the eighteenth century actually were, let alone give figures for the alleged increase. Instead, they have inferred a growing population from the evidence of chiefs' genealogies and of oral traditions about tribal fission and migration. Yet assuming (what is itself doubtful) that the genealogies and traditions as we have them are reliable sources for eighteenth century history, it is not at all certain that they reflect a rapid growth of population. By their very nature, genealogies tracing descent from an apical ancestor show more branches in the later generations than in the earlier ones. Similarly, oral traditions are likely to report the more recent political segmentation and omit the more remote. It is therefore dangerously easy to derive from the genealogies and traditions an illusory impression of cumulative expansion within a growing population, when in fact there may have been only a series of repetitive cycles within a more or less stable population.

A second reason for doubting this insight is that even if the alleged population increase did occur, a causal link between it and the development of the kingdom has not been demonstrated. Stevenson (1968) has certainly claimed (to my mind with a lot of special pleading) that 'state-formation' is positively correlated with high population density in several African societies. But, as Stevenson himself is careful to emphasize, correlations are not causes and, in any case, he concludes (1968:52) that the Zulu kingdom is a 'dubious case' of the correlation.

A third reason for doubt is that even if a causal link did obtain, it is unlikely to have been of the kind asserted by Professor Gluckman and, in at least some instances, by his followers. For they have treated the assumed population increase as one of those 'key causes' on which MacIver commented (1942:113-4) 'of all the devices by which men have evaded the full problem of social causation the most prevalent by far is that which designates some one factor or complex of factors as peculiarly, exclusively, or dominantly determinant'. The full problem of the rise of the Zulu kingdom is indeed evaded by those who attribute it mainly to an increase in population.

It is also evaded by any other explanations which rely on 'developments entirely internal to Bantu society', for they seriously misrepresent the emerging situation in southern Africa during the late eighteenth century. Quite apart from the more recent claim by Smith (1969) that trade with Delagoa Bay contributed to the 'internal growth and consolidation' of the northern Nguni chiefdoms (and I find the evidence adduced for this 'trade hypothesis' almost as suppositious and inferential as that for the 'population hypothesis'), the very distinction between internal and external developments betrays an assumption about the process of social change that hardly accords with the claim of implementing a 'new approach' to the study of South African history. The assumption is essentially similar to one made by Malinowski several decades ago, when he insisted that European and African cultures in contact with one another were nevertheless 'distinct orders of cultural reality' (Malinowski 1945:64).

Ironically enough, it was Professor Gluckman who exposed the defects of Malinowski's approach and offered as an alternative the concept of 'a single social field' within which Europeans and Africans interacted (Gluckman 1949:7, 13). Twentieth-century South Africa was, Gluckman argued, an especially clear example of such a social field, but he also applied the concept to the events in Natal during the early nineteenth century when 'the field of reality in which these events occurred . . . extended in space-time to the Cape'. The extension of the field could proceed even further 'to the whole creation

of the Zulu nation under Shaka. Thus, in reality, events in the Cape
were brought into interaction with events in Zululand and with its
history' (Gluckman 1949:20).

If recent historians had favoured such broader anthropological
insights, then they might have seen that the events precipitated by
Dingiswayo also occurred in a field of social relationships extending
from the Cape to Zululand. That, at any rate, is how I see them precisely because the traditions about Dingiswayo suggest that I should.
One reason why others have not seen the events in the same way may
be because their attention has been distracted by increasingly specu-
lative theories which seek to explain why the events occurred, when
it is still not clear what actually happened. My attempt to clarify
some of the events leaves many others obscure and future efforts of
both historians and anthropologists might best be devoted to elucidat-
ing them, before the even more difficult task of explaining them is
resumed.

## NOTES

[1]Here and elsewhere in this paper I use the term 'Zulu' anachronistically to
mean the whole indigenous population of what came to be the 'Zulu kingdom',
inhabiting 'Zululand'.

[2]Professor Webb and Mr Wright are currently effecting a major improvement
in the quality of the sources for Zulu oral history by editing and translating
James Stuart's voluminous original notes of what his informants told him.
Unfortunately for my purposes, only one of the brief references to Dingiswayo
in the first volume to be published (Webb and Wright 1976:249) relates to
his early career and it does not contain any new material.

[3]The material was collected while I was a Research Officer of the former Rhodes-
Livingstone Institute for Social Research, Lusaka.

[4]Much of this item in the Shepstone collection (in the Killie Campbell Africana
Library, Durban), entitled 'List of Zulu Tribes and their History', is i dentical
with the compilation published in Bird's *Annals of Natal*, Vol. I, 124-53, but
the information concerning Timuni was there omitted, presumably because it
did not relate to the time of Jobe's reign.

[5]Besides this patronymic evidence, there is the statement by one of James
Stuart's main informants, Jantshi, that 'Ndhlovu's and Mruyi's father Timuni
. . . got his information from the same person I myself did, viz. my father'
(Webb & Wright 1976:188). Since Jantshi's father was Nongila who 'was a spy
under Senzangakona, Tshaka, Dingana and Mpande' and who 'crossed into
Natal in Mpande's reign' (ibid.: 174), Timuni's potential status as a knowledgeable informant is enhanced by his alleged contact with such an original source
of Zulu tradition as Nongila.

<sup>6</sup>Although *eRini* does, in its narrower sense, denote Grahamstown, it also has a wider sense in which, according to one of Stuart's other informants, 'the Cape is called *Erini* by natives' (Webb & Wright 1976:220). Matshwili was therefore not necessarily specifying Grahamstown as the place to which Dingiswayo supposedly went and so should not be accused of the kind of anachronism to which Bryant (1929:91) drew attention.

<sup>7</sup>There is an English rendering of this episode in Stuart's own unpublished papers (File 53, Item No. 4) in the Killie Campbell Library. I made use of this rendering in a previous paper (Argyle 1977).

## REFERENCES

ARGYLE, W. J. 1977 – Who were Dingiswayo and Shaka? Individual origins and political transformations, in *The Societies of Southern Africa in the 19th and 20th Centuries*, Vol. 7, Univ. of London: Inst. of Commonwealth Studies.

BROOKES, E. H., C. DE B. WEBB. 1965 – *A History of Natal*. Pietermaritzburg: Univ. of Natal Press.

BRYANT, A. T. 1929–*Olden Times in Zululand and Natal*. London: Longmans, Green.

CALLAWAY, H. 1868 – *Nursery Tales, Traditions and Histories of the Zulus*, Vol. I. London: Trübner.

CARBUTT, H. L. 1879 – The story of Ngangezwe and Mnyamana. *Folk-Lore Journal* **1**, iv, 84-97.

FYNN, H. F. 1888 – History of Godongwana (Dingiswayo) and (in part) of Chaka, in *Annals of Natal*, Vol. I, (ed.) J. Bird. Pietermaritzburg: P. Davis.

———— 1950 – *The Diary of Henry Francis Fynn*. Pietermaritzburg: Shuter & Shooter.

GLUCKMAN, M. 1940 – Analysis of a social situation in modern Zululand. *Bantu Stud.* **14**, 147–74.

———— 1949 – *An Analysis of the Sociological Theories of Bronislaw Malinowski*. Rhodes-Livingstone Paper No. 16. Cape Town: Oxford Univ. Press.

———— 1960 – The rise of a Zulu empire. *Scient. Am.* **202**, 4, 157–68.

———— 1974 – The individual in a social framework: the rise of King Shaka of Zululand. *J. Afr. Stud.* **1**, 113–44.

HATTERSLEY, A. F. 1959 – *The British Settlement of Natal*. Cambridge: Cambridge Univ. Press.

HENIGE, D. P. 1974 – *The Chronology of Oral Tradition*. Oxford: Clarendon Press.

KRIGE, E. J. 1936 – *The Social System of the Zulus*. London: Longmans, Green.

MACIVER, R. M. 1942 – *Social Causation*. Boston: Ginn.

MALINOWSKI, B. 1945 – *The Dynamics of Culture Change*. New Haven: Yale Univ. Press.

MARKS, S. 1967*a* – The rise of the Zulu kingdom, in *The Middle Age of African History*, (ed.) R. Oliver. London: Oxford Univ. Press.

———— 1967*b* – Historians and South Africa, in *Africa Discovers Her Past* (ed.) J. D. Fage. London: Oxford Univ. Press.

———— 1970*a* – African and Afrikaner history. *J. Afr. Hist.* **11**, 435–47.

———— 1970*b* – *Reluctant Rebellion*. Oxford: Clarendon Press.

MOODIE, D. 1960 – *The Record*. Cape Town: Balkema.
OMER-COOPER, J. D. 1966 – *The Zulu Aftermath*. London: Longmans, Green.
———— 1969 – Aspects of political change in the nineteenth-century Mfecane, in *African Societies in Southern Africa* (ed.) L. Thompson. London: Heinemann.
———— 1976 – The Nguni outburst, in *Cambridge History of Africa*, Vol. V. Cambridge: Cambridge University Press.
PROCEEDINGS. 1852–3 – *Proceedings and Report of the Commission Appointed to Inquire into the Past and Present State of the Kafirs in the District of Natal*. Pietermaritzburg(?).
RAGLAN, LORD. 1949 – *The Hero*. London: Watts.
REPORT. 1882 – *Report of the Natal Native Commission, 1881–1882*. Pietermaritzburg.
SAMUELSON, R. C. A. 1929 – *Long, Long Ago*. Durban: Knox.
SHEPSTONE, T. 1888 – The early history of the Zulu-Kafir race of south-eastern Africa, in *Annals of Natal*, Vol. I, (ed.) J. Bird. Pietermaritzburg: P. Davis.
SMITH, A. 1969 – The trade of Delagoa Bay as a factor in Nguni politics 1750–1835, in *African Societies in Southern Africa* (ed.) L. Thompson. London: Heinemann.
STEVENSON, R. F. 1968 – *Population and Political Systems in Tropical Africa*. New York: Columbia Univ. Press.
STUART, J. 1913 – *A History of the Zulu Rebellion 1906*. London: Macmillan.
      1924 – *uBaxolele*. London: Longmans, Green.
WEBB, C. DE B. & J. B. WRIGHT (eds.) 1976 – *The James Stuart Archive*, Volume 1. Pietermaritzburg: Univ. of Natal Press.
WILSON, M., L. THOMPSON. 1969 – *The Oxford History of South Africa*, Vol. I. Oxford: Clarendon Press.

# THE EARLY HISTORY OF THE BUTHELEZI CLAN

*Mangosuthu G. Buthelezi*

This contribution, which I am glad to include in a collection for Professor Eileen Krige whose work I have long admired, outlines the history of the Buthelezi before and after the emergence of King Shaka. It is part of a longer account that I have compiled and I hope to present the remaining parts elsewhere.

## THE BUTHELEZI CLAN BEFORE THE SHAKAN ERA

All the Buthelezi originated at Mcakweni in what is today the Babanango district. The history of the Buthelezi has always been inseparable from that of the Zulu clan, from the pre-Shakan era down to the most recent times, mainly because the Buthelezi came to inhabit an area adjacent to that of the Zulu clan. The Buthelezi area stretched from the Babanango ridge to where it joins the boundary of the Mbuyisa area and further on to the Ntombela area. The Zulu area stretched from the Sikhume ridge right up to Mthonjaneni.

All the Nguni tribes now classified as Zulu were autonomous before Shaka came on the scene and welded most of them into the powerful Zulu nation. Some tribes were stronger than others, but those were fairly peaceful days when 'wars' between tribes, were almost like the modern sport of javelin-throwing. In such 'wars', the enemies gathered and flung long spears in each other's direction. Cheering supporters stood in the background behind each faction ranged against the other; in those days it was even possible for women to join the cheering crowds.

Numerous such skirmishes took place between the Zulu and the Buthelezi, particularly under the rule of Ngwane, the Buthelezi ruler, and of Jama, King Shaka's grandfather; they also occurred during the reign of Phungashe who ruled the Buthelezi during the time of Jama's son, Senzangakhona. Jama had particularly rough treatment from the Buthelezi who not only defeated his Zulu clan, but actually captured him. However, it seems to have been customary then not to kill the ruler if he were captured, so Jama was ransomed from the Buthelezi with some oxen. This episode appears in the praises of Ngwane, the Buthelezi ruler:

*uNgwane ngwati wabamba ngasemazibukweni*
*Obambe uJama wamyekelela*
*Waze wahlengwa ngezimagodla*
*Wamphinda wambamba wamyekelela*
*Wahlengwa ngezimagodla*
*Wabadle uJama wamyekelela*
*Waze wahlengwa ngezimagodla*

A not too free translation of these lines would be:

Ngwane who seized near the drifts in the river
Who seized Jama and then let him go
He [Jama] was ransomed with oxen which had long, winding horns.
He again seized him and let him go
He was freed after payment of oxen with long, bending horns.
Each time he seized Jama he let him go
When he was redeemed with a ransom of oxen with long, bent horns.

This stanza in Ngwane's praises, with its repeated emphasis on the capture and redemption through cattle, may represent a simple, bloodless way by which booty was commonly extracted from a defeated clan. The description of the cattle as having long, winding or bending horns expresses the idea that the beasts paid were large, old ones, whose horns had grown accordingly. There are other such episodes recorded in similar lines from Phungashe's praises, where not only poor Jama appears, but also Senzangakhona and Malambule, the ruler of Ngonyameni [the capital of the Chunu clan]:

*Isiphungaphunga esiphungwe ngabasekhaya*
*Saphungwa ngabasekwendeni*
*Ibamba elibambe uJama lamyekelela*
*Wahlengwa ngezimagodla*
*Labamba uMenzi lamyekelela*
*Wahlengwa ngezimagodla*
*Labamba uMalambule eNgonyameni*

A translation of this would be:

The driven one who is driven off by those of the family
And is driven off by those who have married.

The captor who seized Jama and then let him go
He was freed with oxen having long, winding horns.
He seized Menzi [Senzangakhona] and then let him go
When he was ransomed with oxen with long, bending horns.
He seized Malambule of Ngonyameni.

In contrast, there are only a few lines in Senzangakhona's own praises which refer to the Buthelezi. One set of these lines is:

> *Khona baza benkungu, Menzi ka Ndaba,*
> *Ngisho abakwaButhelezi siyakubadabula*

Even if they come in large numbers as thick as mist,
  Menzi son of Ndaba,
They, the Buthelezi, we shall split them up.

But this was more the expression of a hope than the record of such an achievement. The other lines from Senzangakhona's praises merely say

> *Uthi lwempundu lwakwaNomgabhi*
> *Obeluhlel' izikhova*
> *Obeluhlel' uPhungashe wakwaButhelezi*

Stake forming the gate-post of Nomgabhi
On which owls perched,
On which Phungashe of the Buthelezi sat.

Despite these encounters, mentioned or implied in the praises, relationships between the two clans do not seem to have been over-embittered at that time, for there were also competitions between them, in the form of *amajadu* which were competitive displays of dancing and dress. At that particular time, the Buthelezi seem to have won most of these competitions. However, this background of rivalry is important, because it helps to explain the punitive attitude King Shaka later showed to the Buthelezi ruler, Phungashe, whom he eventually destroyed. The earlier triumphs of the Buthelezi leaders led them to develop a very arrogant attitude towards the Zulu clan. So Phungashe referred to Senzangakhona as 'Dingiswayo's underling' and also as a 'nonentity who earned a living by selling tobacco and medicinal plants' [i.e. the plant known as *ikhathazo, Alepidea ama-*

*tybica*]. These gross insults were noted by the young Shaka, who never forgave Phungashe for his arrogance, and when Shaka came to power, Phungashe paid heavily for them.

However, there were other aspects to the relationships between the Buthelezi and the Zulu and to explain them I must discuss the composition of the Buthelezi family itself. It will help if I provide the genealogy as it is known to me (see Figure 1).

Like all ruling families throughout history, the Buthelezi clan had its share of internal divisions, even at the height of its power. Many of these divisions had their origins in clashes between the *indlunkulu* (the 'great house') and the *ikhohlwa* (the 'left-hand house'). The distinction between these houses was, of course, a common feature of the social organization of these tribes. However, many families have dispensed with the left-hand house, just because setting up both houses has almost invariably led to internecine clashes, resulting in the death of one or the other of the heirs of the two main houses. Each house usually has internal autonomy and each one wants to be independent of the other, which is where most of the trouble between them starts. Each one tries jealously to guard its independence and anything which it regards as an infringement of its rights or autonomy may be the *casus belli*. As can be seen from the genealogy, Ngwane, the ruler of the Buthelezi, had two such 'house' heirs: Phungashe, the *indlukulu* or general heir, and Mvulane, heir of the *ikhohlwa* house.

Mvulane, in his turn, had two sons, called Khoboyela and Nqengelele, by his wife, Nochugu Mbatha, who was the daughter of Dlekezele, father of the famous Manyosi. When Mvulane died, he was buried at Mcakweni in the present Babanango district. After his death, his younger son, Nqengelele, soon noticed that the general heir, Phungashe, had the habit of slaughtering cattle which belonged to the *ikhohlwa* house of which Khoboyela and Nqengelele were now the heirs. Nqengelele drew the attention of his elder brother to this fact and the gossip about their complaints soon reached the ears of Phungashe. He therefore planned to eliminate them, but the two brothers were alerted to the fact, so they rose early one day before dawn and disappeared. They fled northwards to be as far away as possible from the wrath of Phungashe. They were away for some years, but eventually wanted to return to the area of their birth. They realized, however, that to go to their own home would cost them their lives. They therefore decided to return not to the Buthelezi

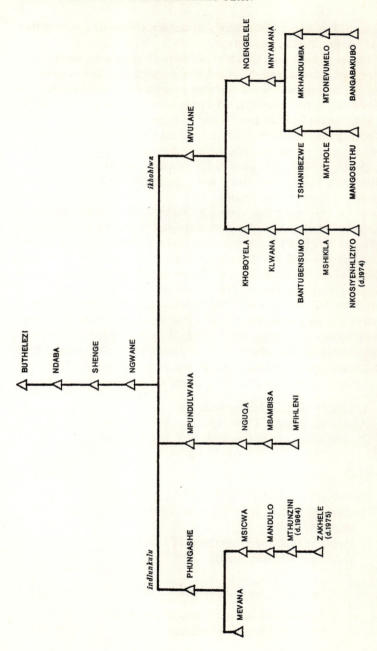

Figure 1. Genealogy of the Buthelezi Lineage

area itself, but to the Zulu ruler's place, KwaNobamba, where they would *khonza*, that is, seek refuge.

However, Khoboyela, the elder brother of Nqengelele, had become a very sickly man and Nqengelele struggled to help Khoboyela along on the journey, while carrying Khoboyela's son, Klwana, on his back. So before they arrived at Nobamba, Nqengelele left them in a gully or cave for shelter. When he himself reached Nobamba, it was during the early part of Senzangakhona's reign and he could not divulge that he was from the Buthelezi ruling family, because he feared that the Zulu, for their own safety, would not allow him to seek shelter with them, since they were then less powerful than the Buthelezi tribe, as we have seen.

Now, at this particular time, and much later, it was a matter of great pride that the Nguni had migrated from the north and to emphasize this fact they would say: *SingabeSuthu* – 'we are Suthu'. This concept is well brought out by James Stuart, one of the greatest authorities on the Zulu people, who recorded oral evidence early in this century from various Zulu informants. In his interview with Kambi ka Matshabana in 1903, Stuart records: 'owing to living north and so in the direction of or close to Basutos, the Zulus came to be spoken of as abeSutu' (Webb & Wright 1976:208). It was not an opprobrious term, but in fact gave prestige to the origins of the Zulu, as may be seen from its occurrence in praise-poems. Thus some ₄ines in King Senzangakhona's praises say:

> *UmSuthu wakwaMashwabada no Nsele*
> *Ngoba washwabada izindlubu zomfowabo namakhasi*
> *Ngoba washwabada izindlubu zika Mudli namakhasi*

meaning

> Suthu of the Mashwabada and Nsele people
> Because he took by force the groundnuts of his brother
>     and their shells
> Because he took the groundnuts of Mudli
>     together with their shells.

Again, in these lines from King Dingane's praises, he is referred to as

> *UmSuthu owadla izinyosi zamukela*
> *Abanye bezidla ziyazalela*

which may be translated,

> The Suthu who ate honeycombs and the bees left
> Other [Suthu] eat them [honeycombs] as they [bees] continue
> to make more honeycombs.

The point is further corroborated by other informants of James Stuart, including members of the Zulu royal house such as Ndlovu ka Thimuni, of the Zulu *ikhohlwa* house; by my mother, Princess Constance Sibilile Magogo ka Dinizulu, the full sister of King Maphumzana Nkayishane ka Dinuzulu and by several informants in KwaZulu who are in their seventies and eighties.

Consequently, when Nqengelele arrived at the Zulu royal court, his need to remain incognito meant that it suited him to say he came from the north, even to the point of saying, 'We are Suthu'. Thus began the legend that he was more Sotho than other Nguni. But the emphasis on coming back from the north was, in his case, a matter of life and death, since he dared not let his return become known to the Buthelezi ruler. The emphasis was repeated in the praises of his sons where references to them as Sotho are very liberally used. For example, Mnyamana, who was later Chief of the Buthelezi and Prime Minister, has the following line in his praises:

> *UmSuthu ongubozimawanguwangu*
> *Zinjengezabefundisi bephum' eSontweni*

> The Suthu who has multi-coloured garments
> Similar to those of Ministers coming out of Church.

Again, the praises of Maphovela, Mnyamana's *ikholhwa* heir, include the line

> *UmSuthu ongube zibomvu*
> The Suthu with red robes.

Such references can also be found in the praises of other sons of Mnyamana, but I have cited enough examples to show how they were carried on. If I have laboured the point that such references originated in Nqengelele's need to conceal his identity and were then prestigious rather than opprobrious, it is because Bryant has misled a number of people by not dealing with the issue in depth and because it has even been used for political ends in attempts to denigrate myself and my family amongst the Zulu.

Besides concealing his own identity, Nqengelele did not tell anyone that his brother Khoboyela was hidden in the gully, a short distance from the Nobamba royal residence. Of course, he realized that his brother would starve to death without his assistance, so he offered to go out to collect dried cow-dung [*amalongwe* – used as fuel] for Senzangakhona's mother, Mthaniya. In the basket [*iqoma*] he carried ostensibly for this purpose, he hid food for his brother and the child, Klwana. Nqengelele did this for quite a while, but his brother eventually died. He was therefore left with the task of bringing up his brother's son and heir, Klwana, for whom he ultimately had to *konza* [seek refuge] as well.

As time went on, Nqengelele was able to perform various valuable services for the Zulu. Because he had had to look after his sickly brother, he had acquired medical knowledge and skill. At that time tape-worms were an epidemic affliction at the Zulu royal court where it was then fashionable to eat *isichafuchafu*, a mixture of milk straight from the cow with ground, boiled mealies or corn. Nqengelele had been appalled to see that even those who milked the royal herds had to have small twigs next to them to remove the protruding worms while they milked. He therefore recommended that the milk should first be poured into gourds, so that it would curdle and turn sour, thus eliminating one cause of the tape-worm epidemic. He also used his knowledge of herbs to introduce the fern known in Zulu as *umkhoma-khoma* (*Nephrodium athamanticum*) as a remedy for tape-worm. Its efficacy is accepted even by modern medicine. Nqengelele is further credited with introducing the recipe for Zulu beer to the Zulu royal court. There is a story that the Zulu ruler heard people making a noise and when he enquired about it was told that Nqengelele was responsible, having used malted corn to make a product called *utshwala* which had made people feel happy and talkative.

Another domestic improvement came about after he found that some of Senzangakhona's wives and fiancées did not empty the night-pots at a distance from the huts when it was raining, but placed them in a row behind the huts. Nquengele disapproved of this neglect and remonstrated with them so that the pots were taken out of sight before the Zulu King came out in the mornings. It was not his function to see to such matters, but it was one of the useful hygienic measures he introduced into the Zulu royal court. It is also said that he violent-

ly rejected the advances made to him by some of the girls of the
royal enclosure [*isigodlo*], thus avoiding a frequent cause for the
downfall of men who served at the royal court.

It was not, however, only in the domestic sphere that he made
himself useful. He also showed great bravery in war and in one
skirmish he attacked his adversary with a short spear at close range,
using a basket [*iqoma* or *isixaxa*] as a shield, an episode echoed in the
line from his praises

'*Umkhono ovikel' isibili*

The arm which shielded the body

because he had no proper shield to ward off the blows.

Thus, as the fortunes of his own people, the Buthelezi *indlunkulu*
house at Mcakweni, waned, those of Nqengelele were in the ascen-
dant. There was, however, one episode which might have marred his
fortunes. This was the death of Senzangakhona's mother, Queen
Mthaniya, who was one of the Sibiya clan and whose father was
Zingelwayo. Nqengelele, as we have seen, performed domestic services for her from his arrival at the royal court and is said to have later
received the infant Shaka in his hut at night, when this future leader
of the Zulu was secretly brought there, so that Mthaniya could see
her grandchild without Senzangakhona knowing about these visits.
Some years later, Queen Mthaniya died under unusual circumstances
and while still in the prime of her life. It seems that since she was
still relatively young when her husband, Jama, died, she had to enter
an *ukungena* [leviratic] union with one of the other male members
of the Zulu royal lineage. However, the young king Senzangakhona
frowned on this arrangement, because he thought that it derogated
from his own status. His mother in turn took exception to her son's
attitude which she interpreted as impudence on his part. She therefore
began to prepare to eliminate him, saying to other women that since
the man with whom she had the *ukungena* union was also of royal
blood, the two of them were quite capable of producing another
King, just as she and Jama had produced the present King, Senzangakhona.

Her plans to eliminate him were discussed during the night between
the Queen and one of the women of the *isigaba* [servants' quarters].
Unfortunately for them, Funjana, another servant girl who shared
the hut with the Queen Mother, only pretended to be asleep, while

lying with her head covered by a skin blanket. Through the perfora-
tion left by the wound which killed the beast, she could observe the
two women plotting and overheard the plans they made to send a
pot of poisoned beer to Senzangakhona the following morning. This
would be possible because there had not yet been an open breach
between mother and son, so when Mthaniya brewed beer, she still
sent a special pot called *ukhamba lomhlolo* to her son, who, in return,
sent back beer from his own brewery. This time the girl who was to
carry the beer to Senzangakhona would pretend to be in a hurry to
go outside to relieve herself and then she would flee without taking
the traditional first sip of the beer she had brought, as is the Zulu
custom.

Funjana, the Queen's servant, got up before dawn and went to
the King's place where she demanded admittance to the King's hut.
Senzangakhona was surprised to recognize the voice of the girl demanding entry as that of Funjana, his mother's servant. She asked
to speak to him alone and then divulged all his mother's plans to
eliminate him.

When the beer arrived from the Queen Mother, Senzangakhona
made arrangements to have it emptied in another pot and had this
pot with the poisoned beer in it sent back to Mthaniya. The story
goes that when the girl arrived with the beer, the Queen Mother had
just returned from relieving herself. She did not even wait for the
traditional first sip to be taken, but took gulps of this beer brought
from her son, little imagining that it was the same poisoned beer
which she had sent to him. Her accomplice, the woman from the
servants' quarters, shared the same beer. Immediately they both felt
painful spasms in their stomachs. At first they were mystified, but
then they began to perspire; the Queen Mother asked what had
happened to Funjana who had not even emptied her night-pot that
day. She suspected that Funjana was the one who had given the plot
away, but by that stage her life was ebbing and both she and her
accomplice died soon afterwards.

At first there was consternation when Senzangakhona and people
at his place continued to sing and dance even after hearing the first
sounds of wailing from the direction of his mother's place. But then
the whole mystery of the Queen Mother's death was resolved. The
King's uncle with whom Mthaniya had been joined in the *ukungena*
union was also killed. It was assumed that he must have known
about her plans to poison the King which had been meant to ensure

that their relationship could flourish without any interference from Senzangakhona.

This episode initially had a traumatic effect on Nqengelele and others who, like him, had been closely associated with the Queen Mother. But their feelings calmed down when her plot against her son was revealed to them. Nqengelele's rise to prominence was therefore not damaged. Indeed, one feature of his earlier attachment to her service contributed after her death to a further advance in his career. That was his contacts with Shaka and Shaka's brothers when they were children and it was these contacts which explain the remark of one of Stuart's informants that Nqengelele was 'a man of the locality [who] was Tshaka's "father". Tshaka and his brothers grew up in his charge' (Webb & Wright 1976:190). Since, indeed, Shaka had met Nqengelele whenever he had visited his grandmother, Queen Mthaniya, who had sworn Nquengelele to secrecy about these visits, Shaka knew what a pillar of strength Nqengelele had been to his grandmother. He also learned then, or later, of Nqengelele's skill in herbs, of the reforms he introduced to the routines of the royal court and of his prowess in attacking an enemy *amahlange*, that is in close combat, instead of throwing spears from a distance. Shaka himself was, of course, also full of ideas on revolutionary methods of fighting which he eventually introduced in his own armies, so it is not surprising that he greatly admired Nqengelele.

Shaka was, moreover, fascinated by the similarities between Nqengelele's background and his own. Just as Nqengelele had fled from the royal court of the Buthelezi to escape death and had finally found shelter in another royal court, so, too, Shaka had had several brushes with death as a youth, before he finally found shelter at the royal court of the Mthethwa ruler, Dingiswayo. There he, too, had first done domestic chores, such as looking after Dingiswayo's cattle, before he distinguished himself by such feats as killing a leopard and the madman feared by the whole Mthethwa tribe.

A final bond between them was that they both had grievances against the Buthelezi ruler, Phungashe, who, as we have seen, had offended the Zulu clan with a barrage of insults which Shaka never forgot. The Buthelezi were therefore amongst the first tribes to experience the devastating warfare of Shaka. I must now turn to those experiences and their consequences.

## THE BUTHELEZI AT THE DAWN OF THE SHAKAN ERA

When Shaka came to declare war on the Buthelezi, Phungashe reacted as if it were going to be a picnic and let his contempt for the Zulu tribe surface again. He had no idea of what was in store for him and his army. Shaka led his own army (which was quite a new thing for a ruler to do) against the Buthelezi and, using the new methods, his regiments scattered the Buthelezi, killing them in large numbers, including women and children. The Zulu also seized the cattle as booty, which was then the custom.

Phungashe himself managed to escape and, since he was a friend of the ruler of the Ndwandwe tribe, Zwide, he fled to the Ndwandwe area across the Black Mfolozi river, in what is today the Nongoma district, named after Zwide's headquarters. Zwide could not understand how so great a chief as Phungashe could be defeated and driven away by someone he considered to be an upstart, a 'mere lad', as Phungashe himself confirmed. However, he must have been more astonished than sympathetic, because Phungashe was treacherously assassinated at the instigation of his supposed friend, Zwide.

It is not clear to me if Nqengelele actually participated in this battle against his own people. It seems that he may have done so, perhaps in a spirit of revenge, because there is in his praises the line:

> *Umkhonto ukubuya nobende*
> *Kwezika Phungashe wakwaButhelezi*

The spear which pierced, bringing back part of the spleen
Amongst those of Phungashe of the Buthelezi.

In any event, the death of Phungashe meant the end of the dynasty of the *indlunkulu* house of the Buthelezi and the ascendancy of the *ikhohlwa* house, now led by Nqengelele. It is true that Phungashe left a general heir called Msicwa, but it seems that he was soon eliminated. This happened after Mzilikazi Khumalo had been sent on a raiding expedition by King Shaka and then fled with the booty. Nzobo, of the Ntombela clan, was therefore instructed to raise a regiment from the remnants of the Buthelezi which was then sent to follow Mzilikazi. While all the able-bodied Buthelezi were away on this wild-goose chase after Mzilikazi, Shaka sent the same Nzobo Ntombela to murder Msicwa. He arrived at Msicwa's place hiding a spear under his *isiphuku* (skin blanket). Nzobo then pretended to be giving snuff to Msicwa who put out his hand to receive it, whereupon Nzobo killed him. There is actually some controversy about whether it was Msicwa or his brother, Mevana, who was thus killed by Nzobo. In Nzobo's own praises it is Mevana's name that is mentioned:

uDambuza mthabathe uvundisa izintaba zakwa Mashobana
uMevana onjengowakwa Buthelezi

Dambuza, take him [uMevana?] and enrich the hills of Mashobana uMevana who is like one of the Buthelezi.

In any case the dominion of the *indlunkulu* house was ended.

## THE BUTHELEZI AT THE ESTABLISHMENT OF THE ZULU KINGDOM

After Shaka had defeated Phungashe and succeeded to the Zulu kingship, he proceeded to defeat many other tribes which he subsequently merged into his own army, so that he grew ever more powerful. However, he had not yet faced Zwide, the Ndwandwe ruler who had a powerful army. By this stage, Nqengelele had become Shaka's closest adviser on military matters, as well as others. He therefore played a very important part in the eventual battle between the armies of Shaka and Zwide. In particular, he acted as an intelligence agent before the battle began. He discovered that one of the secrets of the previous invincibility of Zwide's army was that it was always well fed and ate a lot of meat. Nqengelele passed on this information to Shaka and advised him to destroy food supplies to weaken Zwide's army in any final battle.

Further, Nqengelele went to see Zwide's military commander, Noju, and assured him that the Ndwandwe would easily defeat Shaka's army. At the same time, he advised Noju that the Ndwandwe army should all shave their heads so that they could easily distinguish each other from the enemy in the forthcoming battle. The real intention of this advice was just the opposite, to ensure that Shaka's army could easily identify the Ndwandwe. Noju fell for this deception.

Nqengelele's plan was put into operation and Shaka ordered that food should be destroyed all the way to Mhlatuze to ensure that the

Ndwandwe army would starve. In the actual battle, Shaka's army was easily able to recognize the members of the Ndwandwe army by their shaven heads. Nqengelele was himself present at both the Mhlatuze encounter, where he distinguished himself, and at the battle of Gqokli Hill. In this latter battle, Nqengelele's eldest son, Somalume, was one of the most outstanding warriors. Somalume was such a strong and brave young man that the animal hides for his shields were not softened or treated at all, but merely dried out and the shields cut from them straight away. So great was his prowess as a warrior that even Shaka was uneasy about him.

Nqengelele's own status was enhanced by his part in the defeat of the mighty Zwide to the point where one of Stuart's informants could comment that 'Nqengelele was a dominant figure who commanded the attention of the whole nation: when he spoke no one else would speak, only the king would speak' (Webb & Wright 1976:12). In recognition of Nqengelele's services, Shaka gave him a stretch of land from what is now Mahlabatini district through Vryheid, Louwsburg and right across the Phongola river into what is today the Piet Retief district in the Transvaal. In this area there were situated the military kraals of Mbelebeleni, Ebaqulusini, Impangiso, Uguqu, Ezembeni, Ozweleni. Nqengelele was also given a number of girls from the *isigodlo* to marry as wives and a number of cattle.

These gifts were, however, not without unfortunate consequences. His son, Somalume, was unwilling merely to bask in the sunshine of Nqengelele's fame. Since Somalume had distinguished himself in battle in his own right, he demanded land for himself as a reward. This demand confirmed Shaka's fears about what Somalume might eventually do. He therefore ordered Somalume to be killed for this act of defiance and insubordination. Even the people who were sent to kill him were scared to do so and only did it when Somalume himself threw away his shield and spears and beckoned them to kill him.

Despite this episode, the position accorded to Nqengelele by Shaka marked the supersession of the senior house of the Buthelezi by a junior house, just as Zulu, a junior son of Malandela, had earlier superseded Qwabe who was the senior son and general heir in the Zulu clan. Members of the Buthelezi now regrouped around Nqengelele, though it was not until the reign of Mathole in the 1920s that the *indlunkulu* heir, Mthunzini, son of Mandulo son of Msicwa, moved from Nquthu to Mahlabatini. He there became one of the Councillors of Chief Buthelezi and also served under me [Mangosuthu in the genealogy] before he died in 1964. At the time when Mthunzini moved to the Buthelezi area, there were even rumours that he had come to take over. However, these rumours were a source of amusement to Mathole, since the Buthelezi area which he had inherited was not where the Buthelezi originated but was, as we have seen, awarded to Nqengelele for the services he had rendered.

In his success, Nqengelele did not forget his nephew, Klwana, whom he had brought up, and put him in charge of one portion of this very wide area known as Ngotshe, where Klwana ruled a section of the Buthelezi and built himself a place called Embongom-bongweni. Nqengelele's acknowledgement of Klwana was to lead to further complications amongst the Buthelezi later which I describe below.

In the meantime, Nqengelele had further chances to show his wisdom. A major one came when Shaka's mother, Queen Nandi, died. It is well known that on her death Shaka almost became mentally unbalanced and ordered the death of many of his subjects. One reason for killing some of them was because they wailed a traditional exclamation of grief:

*Maye  Babo*
*Yebuya Mama*

Alas,  father
Alas, mother.

Shaka argued that these laments were for their own parents and not for his mother's death. When Nqengelele heard of this interpretation, he sent messengers along all the routes leading to Nandi's place. He told them to advise people not to wail with those words, but to use instead

*Maye ngonina we Nkosi*

Alas, the loss of the King's mother.

Since those who did not shed tears were also killed, Nqengelele also sent messengers everywhere to advise people that they should sprinkle snuff into their eyes, so that tears would flow and they would escape being put to death for not weeping. In addition to Gala ka Nodade of the Biyela clan who asked the King to be firm enough to stop the

killings, Nqengelele also implored the King to allow people to cultivate their land, or the nation would perish. Thus Nqengelele became

> *Inyoni ka Makhala*
> *Eyakhalela uZulu*
> *Nyakana uZulu engasenakulima kithi kwaBulawayo*
> *Eseyakulima ngensimb' edl' amadoda*

of which a free translation is

> The bird that cried out
> It cried out for the Zulu
> During the year Zulu could not cultivate at Bulawayo
> Except with the iron [spear] that eats men.

Nqengelele lived to a great age and was able to build several
homesteads for himself in addition to Nsukaze which Shaka built for
him and which was where Nqengelele eventually died, when it was
situated a few miles north of the White Mfolozi. He was buried near
the Ndlovana stream in Mahlabatini. His other kraals included
Embekamuzi, Entendeka, Emhlabaneni, and Ezidwadweni.

Besides Somalume, he had numerous other sons: Mnyamana [the
only one shown on the genealogy], Somfongoza [the full brother of
Mnyamana], Mbangambi, Santinge, Ngoza, Nobiya, Majiya,
Nkanyana, Mziyikazi, Mqayikane, Zidunge, Faku, Qhwadise,
Sonkeshana, Ziyankomo, Mbozisa, Mthutheni and Mzingaye.

Somfongoza died during Nqengelele's lifetime, as did Mqayikane.
This left, as Nqengelele's heir, Mnyamana, who was still a fairly
young man when Nqengelele died. Consequently, Klwana, the son
of Khoboyela and himself a great warrior, looked after his cousin,
Mnyamana, and took charge of the whole area. It soon became
obvious that Klwana in fact wanted to inherit Nqengelele's estates
and area, on the grounds that his father, Khoboyela, had been older
than Nqengelele. He therefore devised a plan to kill Mnyamana
which involved going to a precipice and sending for Mnyamana to
come there. However, his intention was plain to Mnyamana who
immediately fled. He stopped to sleep at the home of Dikana Mbatha,
since the Mbatha were the group from which Nqengelele's mother,
Mochugu, came. Dikana there slaughtered a young ox for Mnyamana
who was in a hurry to report Klwana's attempt on his life to Mpande
(who was by then King) at Nodwengu.

Since Klwana had been a distinguished warrior under Shaka, Dingane and Mpande, the King ordered Klwana to be killed only after he had himself confirmed what had been reported to him. He obtained confirmation in a typically unaggressive way that was part of his nature. He sent for Klwana and questioned him while Mnyamana was hidden at the back of the hut under some blankets. Mpande asked Klwana if Nqengelele had left no heir so that Klwana was now the sole heir. When Klwana said that was so, he himself had displayed his ambitions and confirmed Mnyamana's story of the attempt to kill him. It was a great shock to Klwana, when the blankets were removed and Mnyamana's presence was revealed. Since Klwana had convicted himself, Mpande ordered that he be put to death. Some lines in Mpande's praises that refer to Klwana are

*Isihlahla somtshungu sombhelebhele*
*Sigawulwe wuKlwana waseMbongombongweni*

meaning literally

The tree of the Capsicum species
Which was chopped down by Klwana of Mbongombongweni.

These species of tree have bitter fruits, so the implication of the lines is that Klwana provoked Mpande [represented as a tree] to the extent that he ordered the killing of Klwana.

The whole episode had important consequences for the later history of the Buthelezi in that further acts of vengeance between the two 'houses' of Khoboyela and Nqengelele flowed from it. That, however, is one of the themes which I hope to take up on another occasion. For the time being, I shall leave my account of the Buthelezi at this point, where Mnyamana was just beginning his own distinguished career in succession to his father, Nqengelele, who had raised himself by his own ability and energy to a position that was important not only for the Buthelezi but for the Zulu nation as a whole.

## REFERENCES

WEBB, C. DE B. & WRIGHT, J. B. (eds.) 1976 – *The James Stuart Archive, Vol. I.* Pietermaritzburg: Univ. of Natal Press.

# HOUSEHOLD COMPOSITION AND MARRIAGE IN A WITWATERSRAND AFRICAN TOWNSHIP

*Max Marwick*

## INTRODUCTION

During the first half of 1961 I directed a social survey of nearly 500 households in one of the two principal ethnic divisions of a Witwatersrand African Township. My objective was to establish the main features of a population, whose social characteristics were largely unknown, so that subsequent, more intensive research could be based on quota samples designed to approximate the initial sample and thus provide a reasonably good representation of the universe. However, my decision to become a voluntary exile from South Africa led to the abandonment of plans for the later phases of the project. In 1967 I prepared a fairly comprehensive report on the survey for my main sponsors[1], but I have not hitherto published any of its results because, firstly, my anthropological (as opposed to sociological) biases make me sceptical about 'door-knocking' sociography unaccompanied by more intensive investigation, and, secondly, my distance from the research field has raised several problems.

Two considerations now reduce my diffidence about publication. First, Professor A. A. Dubb of the University of the Witwatersrand has expressed an interest in taking over my research material and supplementing it with follow-up studies in the Township where it was originally gathered. Secondly, I am glad of the opportunity to join with colleagues in paying tribute to Emeritus Professor Eileen Krige and, inseparably, to the memory of the other partner in the well known and widely respected Krige team; for there are few people to whom I am as indebted as I am to Eileen and the late Jack Krige, whose encouragement and help at critical stages in my career were of great benefit and whose insistence on the highest standards of scholarship and teaching have been inspirational to all who have had the good fortune to work with either or both of them.

Although the survey represents the first part of an uncompleted project, some useful information can be extracted from its results in regard to the nature of the social changes that occur when rural subsistence cultivators and herdsmen move to the urban areas and become involved in a modern industrial system. In what follows I shall focus attention on changes that the survey reveals in the spheres of domestic organization and marriage.

The Township referred to in this paper had been established (by one of the Reef municipalities) some twelve years before the 1961 survey. It was about 30 km by a relatively traffic-free route from my home in Johannesburg. All but its three oldest sections had been subject to the Government's policy of ethnic grouping, and I was able to devote my attention to those parts of it which, nominally at least, were classified as Nguni. This ethnic division, which includes such designations as Bhaca, Mpondo and Xhosa (Cape Nguni), Zulu (Natal Nguni) and Swazi, is more familiar to a Natal-born person such as myself, and is a section of the South African population about whose traditional ways of life there are good ethnographic accounts.

Given the survey's aim at the time, unstratified random sampling seemed to be the most appropriate procedure; and a fairly comprehensive interview schedule, the most appropriate research instrument. The relevant sections of an up-to-date Voters' Roll for the Township's Advisory Board elections provided the sampling frame from which, by using tables of random numbers, my research assistants[2] and I drew 500 Nguni households together with a small reserve list from which further households could be drawn as substitutes for those in the original sample whose members, after repeated attempts, could not be contacted or were not willing to be interviewed.

The interview schedule[3] made provision for a fairly conventional investigation of households and of persons within them aged 15 and over. The total population of the sample households was just under 2 200; and, of these, 586 males and 580 females were aged 15 and over.

Thanks to the reputation among Township residents of the University of the Witwatersrand, of which I was a member at the time, the rapport established by the interviewers (most of whom were teachers in Township schools) and the enthusiasm and skill of my research assistants, the response on the part of the residents was excellent; and, with comparatively little resort to our supplementary sample list, we were able to obtain returns for 492 households, having aimed at 500. This represented a sampling fraction of about one-eighth.

Although, as mentioned above, little was known in advance about the population from which the sample was drawn, there were two respects in which it could be checked against its universe. It was found, first, to be distributed in the named sections of the Township in proportions similar to their respective populations; secondly, it was found to yield a mean of persons per household not inexplicably different from the one computed for the Township as a whole by the Township Manager's Office.

During the long-drawn-out process of tabulation, the data were coded and transferred at first to punched cards intended for use with a card-sorting machine; then, as the possibility of computer tabulation presented itself, they were transferred to a fresh deck of cards, involving a revised code more appropriate to this kind of treatment.[4] These changes sometimes led to the loss – in the cardboard salad produced by a malfunctioning sorter – of some of the household records, since it was occasionally impossible to re-establish the link between a destroyed card and the schedule from which it had been punched. One outcome of these accidents is that, in the tables included below, the total number of households varies between 492 and 486, according to the stage of the research at which the table concerned was drawn up.

CHARACTERISTICS OF TOWNSHIP HOUSEHOLDS

As Tables 1 and 2 show, there proved to be some statistical justification for referring to households in the sample as 'Nguni'; for all but 16 per cent of the household heads identified themselves as of Nguni ethnic origin, and, in all but 10 per cent of households, the first language returned belonged to this classification. There was an interesting tendency for Natal Nguni (Zulu) to be returned as the home language, not only of households with heads of this ethnic category, but also of some of those whose heads belonged ethnically to the other two divisions of the Nguni (i.e. Cape Nguni and Swazi) and to non-Nguni classifications. Thus in Table 2 there is a marked coincidence of ethnic origin and home language. This statistical association is reflected in high frequencies in the diagonal cells and in an overall $x^2$ of 649,293 (p < 0,001; C = 0,74)[5]. However, of the 129 cases in cells not on the diagonal, only 12 are not in the column representing Natal Nguni as a home language. This tendency suggests a shift towards using the language of the majority, and it may also be related to the fact that Swazi is often written in Zulu orthography.

TABLE 1

COMPARISON OF ETHNIC CLASSIFICATION OF HOUSEHOLDS BY
HEAD'S ORIGIN AND BY FIRST HOME LANGUAGE REPORTED

| Ethnic Classification | Origin of Head | | Home Language | | Difference |
|---|---|---|---|---|---|
| | f | % | f | % | % |
| Natal Nguni | 213 | 43,83 | 320 | 65,84 | +22,01*** |
| Cape Nguni | 105 | 21,60 | 92 | 18,93 | − 2,67 |
| Swazi | 88 | 18,11 | 24 | 4,92 | −13,19*** |
| Non-Nguni | 80 | 16,46 | 50 | 10,29 | − 6,17*** |
| | 486 | 100,00 | 486 | 100,00 | 0,0 |

*** p < 0,001

TABLE 2

ETHNIC ORIGIN OF HEAD AND FIRST HOME LANGUAGE

| Ethnic Origin of Head | First Home Language | | | | Total |
|---|---|---|---|---|---|
| | Natal Nguni | Cape Nguni | Swazi | Non-Nguni | |
| Natal Nguni | 203 | 1 | 2 | 7 | 213 |
| Cape Nguni | 14 | 90 | 1 | 0 | 105 |
| Swazi | 67 | 0 | 21 | 0 | 88 |
| Non-Nguni | 36 | 1 | 0 | 43 | 80 |
| | 320 | 92 | 24 | 50 | 486 |

$x^2$ = 649,293; p < 0,001; C = 0,76

There appear to be two reasons why the Nguni sections of the Township were not 'ethnically pure' in the sense that 16 per cent of the
households were not of this extraction. First, the Township's two
main ethnic divisions, Nguni and Sotho, were large, and people
belonging to smaller ethnic divisions, e.g. Venda, for whom no

specific provision had been made, were sometimes distributed among them. Secondly, as Table 3 shows, there were some 'mixed marriages' in which the ethnic origin of the household head differed from that of his spouse; and in some cases her language may have been adopted as the home language. As Table 3 indicates, marriages were overwhelmingly between persons of the same ethnic origin.

TABLE 3

ETHNIC ORIGIN OF HOUSEHOLD HEAD BY THAT OF HIS SPOUSE

| Ethnic Origin of Spouse | Ethnic Origin of Head | | | | Total |
|---|---|---|---|---|---|
| | Natal Nguni | Cape Nguni | Swazi | Non-Nguni | |
| Natal Nguni | 101 | 10 | 18 | 12 | 141 |
| Cape Nguni | 13 | 39 | 6 | 7 | 65 |
| Swazi | 23 | 9 | 28 | 7 | 67 |
| Non-Nguni | 24 | 20 | 11 | 38 | 93 |
| No current marriage and no information | 52 | 27 | 25 | 16 | 120 |
| | 213 | 105 | 88 | 80 | 486 |

$x^2 = 172,617$; $p < 0,001$; $C = 0,51$

Since marriage was one of the normal qualifications for being housed in the Township, it is not surprising to discover that, as Table 4 shows, a very high proportion of household heads fell into this category of conjugal status. Of the 48 female household heads, nearly two-thirds were widowed and a quarter were not currently married for some other reason.

If it is borne in mind that the Nguni traditionally lived in homestead units occupied by extended families defined by patrilineal descent, patrivirilocal residence and polygyny (Hunter 1936:15ff.; Krige 1936:39ff.; Hoernlé 1937:74–76, 82–83; Kuper 1947:36ff.; Hammond-Tooke 1962:35ff.), the social composition of Township Nguni households affords striking evidence of at least their outward change, though it does not necessarily imply that the people concerned have changed their values so much as come to terms with the inescapable conditions of urban life.

TABLE 4

CONJUGAL STATUS OF HOUSEHOLD HEADS

| Conjugal Status | Male Heads | Female Heads | Total |
|---|---|---|---|
| Married* | 398 | 6 | 404 |
| Widowed | 14 | 30 | 44 |
| Not currently married† | 30 | 12 | 42 |
| | 442 | 48 | 490 |

$x^2 = 218,050$; p < 0,001

*Includes 17 *de facto* married.

†Includes never married, divorced, separated and deserted.

Since a careful record had been made of the precise relationship of every member of each household to its head, it was possible to draw genealogies which could be used for classifying households (by hand rather than by computer) according to their social composition. The broad categories into which they fell are shown in the upper half of Table 5. In the lower section of this table, the percentage distribution of Township households in categories of social composition is compared with percentages derived from Hammond-Tooke's survey of 29 homesteads among the Bhaca, with those derived from the 1951 British census and with those found in a sample of 344 households in 'New Town', Victoria. 'New Town' is an outer suburb of the Melbourne Metropolitan Area, which, like the Township, was a new housing estate, about twelve years old when studied, and occupied predominantly by manual workers and their families. In this table, evidence of at least external change is to be found in the fact that the first four categories in the Township, accounting for 71 per cent of households, constitute kinds of social composition one would expect to encounter among any modern group of urban dwellers. Even the remaining categories, 'extended family' and 'others' are to be found in modern populations elsewhere, though not in as high proportions as they occur in the Township. Although Hammond-Tooke's sample is too small for safe generalization, it is interesting to note how the Township Nguni sample falls between the position of the rural Bhaca (who have changed considerably from the traditional Nguni system, particularly in their shift away from polygyny) and some of the modern populations represented.

TABLE 5

SOCIAL COMPOSITION OF HOUSEHOLDS TOGETHER WITH
COMPARABLE DISTRIBUTIONS FROM SELECTED STUDIES

| Social Composition | Township Sample, 1961 | | | % |
| | Households with | | Total | |
| | Male Heads | Female Heads | | |
|---|---|---|---|---|
| Persons living alone | 37 | 5 | 42 | 8,54 |
| Couple without children | 46 | 0 | 46 | 9,35 |
| Single parent and child(ren) | 13 | 15 | 28 | 5,69 |
| Couple with child(ren) | 234 | 0 | 234 | 47,56 |
| Extended family | 101 | 30 | 131 | 26,63 |
| Others* | 11 | 0 | 11 | 2,24 |
| | 442 | 50 | 492 | 100,00 |

| Social Composition | For Comparison | | | |
| | Township 1961 (N = 492) | Bhaca 1949? (N = 29) | 'New Town' 1966 (N = 344) | Britain 1951 (N = 14,5 mill.) |
|---|---|---|---|---|
| Persons living alone | 8% | 0% | 0% | 10% |
| Couple without children | 9% | 4% | 3% | 22% |
| Single parent and child(ren) | 6% | 14% | 4% | 48% |
| Couple with child(ren) | 48% | 41% | 86% | |
| Extended family | 27% | 41% | 5% | 20% |
| Others | 2% | 0% | 2% | |
| | 100% | 100% | 100% | 100% |

*This category in the Township was made up of polygynous households (2), households containing unrelated persons (2), the head and his sibling(s) only (3), and the head and his nephew, cousin or affine only (4).

*Sources:*
Bhaca: Hammond-Tooke, 1962:38–9.
Britain: *Britain: An Official Handbook*, 1964, 21.
'New Town', Victoria, Australia: Sample survey conducted by the Department of Anthropology and Sociology, Monash University; figures kindly extracted by Mrs. L. Bryson and Miss. I. Speed.

The 'extended family' category in the Township sample, comprising 131 households, is worth further analysis. Table 6 summarizes the types of relationships to the head that may be regarded as converting a household in one of the first four categories of Table 5 into what is here referred to as an 'extended family'. It should be noted that Table 6 summarizes relationships and not households, and that its totals can therefore be reconciled with the entries in the fifth row of the upper section of Table 5 only if subtractions are made in respect of the 21 households in which there were two extending relationships and the three in which there were three.

Extending relationships may be lineal, as when a parent of the head or of his wife is present or when children of one or more of the head's children are included; or they may be collateral, as when the household includes relatives who are linked to the head through one of his or his wife's siblings or one of the siblings of one of their lineal ancestors. Lineal extensions of both types, ascendent and descendent, are not unknown in the households of modern societies, and collateral extensions are also found. A closer examination of Township households occupied by extended families shows, however, two special features. The first, an emphasis on relationships through males, is in accord with traditional patriliny. The second, a high frequency of illegitimacy, while representing a shift away from tradition, is a trend common in recently uprooted populations (see, for instance, Smith 1956:142–3, 221, 226–8). These two features, one in line with tradition and one departing from it, can exist side by side in the same series of households. This pattern is reflected in Table 7, the first contingency table derived from Table 6, where there is an extremely significant[6] association between extension through males in the head's generation and through females in his children's generation ($x^2 = 37,420$; p < 0,001).

TABLE 6

KINDS OF EXTENDING RELATIONSHIPS IN THE 131 HOUSEHOLDS
COMPRISING EXTENDED FAMILIES

| Relationship to Head | Number | ANALYSIS | | | |
|---|---|---|---|---|---|
| | | Through a Male* | Through a Female° | All Links Legitimate | Some Links Illegitimate |
| *Lineal:* | | | | | |
| Father | 3 | 3 | | 3 | |
| Mother or mother's mother | 17 | 17 | | 17 | |
| Wife's mother or mother's mother | 2 | | 2 | 2 | |
| Son's child(ren): | | | | | |
| legitimate | 9 | 9 | | 9 | |
| illegitimate | 5 | 5 | | | 5 |
| Daughter's child(ren): | | | | | |
| legitimate | 10 | | 10 | 10 | |
| illegitimate | 43 | | 43 | | 43 |
| | | | | | |
| *Collateral:* | | | | | |
| Patrilateral†: | | | | | |
| legitimate | 26 | 26 | | 26 | |
| illegitimate | 19 | 19 | | | 19 |
| Matrilateral†: | | | | | |
| legitimate | 14 | | 14 | 14 | |
| illegitimate | 10 | | 10 | | 10 |
| | 158 | 79 | 79 | 81 | 77 |
| | | | | | |
| Correction for counting 2 relationships in 21 households and 3 in 3: Subtract | 27 | | | | |
| Households comprising extended families: reconciled with Table 5 | 131 | | | | |

*Through a male head, or his son.

°Through a female head or the wife of a male head, or his daughter.

†Patrilateral and matrilateral are here used with the Head's children as the point of reference, i.e. patrilateralr elatives include the cognates of a male head, and matrilateral relatives include the cognates of the wife of a male head or the cognates of a female head.

TABLE 7

MODE OF EXTENSION OF 158 RELATIONSHIPS IN 131 EXTENDED
FAMILIES BY GENERATION

| Generation involved | Extending Relationship | | Total |
| --- | --- | --- | --- |
| | Through Male | Through Female | |
| Head's | 65 | 26 | 91 |
| Children's | 14 | 53 | 67 |
| | — | — | — |
| | 79 | 79 | 158 |
| | — | — | — |

$x^2 = 37,420; p < 0,001$

The tendency for extension to be through females in the junior generation is attributable to the greater frequency with which the illegitimate children of daughters rather than of sons are included in the household (see Table 8, where $x^2 = 9,121; 0,01 > p > 0,001$).

TABLE 8

LEGITIMACY AND ILLEGITIMACY OF HEAD'S SONS' AND
DAUGHTERS' CHILDREN RESIDING IN HIS HOUSEHOLD

| Head's | Legitimate | Illegitimate | Total |
| --- | --- | --- | --- |
| Sons' children | 9 | 5 | 14 |
| Daughters' children | 10 | 43 | 53 |
| | — | — | — |
| | 19 | 48 | 67 |
| | — | — | — |

$x^2 = 9,121; 0,01 > p > 0,001$

These figures are in line with the fact that in certain households there seems to be developing the type of social composition noted particularly among Negro families of the Caribbean area (see, for instance, Smith 1956: loc. cit.). In other words, there seems to be a shift from the traditional Nguni patrilineal descent and patrilateral emphasis to a form of domestic organization in which the mother-child relationship, of fundamental importance in any society (even in traditional Nguni society where a man's mother's rank was, in a polygynous family, a secondary determinant of his status), is thrown into sharp relief when, owing to a breakdown in tradition, the father's role becomes peripheral to the domestic group. However, only a small minority of households in our sample show this tendency, since they make up but a fraction of the 27 per cent of households occupied by extended families (see Table 5, upper section, fifth row).

If we give due attention to the 71 per cent of Township households approximating types commonly found in modern communities (see table 5, lower section, first four rows), the essentially modern character of Township household composition becomes clear. The changes revealed by the survey and by comparative reading of Nguni ethnography may be summarized by saying that the shift in the social composition of the domestic group has been from an extended family defined by patrilineal descent, patrivirilocal residence and polygyny to complete and incomplete forms of the nuclear family, along with a somewhat larger than normal proportion of extended families, among a few of which traditional principles of social organization have been superseded by the more elemental link between mother and child. Examples of household genealogies are reproduced in Figure 1.

CHANGING MARRIAGE PATTERNS

The social homogeneity characteristic of marriage partners found in most societies (and already noted in our sample in respect of ethnic origin – see above, Table 3) is to be found in the Township. Table 9 shows that, even allowing for the effects of the intervening factor of age, there is, between the parents of both males and females of 15 years and over, in our sample, considerable homogeneity in respect of occupational and educational status; and that, between persons of both sexes in the sample and their spouses, there is homogeneity in regard to stabilization in urban residence. In brief, it might be cautiously concluded that, in the Township, marital homogeneity is being expressed in modern forms.

Other modern influences are to be detected in a comparison of the current marriages of older and of younger members of the sample.

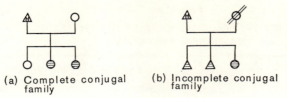

(a) Complete conjugal family

(b) Incomplete conjugal family

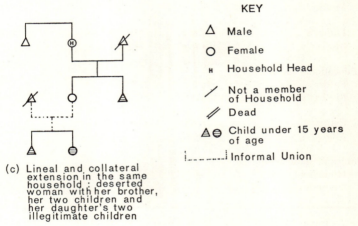

KEY

△ Male

○ Female

H Household Head

/ Not a member of Household

// Dead

△⊖ Child under 15 years of age

⌐......⌐ Informal Union

(c) Lineal and collateral extension in the same household : deserted woman with her brother, her two children and her daughter's two illegitimate children

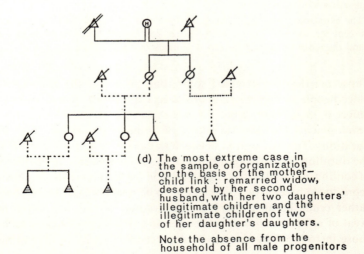

(d) The most extreme case in the sample of organization on the basis of the mother–child link : remarried widow, deserted by her second husband, with her two daughters' illegitimate children and the illegitimate children of two of her daughter's daughters.

Note the absence from the household of all male progenitors

Figure 1.  Some Examples of Household Social Composition in Township

TABLE 9

VARIABLES REFLECTING THE POSSIBLE HOMOGENEITY OF
MARRIAGE PARTNERS

| Variable | Sex of Ego | Coefficient of Contingency* | |
|---|---|---|---|
| | | With Age† | Between Marriage Partners |
| Occupational status: | | | |
| Father's | Male | −0,37 ⎫ | +0,63 |
| Mother's | Male | −0,41 ⎭ | |
| Father's | Female | −0,37 ⎫ | +0,63 |
| Mother's | Female | −0,38 ⎭ | |
| Educational status: | | | |
| Father's | Male | −0,33 ⎫ | +0,58 |
| Mother's | Male | −0,36 ⎭ | |
| Father's | Female | −0,29 ⎫ | +0,44 |
| Mother's | Female | −0,33 ⎭ | |
| Index of stabilization: | | | |
| Household head's ⎫ | | −0,38 | +0,42 |
| His spouse's ⎭ | | | |

*See footnote 5. (Also, + = same direction of association; − = opposite direction of association.)

† The association with age is that for Ego's age for all entries in this column except the last which is the coefficient of contingency between the head's age and the mean of his and his spouse's index of stabilization.

Those marriages contracted some time back (i.e. the marriages of older people or the marriages of longer duration) were found to be different in several respects from those representing more recent developments (i.e. the marriages of younger people or of shorter duration). The association between the age of a married person and the duration of his/her current marriage was reflected in coefficients of contingency of 0,50 for males and 0,54 for females (from a table not reproduced here). The comparisons to be made below are, of course, rather crude because they take no account of the differential survival of either persons or marriages and thus neglect biases such as those introduced by the inevitable over-representation among marriages of longer duration of those with characteristics conducive to their survival. In the analysis that follows, the tables on which our tentative conclusions will be based will be those for the current marriages of males aged 15 and over in our sample. Corresponding tables for females gave very similar results – for the reason that, by and large, they referred to the same set of marriages.

Four hundred and nine, or 70 per cent, of males aged 15 and over reported being currently married, and the corresponding figure for females was 377, or 65 per cent. The analysis did not take into account previously existing marriages, in which 67 men (11 per cent) and 85 women (15 per cent) reported having been involved at least once. Being small in number, the previous marriages, had they been included, would have only slightly increased the reliability of the results in some respects but would have complicated the analysis in others.

The more obvious changes revealed by comparing marriages of longer and shorter duration had to do with the custom of bride-wealth (*lobolo*). An urban-dwelling population cannot be expected to keep large herds of cattle from which to make marriage payments; and money has come to be substituted for them. This is a well-known trend that has affected Africans, even some of them in rural areas, for some generations. Perhaps the surprising feature about Table 10, which illustrates this trend, is the fact that even recently contracted

TABLE 10

FORM TAKEN BY LOBOLO IN MEN'S MARRIAGES ACCORDING TO THEIR DURATION

| Form of Lobolo | Duration of Marriage | | | |
| --- | --- | --- | --- | --- |
| | 0–9 years | 10–19 years | 20+ years | Total |
| Involving cattle | 54 | 71 | 59 | 184 |
| Not involving cattle (usually involving money) | 124 | 61 | 10 | 195 |
| Unknown (possibly *de facto* marriage) | 22 | 7 | 1 | 30 |
| | 200 | 139 | 70 | 409 |

$x^2 = 60,004$; p $< 0,001$; C $= 0,36$

marriages still include about a quarter which have been formalized by the transfer of cattle rather than of money. The table as a whole, however, shows clearly that the trend has been for cattle to be displaced by money as the currency of *lobolo*.

Since, as Mrs Brandel-Syrier has suggested (1958), *lobolo* has acquired new functions in urban areas, it is not surprising to find that this custom, previously one of the fundamental features of a markedly patrilineal, cattle-keeping people, is still observed – or reported to be observed – by almost all Nguni residents in the sample. Our data suggests that there are only two senses in which this custom may have declined. Firstly, there is a statistically reliable decline over the years (of decreasing duration of marriage) in the value of *lobolo* (see Table 11). Secondly, as the last row of Table 10 suggests (though not very reliably, given the small row total), there is probably an increase in the proportion of *de facto* marriages in which formalities of any kind are dispensed with. The second of these trends is well known among urban Africans, and it is conceivable that, for obvious reasons, it is more marked than our data show.

The first of these trends, a decline in the value of *lobolo*, is based on safer evidence which merits closer scrutiny. Table 11 shows the association between duration of marriage and the value of *lobolo* to be significant at the level of $p < 0,001$ and positive ($x^2 = 52,426$; $C = 0,34$) which means that the longer-existing marriages were contracted with larger amounts of *lobolo* than the more recently contracted ones. It should be explained that comparisons between the amounts of *lobolo* in cattle and in money were made possible by converting money payments into the equivalent of beasts, using the conventional ceremonial value of R20 per beast. Had the market value been used, the decline in the amount of *lobolo* would have been even more striking. This adjustment is, of course, a questionable one because of problems relating to converting from one sphere of exchange in a multi-centric economy to another (see Bohannan 1963:248–65). However, even if an estimate based on the market value of cattle in terms of real income had been used, it seems likely that the same conclusion would have been reached, i.e. that there has been, not an increase in the value of *lobolo* as several writers have suggested (see, for instance, Brandel 1958:35; Longmore 1959: 66; Mathewson 1959:75), but a decline.

TABLE 11

VALUE OF LOBOLO IN MEN'S MARRIAGES ACCORDING TO THEIR
DURATION

| Amount of Lobolo in Beasts (1 beast taken as equal to R20) | Duration of Marriage | | | Total |
|---|---|---|---|---|
| | 0–9 years | 10–19 years | 20+ years | |
| Less than 10 | 123 | 79 | 17 | 219 |
| More than 10 | 54 | 53 | 52 | 159 |
| Unknown | 23 | 7 | 1 | 31 |
| | 200 | 139 | 70 | 409 |

$x^2 = 52,426$; $p < 0,001$; $C = 0,34$

Such a decline was confirmed by another of the computer tables (not
reproduced here) in which, again using the ceremonial value, the
amount of *lobolo* was cast against whether it took the form of cattle
or money; and a particularly strong association emerged between
larger amounts and the *lobolo* being paid in cattle, and correspondingly, between smaller amounts and *lobolo* being paid in money
($x^2 = 202,727$; $p < 0,001$; $C = 0,59$).

The association between declining amounts of *lobolo* and increasing
stabilization in urban residence (table not reproduced here) is probably too slight ($0,025 > p > 0,01$) not to have been affected by hidden
intervening variables. The possibility that increasing urban affluence
might have been associated with a rise in the value of *lobolo* was not
supported by our data, since the association (at the level of $0,005 > p
> 0,001$ among the 382 men in respect of whom relevant information
was available – again from a table not reproduced here) between
amount of *lobolo* and income was opposite to the trend that such an
hypothesis would require.

One of the findings with a safe statistical significance ($p < 0,001$;
$C = -0,26$, from a table not reproduced here) is one which shows
that women with higher educational status tend to have been *lobola*'d
with smaller amounts of cattle and/or money. This finding has some
bearing on Mrs Brandel-Syrier's suggestion (1958) that profession-
ally trained women command higher amounts of *lobolo* because one

of the new functions of *lobolo* in urban areas is to transfer their earning capacity to their *lobolo*-paying husbands. The failure of our data
to confirm this suggestion could possibly be because they refer to
years of education in general rather than to specific professional
training. Our interview schedule included a question about special
training, but too few persons reported it (four per cent of males and
four per cent of females) to warrant tabulating the results against
such variables as the value of *lobolo*.

Is the homogeneity of marriage partners thus far noted in ethnic
origin (Table 3), in education and occupational status and in stabilization in urban residence (Table 9), to be found in other aspects of
modern urban African marriage? Is a greater homogeneity developing between marriage partners in respect of age and education and
a greater heterogeneity in respect of religious affiliation? Various chi-
square tables were called for in the computer programme in an attempt to answer these and related questions. There were no statistically significant differences between longer-existing and more recently
contracted marriages in respect of relative age of husband and wife,
relative education or relative religion. Nor was there any discernible
trend in the method of formalizing marriage, i.e. the addition to
traditional *lobolo* of religious or civil ceremonies was as characteristic
of marriages contracted some years ago as of those contracted recently. One reliable trend to emerge was an increase in age at marriage in
the more recently married divisions of our sample, this being at a
higher level of significance for women ($x^2 = 23,927$; $p < 0,001$; C =
0,24) than for men ($x^2 = 16,580$; $0,005 > p > 0,001$). The nature of
the data on which this finding rests precludes any speculation about
its possible cause.

CONCLUSION

In this paper the results of a social survey have been reviewed for the
light they can throw on changes in domestic organization that
Africans undergo on moving from traditional subsistence activity to
participation in modern urban industrial life. The analysis has shown
that the patterns of domestic organization move in the direction of
those normally found in modern industrial societies; and that marriage shows an interesting mixture of emerging new trends and surviving but changed traditional features.

## NOTES

[1] The South African National Council for Social Research to whom grateful acknowledgement is made. My thanks are also due to the University of the Witwatersrand and Monash University for further assistance, both in finance and in free computer time; to Mrs Mia Brandel-Syrier, who generously shared with me her very considerable research experience in the Township; to the Manager and the residents of the Township who were unfailing in their kindness during all stages of the project; to Miss Lyndal Montgomery of Griffith University, who obligingly and efficiently prepared the tables accompanying this paper; and to Dr W. Roy Cook for commenting on a draft of this paper.

[2] When senior undergraduates, Miss Vera Picker and Miss Olga van Rijswijck (now Dr Olga Gostin) worked as part-time research assistants, and on my behalf gained valuable advice on sampling from Prof. Schlemmer then of the Witwatersrand University Department of Sociology; and Miss Valetta Dlamini, B.A., and Miss Gloria Luk Sun, B.A., worked full-time on field research and tabulation respectively. I was indeed fortunate in having the enthusiastic and able help of all these young people.

[3] Dr J. Clyde Mitchell, then Professor of African Studies at the University of Rhodesia, gave me some excellent advice on both the form and the content of questions. I am grateful to him and to Mrs Masekela and Mr Kokgato who very kindly tried out an earlier draft of the schedule and advised me on its revision.

[4] In matters relating to tabulation and computing, I received generous help in Johannesburg from Dr Henderson of the Witwatersrand University Computing Centre and from Mr Langschmidt of Messrs Market Research Africa (Pty.) Ltd; and in Melbourne from Mr Oscar Roberts, then of Monash University.

[5] When referring to the statistical reliability of results, I follow the accepted conventions, i.e. in this paper 'significant' refers to the situation in which there is a probability of between 5 and 1 per cent that an observed difference or similar outcome could occur as the result of chance alone $(0,05 > p > 0,01)$, this being sometimes shown by a single asterisk; 'very significant' is used when the probability lies between one in a hundred and one in a thousand $(0,01 > p > 0,001$, two asterisks); and 'extremely significant', when the probability is less than one in a thousand $(p < 0,001$, three asterisks). In most instances where $p < 0,001$, I have in addition computed the contingency coefficient, C, which is a measure of strength (as opposed to the mere existence) of the association between the variables being considered, and which is similar to a correlation coefficient, which it approaches in value when the population may be assumed to be normal (Tippett 1948:203).

[6] See note 5.

## REFERENCES

BOHANNAN, P. 1963 – *Social Anthropology*. London: Holt, Rinehart and Winston.

BRANDEL, M. 1958 – Urban lobolo attitudes. *Afr. Stud.* 27, 34–51.

HAMMOND-TOOKE, W. D. 1962 – *Bhaca Society*. Cape Town: Oxford Univ. Press.

HOERNLÉ, A. W. 1937 – Social organization. In I. Schapera (ed.) *The Bantu-Speaking Tribes of South Africa*. Cape Town: Maskew Miller.

HUNTER, M. 1936 – *Reaction to Conquest*. London: Oxford Univ. Press.

KRIGE, E. J. 1936 – *The Social System of the Zulus*. London: Longmans Green.

KUPER, H. 1947 – *An African Aristocracy*. London: Oxford Univ. Press.

LONGMORE, L. 1959 – *The Dispossessed*. London: Jonathan Cape.

MATHEWSON, J. E. 1959 – Impact of urbanization on lobola. *J. for Racial Affairs* **10**, 72–6.

SMITH, R. T. 1956 – *The Negro Family in British Guiana*. London: Routledge and Kegan Paul.

TIPPETT, L. H. C. 1948 – *The Methods of Statistics: An Introduction Mainly for Experimentalists*, 3rd ed. London: Williams and Norgate.

# FAMILIES WITHOUT MARRIAGE:
## A ZULU CASE STUDY

*Eleanor Preston-Whyte*

As a student of Professor Eileen Krige I soon became aware of her deep interest in kinship and of the importance which she placed on detailed field studies of it. The paper which I offer to this collection in her honour deals with a vital area of kinship – that of family and household composition and interaction. Much of the material upon which I will draw was collected during fieldwork done under the direction of Professor Krige amongst Zulu women in Durban. It was she who encouraged me both then and later to investigate the process of innovative and adaptive change in African urban family and domestic life to which her own study of marriage and familial relations in three Pretoria townships had contributed some forty years previously (Krige 1936).

More recent material on African urban family life in South Africa is rather scarce. Eileen Krige's work, together with that of Hunter (1932) and Hellmann (1935, 1937, 1948), did give us a good idea of the trends in the nineteen thirties and early nineteen forties in East London and on the Witwatersrand, while Levin's work on Langa (1947) provided a picture of marriage in the Cape Town area at the same period. Since then Pauw's detailed and painstaking investigation of East Bank Location in Port Elizabeth, which was published in 1963, has come to be the standard work upon which writers dealing with the urban African family draw (Hellmann 1971; Dubb 1974). This study, which was based upon a sample survey of household composition, raised many fascinating questions about the structure and development of African families and households in town. One of the issues on which both Pauw and Mayer commented was the emergence amongst the African population of the so-called 'matrifocal' family (Pauw 1963: 155–6; Mayer 1963: viii).

Pauw found that a significant proportion of the households in his sample were headed by women and was at pains to compare them with, and distinguish them from, 'matrifocal' households that are so prominent in the Caribbean. It was, of course, in relation to a large proportion of Negro families in one Caribbean population that R. T. Smith coined the term 'matrifocal' in 1956. It is now clear

55

that he meant this term to refer not so much to the structure of these families and households – that is, that they might exist without a husband/father – as to the nature of the pattern of domestic authority which was exercised by a dominant woman. He has recently (1973) pointed out that, by his original definition, matrifocality is characteristic even of conjugal households so long as it is the women, rather than the men, who make the major decisions and are largely responsible for the support and running of the domestic units. Unfortunately, the term 'matrifocal' had already been widely used purely in the structural sense to characterize households established by women in the absence of marriage or any lasting consensual union, and this usage has led to some confusion in the literature (Solien 1960; Kunstadter 1963; Randolph 1964; Gonzalez 1969; Farber 1972). Pauw was well aware of the distinctions originally made by Smith and both he and Mayer pointed out that they found no overall trend towards 'matrifocality' in the organization of interpersonal relationships within conjugal families and households in East Bank. However, in those cases where there was no male head present the major burden of support, direction and decision-making usually fell on the women who headed the households. The question then becomes not so much one of 'matrifocality' as of the extent to which female-headed households occur amongst Africans in South African urban areas and of the factors which bring them into being.

It can be said immediately that such households, though common, are not in the majority. Although Pauw found in East Bank that 42 per cent of the households had female heads (1963: 147), an estimate made by the West Rand Bantu Administration Board in 1960 for Soweto put the proportion of female-headed households at only 14 per cent. By 1970, however, the proportion of homes registered in the name of women in Soweto had risen to 22 per cent while in Eastern Bantu Township, one of Johannesburg's oldest African areas, a figure of 41 per cent female-headed households has been recorded (all figures quoted from Hellman 1971b: 12).

The most frequent type of household in most urban areas is based upon the nuclear family composed of a man, his wife and their children. Relatives or dependants of either the man or woman may also reside in the house and grandchildren of the conjugal pair may be present (Hellmann 1971a: 69; Dubb 1974: 457). Fifty-three of the 109 households in Pauw's sample were of the above complex nuclear type (1963:144) and the proportion is probably much higher in recently built townships and in areas where houses are allocated only to married couples. The most frequent extension of the nuclear unit includes the children of unmarried daughters of the head so that there is a definite tendency for the household to contain more than two generations (Pauw 1963:144–54; Hellmann 1971a:169, 1974:16). In all these cases, the household is formed around a middle-aged or elderly conjugal pair whose marriage is stable and endures over time. Authority rests with the father and what Mayer (1973:viii) calls the patriarchal and patrifocal ethic dominates familial interaction.

In contrast to households with male heads are those headed by women who have been widowed, separated or divorced, and by women who have never married but have usually borne and are rearing children without the permanent assistance of an unrelated male. Of the 109 households in Pauw's sample 46 were headed by women. Many of these households were also multigenerational and since authority usually rested with their female heads (1963:149–152), they were also necessarily matrifocal in the original sense of the term. It is important to note that 33 of the 46 female heads in Pauw's sample had acquired their domestic authority only when they were widowed, divorced, or abandoned by their husbands. As Pauw commented the women concerned were, on the whole, not young and these cases, therefore, represented a common stage in the developmental cycle of the normal nuclear family, resulting from the death or withdrawal from the unit of the husband and father. The households of the women who had never married (accounting for 13 of the 46 female headed households in the sample) he put in a distinct category and suggested that they might indicate the emergence of a new type of urban family. The women concerned were, on the whole, younger than the women heads who had once been married (1963: 147) and it is probable that they were women who, having had children early in life, did not marry, but, on the death of their parents or other kin on whom they had been dependent, set up their own households. To quote Pauw (1963:140), 'there are unmarried mothers who never get married, but nevertheless families develop around them which never pass through a stage of being a complete elementary family'.

My own fieldwork, undertaken in Durban and its surrounding African townships during the late nineteen sixties and early nineteen seventies, tends to confirm Pauw's suggestion that there is a distinct type of family centring on a woman and her children. In the city there are large numbers of African women who are earning their own living and many are rearing children in the absence of marriage or any form of lasting informal union. Some of them would prefer to be married, but others regard marriage with mixed feelings, predominant amongst which is a fear of losing the independence and freedom they experience as wage earners in town. Hellmann (1974: 19) has recently commented on similar sentiments expressed to her by Soweto women.[1] These views show that such households or as I would like to call them, families, consisting of women and their children, can be viable in town, where females may earn money with relative ease. The major problems for these families are finding a place to live and organizing domestic routines so as to cater for the usual functions of the conjugal family. The case studies which I will present later show how these problems are faced and, up to a point, resolved.

Although it is useful for structural and typological studies to distinguish between those households in which the female heads have formerly been married and those in which they have not, I would argue that in functional terms the distinction is less meaningful. Many of the women amongst whom I worked had indeed been widowed, divorced or abandoned by husbands while living in the country and had come to town in order to find support. Their problems were not essentially different from those facing single women who also had to support themselves and their children. Moreover, as the first case study covering a period of some fifty years shows, headship of the same family may devolve from a once married woman to her unmarried daughter, depending on circumstances and the natural progression of age and maturation.

If families headed by women are examined as they develop over time, which is what the case studies allow, then another striking feature of their composition and internal organization is apparent. Apart from being headed by women, many of these families tend to consist very largely of women who are uterine kin. That is, they form round a core of adult females: the head, her daughters, and possibly adult granddaughters who cooperate in the performance of domestic tasks and in providing support for each other and for any children or other dependants they may have. Alternatively, the head may form a family with one or more sisters and their offspring. Unmarried adult sons or brothers of the women may live with the female core and may contribute to its upkeep for longer or shorter periods. It seems, however, that men are drawn away from the household of their mother or sisters when they marry and set up their own households. Looked at over time, the most enduring and certainly the most functionally important social links are therefore between the women and I suggest the term *female-linked*[2] be used to describe such families. For them, marriage is not significant since even if one or more of the women has been married, the union has been broken. Indeed it is largely the absence of husbands to support them which has made the cooperation between the related women necessary. Men are, however, seldom completely absent from the household since the adult women may have lovers who visit them regularly and even live with them for periods. Though these men give financial and other aid to the women and their children, their role in the household is usually ill-defined and transient. Many are married to other women and eventually move away (Pauw 1963: 130–135). Their major contribution to the female-linked family is often the protection they provide when living there and the children whom they father. Marwick has given an example of this type of household elsewhere in this book (see figure on page 47).

The division of labour within female-linked families usually resembles that of the normal conjugal household in that at least one adult woman remains at home caring for the house and any younger children or other dependants incapable of looking after themselves. Other women in the families go out to work, thus taking on the roles of major breadwinners, usually assigned to the men in urban conjugal pairs. Earning money usually takes a woman outside the home, but some African women with houses in the townships let rooms to bring in money (Pauw 1963:32-3), while others make money by brewing and pursuing various illegal activities (Hunter 1932:682). Both these strategies allow them to be at home for a good deal of the time but leave them open to prosecution. Yet even the relative security of wage employment often has such disadvantages as working long hours away from home and travelling great distances to and from their places of work. In Durban the best opportunities of employment for unskilled African women lie in domestic service for which most employers prefer that their employees live on the premises and visit their homes only on weekly off-days and during annual leave. Even nurses may have to live at the hospitals and clinics where they work and teachers may be expected to go and live near the schools to which they are posted. Consequently, many African working women cannot live in the households which they are themselves supporting. This gives rise to a pattern of domestic dispersal to which I would like to draw particular attention. Although most South Africans who employ resident domestic servants know that their employees have children and 'families' in the townships, or more frequently in the country, few consider the implications and problems arising from a situation in which a mother is absent from her home and children for most of her life. Even amongst administrators and others who are most concerned with the effects of migrant labour, there is little awareness that the problems caused in rural families by male migrancy are increasingly common to families in both town and country which are centred on women and in which women are the labour migrants.

It may seem that the discussion of particular cases which follows is dominated by the problems facing women who were not born in an urban township and have therefore no rights to township houses. These women are a minority in relation to the thousands of urban women who live relatively settled lives in the townships. To some extent this bias to the minority results from the nature of my field work which was amongst women working as resident domestic servants, of whom the majority were migrants to the city. On the other hand, there is the ever present possibility that any urban housewife whose husband dies or deserts her, or even becomes chronically ill, may be faced with similar problems. She may have to assume headship of the household and provide financial support for it. The case-studies that follow are therefore not as unrepresentative as the rather restricted population from which they are drawn may at first suggest.

THE CASE OF ROSIE MAJOLA

The first case centres on Rosie Majola (as I will call her) whom I first met in 1963 when I collected much of her life history. She was then a single woman of 52 who had borne four children, two of whom were still alive and largely dependent upon their mother. Gertrude was about 24 and had a four-year old daughter, while Ntinini was 11 and still at school. Rosie worked as a resident domestic servant in an upper class White suburb of Durban. She had arranged for Gertrude, and her child and Ntinini to live in a house built largely with her money on land belonging to her lover, a Mr Bhengu, in Clermont, an African freehold area some 19 km from Durban. Rosie usually visited Clermont on her weekly day-off and stayed there during her annual holiday. Gertrude and Ntinini in turn visited her fairly regularly on the premises of her employer. Mr Bhengu worked at a butchery near to the house of Rosie's employer and spent most week nights in her room. He had a wife and family of his own in KwaMashu, one of the municipal African townships. I followed the vicissitudes of Rosie and her family for two years while doing full-time fieldwork. In 1975 I contacted her again and brought the story of the family up to date. I present now a case-study of the family which covers some 55 years, from about 1920 to 1975. It represents what Rosie told me about the period prior to 1963 and after 1965, and what I observed during fieldwork. I have divided the whole period into five phases corresponding to changes in the headship of the family and in its location. A skeleton genealogy illustrates each phase.

PHASE I: 1920–1938

Rosie was one of the 11 children of a widow, MaNgcobo,[3] whose husband, when he died in about 1920, left her with no affines willing to take responsibility for her and her nine children (Fig. 1a). MaNgcobo later had two more children by a lover (Fig. 1b–d). Rosie's father, Ben Majola, though he had been born in a tribal area, had decided some time before his death to move nearer to Durban in the hopes of finding employment. He rented a small plot of land from an Indian family on the outskirts of the city and put up a wood and iron dwelling. After his death MaNgcobo continued to live in the shack and earned money for rent and food by doing odd jobs and laundry for neighbouring White farmers. At first she left her eldest daughter in charge of the younger children during the day but as each child reached the age of 10 or 12, he or she also sought paid employment. The boys did gardening and worked intermittently as day labourers on building sites. Three sons eventually abandoned their mother and disappeared to town, while the other was continuously ill and out of work and proved more of a burden than a help to the family. Rosie and her four sisters went into domestic service and, until each of the three elder girls married or left Durban, they contributed a good deal to the family income. Rosie and her youngest surviving half-sister, Mary, never married. Rosie gave her mother some of her wages each month but Mary, who was mentally retarded, could not keep even the most simple job.

Rosie's life has therefore been spent very largely on the premises of a succession of White employers. She started working at the age of 11 when her mother found her a job as a nursemaid to the children of a nearby White family for a few hours each day. She was paid very little and, once she had gained some experience of working for Whites, her mother allowed her to take a resident domestic job where she was fed and clothed, as well as paid a higher wage until, at the age of about 18, she fell pregnant. After the birth of the child she returned to her mother's house where she lived caring both for her own baby and for the younger children in the family. An elder sister who had been living at home with her own child went to work (Fig. 1b). Some two years later this sister had a second baby and in her turn returned home to care for the infant and the other children in the family, while Rosie went back to full-time resident domestic work. At a later date when she was again pregnant Rosie stopped work and went home to live. Towards the end of 1938 the area where the family was living was to be cleared of African tenants. Rosie's two elder sisters married and left the household at about this time. Two other sisters were in resident service, the elder of the two having left her baby to be cared for by Rosie. The youngest sister Mary was also living at home with a baby while the elder sons had deserted the family (Fig. 1c).

PHASE II: 1938–1948

Rosie's mother decided to move into Durban to the Cato Manor shack area. With the financial help of her working children, MaNgcobo put up a small cottage using some of the materials from their original house. She then stopped working and stayed at home caring for her youngest children and her grandchildren – two of Rosie's children, one belonging to a younger sister, and also one and subsequently two borne by the retarded sister, Mary. Rosie returned to resident domestic work and helped to support the household. The old lady let rooms to lodgers and brewed liquor in order to make ends meet. Eventually one of the other daughters married and left home, with her child, while another went to Johannesburg. All the

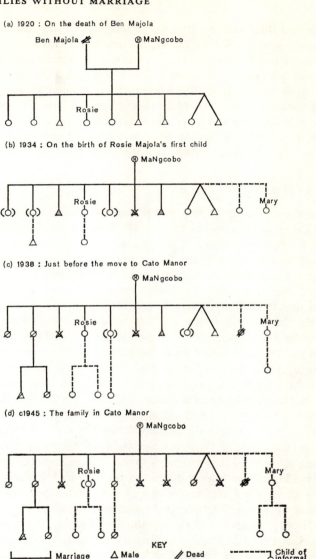

(a) 1920 : On the death of Ben Majola

(b) 1934 : On the birth of Rosie Majola's first child

(c) 1938 : Just before the move to Cato Manor

(d) c1945 : The family in Cato Manor

KEY

Figure 1.  The Case of Rosie Majola 1920–1945

sons deserted their mother. By 1947 it was only Rosie and the retarded sister who looked on the Cato Manor shack as home (Fig.
1d). Rosie visited it on her off-days and over weekends; since Cato
Manor was in the centre of Durban, she was within 20 minutes of it
by bus. It was at this time that Rosie met Mr Bhengu who lived in
the area with his wife. He used to visit Rosie regularly on her employer's premises. Though they were extremely fond of each other
Rosie had no children by Mr Bhengu and they lost touch after
about two years. In about 1948 MaNgcobo died.

PHASE III: 1948–1963

Rosie was working at the time of her mother's death and, because
she was living on the premises of her employers, was not registered as
resident in the Cato Manor house. Since there were no men in the
household and the sister, Mary, was clearly incapable of working, the
municipal authorities allocated the site to another family. Even when
Rosie pleaded to be allowed to keep the site, they refused on the
grounds that there was no man to pay the rental. Rosie, her sister
and their children were left with no secure dwelling place. 'The
family really went to pieces then', remembered Rosie, 'I had to rent a
room in a neighbour's house for my children and my younger sister.'
This arrangement did not work, since the retarded girl could not
care for the younger children adequately and Rosie, in desperation,
paid an old woman living in the same house to care for her children
and sister. This proved prohibitively expensive as Rosie was only
earning R10 per month and had also to find the rent for the room,
as well as food and clothing for the children. Gertrude was then
beginning school and fees and books mounted up. Eventually some
friends made in Cato Manor offered to take the children and sister
to live with their old parents, in one of the African reserves south
of Durban (Fig. 2a). Though Rosie had to send money to them regularly, it was cheaper in the long run than keeping them in Cato
Manor. She felt, in addition, that the children were better cared for
'on the farm' than 'in the slum'.

Rosie remained as a resident servant in Durban but began, at about
this time, to supplement her wages with illicit brewing. She had
two more children. Her employers allowed her to have each of the
babies on the premises for a few months, before she took the child
to join her other children on the South Coast. During this period

(a) 1948–1963 : MaNgcobo dies leaving Rosie head of the family which is dispersed

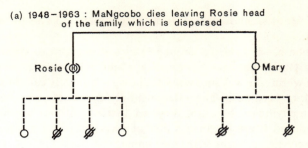

(b) 1963–1973 : Rosie establishes family at Clermont in Mr. Bhengu's house

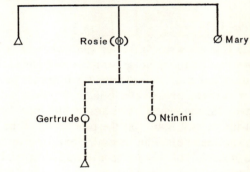

(c) 1973+ : Rosie builds her own house at Groutville

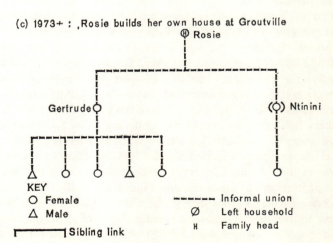

KEY

| | | | |
|---|---|---|---|
| O | Female | ▬▬▬▬ | Informal union |
| △ | Male | Ø | Left household |
| ⌐___¬ | Sibling link | H | Family head |

Figure 2. The Case of Rosie Majola 1948–1973

both of Mary's children died as did Rosie's second and third-born children.

This phase, which lasted about 15 years, was a time of great hardship for Rosie. She was continually plagued by worries over her children whom she was sure were not being adequately cared for. Her sister Mary became ill and later mentally deranged. The costs involved in paying the boarding fees and doctors' bills for her children increased and Rosie began to think of ways to establish a home of her own for them. Because she was unmarried, however, she was not eligible for a township house. A number of plans to board with friends came to nothing.

PHASE IV: 1963–1974

Rosie met Mr Bhengu again in about 1963 when he got a job at a butchery situated near the premises of her employment. By this time he and his family had been moved from Cato Manor to KwaMashu. Mr Bhengu had saved money and bought a plot at Clermont, the one area near Durban where Africans could own land. He was about to put up a small house on the plot in which he intended to let rooms and so make quite an income from his investment on the land. He did not wish his family to live at Clermont because that would mean relinquishing the municipal house which they had been granted in KwaMashu and for which the rent was relatively low. Rosie, who by this time had saved some money from brewing, helped him to pay for the house and furniture on the understanding that Gertrude and Ntinini could live there free of charge. Gertrude had recently run away from school and from the people with whom she was staying in the reserve and was pregnant. Although Rosie's retarded sister, Mary, had been admitted to an asylum, one of Rosie's brothers had reappeared. He was suffering from a chronic illness which made it impossible for him to work and Rosie regarded herself as the only person responsible for him. Mr Bhengu allowed him to live in the Clermont house, where, until his death, he provided some protection for Gertrude and Ntinini (Fig. 2b). From time to time one of Rosie's other sisters who visited Durban or was without a place to live, also stayed in the house. Some of the rooms were let to lodgers. The arrangement suited Mr Bhengu because it meant that the house had not only been speedily completed but it had also been furnished at little cost to himself. In addition Gertrude cared for it and collected the rents. In 1963 Mr Bhengu spent virtually every week night in Rosie's room on the premises of her employers. It was convenient to his work in the butchery where he had to be on duty by 4 a.m. Over weekends he returned to his wife and family in Kwa-Mashu. Rosie's elder daughter, Gertrude, spent most of her time in the Clermont house. She had never taken a full-time job but remained in Clermont caring for her child and younger sister Ntinini. She tried to make money by selling old clothes collected round the neighbourhood of her mother's employment or by dressmaking. She was, however, not very successful despite the expensive sewing machine Rosie bought her and the classes she took to learn how to use it.

Rosie regarded the Clermont house as her home in the 1963–70 period. She was always aware, however, that she and her daughters could be evicted any time, particularly if she ceased to be on good terms with Mr Bhengu or if he should want to accommodate other people in the house. For this reason she could not, she said, give up her resident domestic job. The secure accommodation provided was as important to her as the money she earned from both wages and brewing. She was planning to save not only for Ntinini's education, but as she said, 'put up a place of my own out in Inanda[4] where a friend tells me you can still get land'.

Thinking back on life until then Rosie pointed out that 'I have always fended for myself. I also seem always to have been responsible for somebody – and nobody cares for me'. At the time it seemed as if Gertrude might get married and, she continued philosophically, 'Now if Gertrude does get married she will leave her babies with me and then just as Ntinini is grown up and trained, I will have to educate them!'

PHASE V: 1975 +

When I contacted Rosie again in 1975 her position was in some respects drastically different, and yet in others and indeed in essentials, exactly the same as in the 1960s. She and her daughters had, as she had expected, left the Clermont home and had built and moved into a new house on land bought in Groutville,[5] a rural area situated some 60 km from Durban where tenure is also freehold. The uncertainty of the Clermont arrangement had persuaded her to move. She had also found herself a new lover which had broken her relationship with Mr Bhengu, though they still met and visit-

ed each other occasionally. The ten years had brought considerable changes in Rosie's family (Fig. 2c). Her brother and retarded sister had died and her daughter Gertrude had borne four
more children. The eldest of the children, a boy of 17 had recently
left school and was seeking employment. Two of the others were at
school. Gertrude's proposed marriage had not materialized. Negotiations had continued for some time, but finally broken down over
the payment of *lobolo*. She was living permanently at the Groutville
home with her children. Rosie's younger daughter, Ntinini, had
left school in 1971 when she became pregnant. She had then been
in Standard 9 and Rosie had been bitterly disappointed at the time.
She was, however, very fond of the baby who was living with the
family in their new home. Ntinini was toying with the idea of returning to her studies, but when interviewed she showed little enthusiasm for it. She was then working in her mother's job in Durban,
while Rosie was recovering from a long bout of illness. Although
Ntinini was still in contact with the father of her baby, she had no
intention of marrying him. 'I still write to him as my mother hopes
he will pay damages!' She carefully explained that her current lover
was far more exciting than the baby's father: 'a foreigner with lots
of money and a car – he will take me home to Groutville to visit my
mother at the end of the week,' she said. Ntinini was hoping that
this man would marry her, but as yet knew little of his background or,
indeed, if he was single.

Both Rosie and Gertrude had aged considerably. They were still
involved in various informal money-making activities, but as always
Gertrude was less successful than her mother. She and Rosie brewed
liquor and sold cooked food and their house had come to have the reputation of being a cheerful and inviting *shebeen*.[6] When at home,
Ntinini helped with this trade and was, in addition, a skilful needle-
woman. Her contribution to the family income far exceeded that
of her sister. Her new lover, in addition, was very openhanded and
she managed to get large sums of money from him fairly regularly.
During Rosie's illness it was Ntinini who had taken the initiative
in consulting doctors and it was she who had paid for the consul-
tations. 'How will they manage if I go back to school?' she asked.
She acknowledged, however, the authority of her mother and con-
sulted her in all matters affecting the family. Gertrude, the elder
sister, seemed not to have assumed any decision-making role in the
family. She complained about her younger sister's behaviour: 'she

thinks she is somebody because she got Standard 9', but did not oppose her leadership.

Though I have concentrated on Rosie, because it was she whom I knew well, much of this case could well have been described from the point of view of her mother, who, after the death of Rosie's father, reared and provided for her 11 children and the various grandchildren whom her unmarried daughters brought to live with her. Similarly at some future date, one could write the case from the viewpoint of one of Rosie's unmarried daughters, who will inherit the responsibilities of their mother. What the case study presents, therefore, is the history of a family formed largely of consanguineally related women which has persisted over time, holding together despite frequent changes of residence, the spatial dispersion of its members and even the virtually permanent absence of the woman who in later years was responsible for the major support of the others and for the moral and social continuity of the whole.

There may be those who would hesitate to use the word 'family' in this context. Indeed most recent writers dealing with situations in the Caribbean where a woman raises her children without the help of a permanent male partner, have chosen to refer to female-headed *households*. This has been the convention also with the South African material (Pauw 1963; Dubb 1974; Hellmann 1971a & b; Pendleton 1974), where it is the actual composition or structure of the domestic group which has been of greatest interest. This approach has its advantages, particularly when collecting data on different 'types' of domestic unit, as in a sample survey. If, however, one is interested in process, and the development and adaptation of the domestic unit to changing demands over time (during which the unit may change in composition and location), it is far more useful to use a concept such as 'family' for this carries with it notions of kinship, continuity and also suggests emotional involvement and long-term commitment. As Rosie's case shows, in the South African situation there are furthermore frequent instances where the term 'household' is inadequate, since by no means all members of the functioning unit are living and eating together under one roof. Indeed, the main provider may be absent for all but a few weeks in the year, as in the case of the families of male labour migrants.

Perhaps the major objection to using the word 'family' to describe a social group consisting of women, is that the link between the most important cooperating adults is neither a marital nor even a conjugal one. However, Goodenough (1970) has suggested that the traditional anthropological definition of the family as based upon marriage (however defined in the society concerned) is highly ethnocentric. It may have derived from the unconscious acceptance of the typical middle-class White family (consisting of a man, his legal or common-law wife and their children) as a basic unit in society. This view lies behind much of the earlier literature on the family which portrays the situation of a woman bearing and rearing her children in the absence of marriage, as abnormal (e.g. Clarke 1957; Du Bois 1908; Frazier 1946; Herskovitz 1941; King 1945).

One way to avoid this ethnocentric emphasis on marriage is to look at the family in terms of dyadic relationships between consanguines, an approach by no means new or unusual (e.g. Radcliffe-Brown 1950). In 1960 Adams, using this approach, showed how it makes clear that the family based on the mother-child dyad is not in itself abnormal or peculiar, but, under certain circumstances, is as functional as one based on the conjugal dyad. He was aware that other dyadic relationships might also function in this manner, although he did not discuss them in any detail. In the South African urban situation, what I have called female-linked families can be analyzed fruitfully in terms of dyadic relationships not only between mother and daughter (though these may be the most prominent and frequent), but also between sisters, that is, in terms of sororal dyads.

The cooperation between sisters living in and contributing to a single household headed by their mother is often overshadowed by the dominance of dyadic relationships between each daughter and the mother. In cases where the mother is dead or uninvolved, sisters may cooperate to their mutual benefit as the following case shows clearly.

## THE CASE OF THE DUBE SISTERS

When I first met her, Martha Dube was a single woman aged 38, who had been working in Durban as a resident domestic servant for 18 years and for her current employer for 10 years. She was the younger of two sisters, the only surviving children of a man, Simon Dube, who had, after conversion to Christianity, left the area of his birth to set up a homestead on mission land near Greytown, some 180 km from Durban. It was to this move and simultaneous break with his family that Martha attributed the fact that she and her elder sister, Dorothy, eventually found themselves without kin upon whom they could rely for help or a home.

## PHASE I: 1950–1956

Some years before her father's death the mission land on which the family was living was sold to a White farmer. The latter allowed mission tenants to remain on the land, but made them pay rent for it. At first Martha's father managed to find odd jobs in the vicinity and so earned money for the rent, but as he grew older and weaker he arranged for Dorothy to work in the farmhouse in lieu of rent. In due course, however, Dorothy heard that she could earn a good wage in Durban and left for the city. Martha eventually followed her and the two found work close to each other and met regularly (Fig. 3a).

## PHASE II: 1956–1960

As time went on the Dube parents grew too infirm to be left alone. It was decided that Dorothy must return to the Greytown home to care for them. Although no longer young she had recently fallen pregnant and the subsequent birth of the baby ensured that she remained in the country for some years caring for the infant. Her mother died shortly after the birth and she remained on in the Greytown home caring for her aged father and her child (Fig. 3b).

## PHASE III: 1960 +

Simon Dube died in 1960. Dorothy remained on in the old home with her child. Martha continued to work as a resident servant in Durban and to send as much money as she could home to her sister each month (Fig. 3c). Dorothy did some washing in the vicinity, but could not leave her child alone in order to take a full-time job. Martha was herself still hoping to have a child, and said that if this happened she would return home and care for both children while Dorothy sought full-time work. In commenting on her life she stressed that she and Dorothy were self-sufficient. 'We are lucky as we have a home and as long as we both keep well and I can work, we are all right. In fact, we are happier than some women with husbands who have all sorts of problems . . . and my sister does have a child – if only I could have one as well.'

(a) 1950 : Greytown home supported
        by migrant daughters

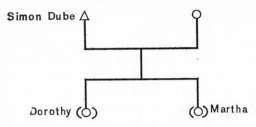

(b) 1956 : Parents age, Dorothy returns home
        with child, Martha supports the family

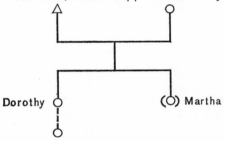

(c) 1960+ : Parents die, and the family is
        based upon a sororal dyad

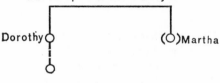

KEY
  O Female              (O) Working as a
  △ Male                    resident domestic
                            servant in Durban
  |_____| Marriage       and sending money
                            home to the family
                            regularly
  |‾‾‾‾‾‾‾| Sibling link  ¦ Child of informal
                          Ǫ union

Figure 3. The Case of the Dube Sisters 1950–1960

The sororal dyad may thus be used quite effectively to solve the problems usually dealt with by either the conjugal or the maternal dyad. This type of arrangement should, however, be viewed as only one of the possible stages in the developmental cycle of female-linked families, rather than a 'type' in its own right. Indeed, in much of Phase III of Rosie's case history cooperation was between herself and her sister Mary (Fig. 2a). Rosie was the dominant partner largely due to the mental state of her sister. After Mary's death, Rosie's family assumed the structure of a female-linked family based on the maternal dyad.

Female-linked families based on the sororal dyad seem to be found less frequently than are families based upon the maternal dyad. Pauw found only two sororal households in his sample (1963:148). There are several possible reasons for this relative rarity. Pauw noted that where sisters lived together with their children in one household, the elder sister, or the one owning the house, was regarded as the senior. My material suggests that there is room for a good deal of tension and conflict in the relationship of sisters cooperating together and particularly where they are living in the same house. The Dube sisters lived apart and only met once or twice a year, but even so Martha admitted to having major disagreements with her sister over domestic matters, particularly over how money should be spent. In the first case, there was clearly a good deal of rivalry between Rosie's daughters despite their age difference. Ntinini, though the the younger, was in 1975 the dominant of the two personalities and during her mother's illness was clearly making the major familial decisions herself. Though Gertrude accepted her leadership, she resented the 'bossiness' of her younger sister. It is possible that between sisters age is not a sufficiently strong principle upon which to base a fixed pattern of hierarchy necessary for organizing a long-lasting cooperation. Unlike the relationship of mother and daughter, where respect and deference are accepted as the due of the mother, that between sisters allows for ambiguity. Rivalries develop over children, how money is to be spent, and indeed, each sister is potentially the head of her own family. This is increasingly the case as her children grow up, require less care and can eventually contribute to an independent household. More research is indicated on this topic, especially the complex interplay of need and dependence versus rivalry and competition in the relationship of sisters living together, both in the presence and in the absence of their mother.

Both the case studies illustrate dramatically the flexibility in the organization of familial and domestic responsibilities in female-linked families. There is no fixed division of labour as in the normal urban conjugal family, where it is the man who goes out to work and the woman who runs the home and cares for the children. Where the family is based on the maternal dyad, it is usually the mother who remains in the house or shack caring for the younger children, as did Rosie's mother, while her daughter seeks work to support the household. The roles of housekeeper and wage-earner may, however, be reversed if the older woman is best equipped to find paid employment, as happened later, when, because Rosie had a secure job with well-disposed employers, her daughter Gertrude remained in the Clermont home. Moreover, women may switch roles with changing circumstances. When one has a young baby, it is the other who seeks work outside the home. This situation of role-switching was well-illustrated in Phase I of Rosie's case history wherein she and her sisters regularly changed roles after the birth of their babies. Similarly, Martha acknowledged to me that it was 'best' for her to work while her sister, who had a young child, cared for the Greytown home.

The fact that different women assume the role of wage-earner at different times, means, of necessity, complementary changes in the assumption of purely internal domestic functions such as decision-making and the rearing of children. A woman who is not living in the household is not completely conversant with the day-to-day problems of running the home and of the tensions and difficulties likely to arise in interpersonal relations. She is therefore not in any position to make many of the decisions which must be based on experience and which often have to be made immediately. The case of the Dube sisters shows how spatial separation affects decision-making in the dispersed family. Martha, though the major bread-winner in the family, was clearly not the head of the family. She in fact left the running of the house to Dorothy who was the elder sister, and could also, by virtue of being 'on the spot', deal best with day-to-day problems. Separation of the order involved in this family, that is between town and country, makes it impossible for a wage-earning woman who visits the home only once or twice a year to be an effective head. An important result of role switching in families such as the Majolas and Dubes is that the children raised in them are often cared for and reared, not only by their own mother, but at times by other women in the family – grandmothers, mothers' sisters or even own sisters. Looked at over time, they may have been reared by not one woman, but by a series of women. This is yet another reason for referring to these families as female-linked.

In laying such emphasis on the dyadic relationships between women in non-conjugal families like those described in the case studies, it may seem that I am neglecting the roles played in these families by the sons and brothers of the women concerned. In African urban areas, adult sons are indeed often found living in households headed by their mothers who have been widowed, abandoned or who have established households for themselves. In each of Pauw's three examples of female headed families, there was an unmarried adult son who contributed to the household income (1963:69, 70, 71) and he found in his sample a general tendency for the adult sons in households headed by women to be older than in male headed households, giving the impression that sons may remain on longer in these households (1963:150) than in conjugal ones.

One factor explaining the presence of an adult son who is a wage-earner is that the administration may then permit the widow to retain the township house which she would otherwise lose after the death of her husband. While the son lives in the house, he is clearly an important member of it both in terms of income and interaction. However, when he marries, he is likely to set up his own household and thus be drawn away from the cooperating unit made up of his mother and probably unmarried sisters. It is my impression that there is no general tendency in town for sons to continue to support their mothers regularly after their own marriages. Should a son bring his wife to his mother's household, the whole character of the family is likely to change. However, one situation in which mother-son links may be maintained is when the one or the other has a business in which the other fulfils an important role. For example, in urban areas women 'doctors' are sometimes protected by adult sons who make their living from assisting their mothers and protecting their interests.

The relationship between an African woman migrant and her growing sons if she lives not in a township, but on the premises of her employers, is often complex and unsatisfactory for the women concerned. In analysing the life histories of older resident domestic servants, it was striking how few were in close or continual contact with their adult sons. Most of the women had left the country while their children were small and when they were old enough to seek work in town, the young men could not live with their mothers, but instead had to find accommodation in hostels or on the premises of their own employers. Women often bemoaned the fact that 'boys don't want to help their mothers today – they spend their money on drink and girls'. Without the focus of an urban household, there is relatively little to keep a son dependent on his mother. He looks to men and women friends for companionship in town and the latter are often chosen to perform domestic tasks such as washing, ironing and sewing for him. So the many factors which hinder migrant women from establishing households in town, also disrupt their relationships with their male children. Men are seldom forced to rely on their mothers, as women are, to help care for children born outside marriage, since these children are usually the responsibility of the women who bear them.

When a man marries and sets up his own household and nuclear family, his wife may regard help given to his mother with some disfavour, since it diverts funds away from their own household. It seems that while the emotional ties between mother and son are initially strong, the relationships into which the young men enter with other women, as girlfriends and wives, draw them away from their mothers. Their marriages and more particularly their founding of an independent household weaken or sever structural links with mothers in town. Pauw (1963:109–110) points to statistics indicating that most men eventually marry, even if it is after they are approaching middle age. In contrast a *small* but significant proportion of women do not marry, but still bear children. It is these women who tend to remain with their mothers and sisters and form the cooperative unit, which I have called a female-linked family, after their brothers have established their own households and families of procreation.

If one considers the relationship between a woman and her brother, a similar picture emerges. Before marriage a man often lives in his sister's household, if his parents are dead and, throughout life, if he is in difficulties he may stay with her and even bring his wife and family to live with her for short periods. When Rosie's younger brother became ill, he made his home in the Clermont household until his death. He was on close terms with Rosie's daughter, whose *malume* (mother's brother) he was, and was treated with love and care by all her family. Marriage, however, draws a brother away from his sister and, once he has his own household, he is merely a visitor to her home. It is true that he often gives gifts to her and her children and is called upon for financial aid and help in crises, but a married brother is like a son, essentially an outsider who helps the female-linked household and family, rather than an integral part of it.

## FEMALE-LINKED FAMILIES AND THE WIDER SOCIETY

Adams, in viewing the family as sets of dyadic relationships, argued that in cases where the maternal dyad is the basis of a significant number of households in a society or section of a society, one should seek what he calls the 'structural correlates' which accompany and explain this situation (1960:46). This entails an examination of the wider social system in order to reveal the circumstances which discourage the development of nuclear families and produce, instead, an emphasis on consanguineal dyads in the construction of many domestic and familial groupings. The approach is implicit in R. T. Smith's work (1956; 1957; 1973) and has also been attempted in a number of the more recent studies of matrifocal or female headed households and families (Gonzalez 1961; 1963; 1969; 1970; Stack 1970; 1974; Aschenbrenner 1975).

In the South African urban situation I suggest that an important factor in the development of what I have called female-linked families is the accelerated pace of African female migration to towns which has characterized the last twenty to thirty years. At one time the disproportionately high African masculinity rate was a feature of most South African cities (for instance, Wilson & Mafeje 1963:4–5). By 1970 women made up 42,5 per cent of the African urban population in the country (Hellmann 1974:14). In most towns many of these women are migrants who have come from the country in search of work. It is important to stress that women migrants fall into a different category from male migrants. Most men return to their rural homes eventually, even if it is after many years of working in town. In contrast only a few of the migrant women who have been away from their country homes for long periods can easily return to them. With the passing of time their parents die and the women become less and less welcome as permanent members of the households of their married brothers or affines. Land cannot be allocated directly to women in most African rural areas and even if a woman persuades a brother or other kinsman to care for her children, or even to allow her to erect a dwelling on his land, she must still work and earn money in order to provide for the upkeep of the home. Thus women who, like Martha Dube or Rosie Majola, eventually rent or acquire land, either from a White farmer or in an area of individual ownership, must continue to work in town to pay for rent and to feed and clothe their children (Preston-Whyte 1973). Many migrant women are forced to remain on in town into old age, earning money, as best they can, and often sending it to dependants living elsewhere.

Widows of townsmen also resist attempts by the administration to send them to the rural areas for they recognize that even if they can find a place to live, there will be no means of support so far from the urban centre and its employment opportunities. Pauw was struck by the large number of women in his sample who fell into what he termed the 'post marital stage' (1963:136, 150). Indeed, 28 of the 46 females who headed households had been widowed as against only 3 of the 63 male heads. Pauw argues that when men are widowed, their households usually break up and the children are sent to relatives. Widows, however, often keep their households together and the family merely passes into another developmental stage, in which the widow is supported by her unmarried sons and daughters. If the woman has unmarried daughters with children, the foundation is laid for the development of a female-linked family based on the long term needs of a widow and those of the daughters who remain unmarried.

It is difficult to estimate exactly how many women do not marry. The number of women bearing children before marriage has been the subject of a good deal of comment (Mair 1969:34; Verster 1965). While, as Eileen Krige showed, many African women marry after the birth of one or two children (1936), there are those who like Rosie, Gertrude and Dorothy, do not marry. As Mayer points out (1963:iii) illegitimacy and matrifocality could be viewed as two sides of the same coin. Certainly the existence of a category of women who had not married, but who were rearing children, struck Pauw forcibly and led him, as we have seen, to postulate the development of a new type of urban family surrounding single women.

The reasons why there should be a category of women in town who do not marry are complex, and I have tried to analyse them elsewhere. Suffice it to point out here that there is evidence to suggest that in town, even when marriages are planned, problems often arise in the course of negotiations between the two families concerned;

the amount of bridewealth demanded by the bride's people may also provide difficulties for the groom and his family. Zulu women come under the stipulations of the Natal Code which fixes bride-wealth and many marriage negotiations come to nothing if the parents of the bride insist on full payment before the marriage takes place. In other cases the parties lose interest in each other during the course of the long drawn out negotiations – as indeed happened in the case of Rosie's daughter, Gertrude (see also Mair 1969:38).

The inadequacy of social security provisions for Africans is a further important factor which draws African women to cooperate with each other. Though they are eligible for disability grants, old age and widows' pensions, and even grants from the child welfare authorities, the benefits are extremely low. There are, in addition, relatively few crèches to help working mothers and, as in other urban situations, there is seldom an extended family system to deal with irregular but recurrent crises such as illness or loss of employ-ment and income. It is in solving these problems that African women have turned to consanguineal kin and in particular to relationships based on the maternal and sororal dyad, and in so doing have re-plicated the mutual assistance and division of labour more usually provided by the conjugal dyad of husband and wife.

Wider socio-political features of South African society also impinge on the type of family and households which develop amongst Afri-cans in town. The movements of all Blacks are circumscribed by legislation and rural Africans moving to town immediately come face to face with the fact that they are regarded for the most part as temporary sojourners in the White city. Therefore, although, as argued above, large numbers of women are effectively urban dwellers, because it is only in town that they can earn money to support themselves and their dependants, it is only with great difficulty that they gain the legal right to live in town permanently and, more important, the right to apply for state and municipal aided urban accommodation. According to section 10 of the Bantu (Urban Areas) Consolidation Act of 1925, as amended by the Bantu Laws Amend-ment Act No. 42 of 1964, country-born African women who are neither the wives nor daughters of urban dwellers gain the right to settle in a White town only after 15 years of uninterrupted residence there, or after having worked for one employer for 10 years. Given the high labour turnover and the liability of Africans to be 'endorsed out' of town after 72 hours unless they have a job, both qualifications are difficult to achieve. Even when they have gained the right to be in town, many women find it almost impossible to find a house in the townships. Preference is given to married couples and, until recently, in some townships unmarried women and widows were not considered eligible for the allocation of a house (Hellmann 1971b:169). Furthermore, any township woman whose husband died could be forced to give up her home, unless she had an adult son to whose name the house might be transferred. In any case the chronic shortage of housing often means that applicants wait years for consideration and for women with only young children a very real problem exists in meeting even the subsidised rents charged for township houses.

The dice would appear to be so heavily loaded against unmarried African women who wish to settle in town that it may seem to the reader surprising that female-linked families exist at all and that they appear, on the evidence of figures quoted earlier in the paper (p.56), to be increasing in number in some areas. One reason is that there are wide variations in the actual application of the relevant Urban Areas Act by different local authorities. In some municipal areas there is, and has for many years been, less rigidity in the control of African housing than others and many individual municipal officers are sympathetic to the plight of widows and unattached women. The women concerned have, furthermore, shown considerable initiative in finding loopholes in the system and exploiting every possible accommodation alternative. Those who are unable to obtain a house rent rooms in the homes of friends, kin and even strangers. Hellmann reported recently that in Soweto while only one-fifth of the registered tenants are women, as high as one-third of all sub-tenants are females (1971a:12). In some townships sub-letting of rooms is illegal and indeed many of the women living in town may be forced to live under illegal conditions for long periods. In some White and multiracial residential areas of Durban, residents permit Africans to live illegally on their premises or else to rent accommodation from them. If discovered both parties are, however, open to prosecution.

Yet another important factor which has facilitated the development of female-linked families over the last two decades has been the spread of shack areas and shanty towns on the outskirts of a number of major urban centres. In Durban, women like Rosie's mother have lived for years in areas such as Cato Manor and more recently in the newly developed shack areas on the north coast (Maasdorp & Humphreys 1975). African women in Durban have also been fortunate in having access to the nearby African-owned areas of Clermont and Groutville where, like Rosie herself, they have been able to put up shacks and houses to accommodate themselves and their dependants. But for these circumstances many Durban women could not have established any kind of secure urban household in which to rear their children.

Women who find it impossible to find accommodation for their families in town have to use the strategy adopted by the Dube sisters. One woman remains in the country, with the children, while another works as a migrant in town. This is a common pattern and, particularly in youth and early middle age, many migrant women belong to this type of dispersed family. A typical first step in the developmental cycle of this type of family is for a single woman to come to town either before or just after the birth of her first child and to send a proportion of her salary home to her parents each month. Widows or women who have been abandoned by their husbands often migrate first at a slightly later age, in most cases after the birth of more than one child. The children may remain either with the kin of the husband or with the woman's own mother or sister. This situation may continue for many years and only be ended when the rural kin who are caring for the children become too old to do so or die. It is at this point that the migrant woman really becomes the focus of a female-linked family and is forced to make new arrangements for the care of the children. In some cases, siblings may take charge of the children in the country, but in the majority of cases the mother seeks to bring them to live in town. If she can find a place to live she establishes an urban household in which she and her elder sons and daughters cooperate in solving the problems of urban life. The major crisis which may befall the family at this stage is the loss of their accommodation. This was well illustrated in Phase III of the Majola family history when Rosie was not permitted to keep the Cato Manor shack.

Similar problems face the township wife who is widowed, but not allowed to keep her husband's house. Single women who have been reared in town may also face accommodation problems when their fathers die. For them the crises may be exacerbated by the fact that they are unlikely to have rural kin upon whom they might rely to house their children. On the other hand, their experience of town life will probably have taught them how to manipulate the administrative system. So-called 'shilling' marriages in which the marriage form is gone through, though the couple have no intention of living as man and wife (Hellmann 1971b:168–9) and female-linked households in shack developments such as those at Cato Manor and Groutville, are often a response to a situation in which the urban administration ignores the existence of 'families without marriage'.

In conclusion, I should like to stress that the cooperation between women, that is, between mothers and daughters, between sisters and even between grandmothers and their grandchildren, which I have described in this essay, presents a marked contrast to the structurally important linkages between agnatically related males upon which Zulu homestead composition and local organization were based (Gluckman 1950) and which can still be seen in the settlement pattern of large areas of rural KwaZulu and Natal today (Reader 1966; Preston-Whyte & Sibisi 1975). Virilocal and patrilocal marriage, while it creates lifelong bonds of cooperation and dependence between male agnates, must of necessity draw consanguineally related women apart. Nguni rules of exogamy separate a daughter from her mother and even her maternal grandmother and unless sisters marry the same man they usually live in different and often geographically distant *imindini* (homesteads). Even in town, mothers, married daughters and sisters who are part of their own nuclear households, often live far from each other. It is only in cases where marriage has not occurred or where it has failed to provide the women with security because of widowhood, separation or divorce, that women cooperate in the solving of common problems. Although the cooperative patterns between African women in town are striking, I do not feel that what I have described can be taken as an indication of a change from patrilineal to matrilineal descent as has been suggested by Professor Wilson (1969:76–7). The arrangements within female-linked families are at present dictated by abnormal problems and contingencies in town and are not part of the wider structural patterns of descent and inheritance in African societies in Southern Africa. The linkages between the women are for their current benefit and for help in the support and rearing of their children; not for the transfer of positions and property between and to men via women as is normal in a matrilineal society. Only the future and further research will indicate whether what I have called female-linked families become a permanent sub-type of urban family, alternative to the conjugal family, or whether they represent merely a temporary adjustment to contemporary problems of migration, rapid change and a politico-administrative system which is weighted, not only against Africans in general, but it seems against African women in particular.

## NOTES

[1]The following report which documents similar sentiments appeared in the *Sunday Tribune* of 13 February 1977:

Catherine Mthwana, the first black South African woman to get a karate black belt . . . started karate three years ago after she became pregnant and was deserted by her lover.

Her father encouraged her and has even built a small gym for her at home.

Catherine has vowed she will never marry. 'What use is it when I now can protect myself and earn something for a living? At least I have a child to boast of', she said.

[2]Professor Wilson has called the type of family that I am discussing 'matrilineal' (1969:77). The use of this term is, however, potentially confusing, since 'matrilineal' is usually associated with institutionalized patterns of descent and inheritance common to and normative within a total society or social group. Yet the type of family to which both she and I are referring occurs only under certain circumstances and does not imply jural relationships between males, as well as females, similar to those found in matrilineal societies. The term 'female-linked' though rather awkward, avoids these connotations of 'matrilineal' and yet indicates the essential elements of this kind of family.

[3]Married women in Zulu society are referred to by their clan names with the preface Ma-. I have kept to this convention despite the change in actual clan name used.

[4]Inanda is a peri-urban area north of Durban where there has recently been rapid shack development (Maasdorp & Humphreys 1975).

[5]Groutville, like Clermont, is one of the few areas where Africans have freehold land rights.

[6]The colloquial word for an illegal bar which sells both home-made and commercial liquor.

## REFERENCES

ADAMS, R. N. 1960 – An inquiry into the nature of the family. In *Essays in the Science of Culture* (eds.) G. E. Dole and R. L. Carneiro. New York: Thomas Y. Crowell.

ASCHENBRENNER, J. 1975 – *Lifelines: Black Families in Chicago.* New York: Holt, Rinehart and Winston.

84 ELEANOR PRESTON-WHYTE

CLARKE, E. 1957 – *My Mother who Fathered Me: A Study of the Family in Three Selected Communities in Jamaica*. London: George Allen and Unwin.

DUBB, A. A. 1974 – The impact of the city. In *The Bantu-Speaking Peoples of Southern Africa* (ed.) W. D. Hammond-Tooke. London: Routledge and Kegan Paul.

DU BOIS, W. E. B. 1908 – *The Negro American Family*. Atlanta: Atlanta Univ. Pubs. No. 13.

FARBER, B. 1972 – *Guardians of Virtue, Salem Families in 1800*. New York: Basic Books.

FRAZIER, E. F. 1948 – *The Negro Family in the United States*. Chicago: Univ. of Chicago Press.

GLUCKMAN, M. 1950 – Kinship and marriage among the Lozi of Northern Rhodesia and the Zulu of Natal. In *African Systems of Kinship and Marriage*. (eds.) A. R. Radcliffe-Brown and Daryll Forde. London: Oxford Univ. Press.

GONZALEZ, N. L. SOLIEN 1961 – Family organization in five types of migratory labour. *Am. Anthrop.* **63**, 1264–1280.

───── 1963 – The consanguineal household and matrifocality. *Am. Anthrop.* **67**, 1541–1549.

───── 1969 – *Black Carib. Household Structure: A Study in Migration and Modernization*. Seattle: Univ. of Washington Press.

───── 1970 – Towards a definition of matrifocality. In *Afro-American Anthropology: Contemporary Perspectives* (eds.) N. E. Whitten and J. F. Szwed. New York: The Free Press.

GOODENOUGH, W. H. 1970 – *Description and Comparison in Cultural Anthropology*. Chicago: Aldine.

HELLMANN, E. 1935 – Native life in a Johannesburg slum yard. *Africa* **8**, 34–62.

───── 1937 – The native in the towns. In *The Bantu-Speaking Tribes of South Africa* (ed.) I. Schapera. London: Routledge and Kegan Paul.

───── 1948 – *Rooiyard: A Sociological Survey of an Urban Native Slum Yard*. Rhodes-Livingstone Paper No. 13. Cape Town: Oxford Univ. Press.

───── 1971a – *Soweto: Johannesburg's African City*. S. Afr. Inst. of Race Relations.

───── 1971b – Social change among urban Africans. In *South Africa: Sociological Perspectives* (ed.) H. Adam. Cape Town: Oxford Univ. Press.

───── 1974 – African townswomen in the process of change. *S. Afr. International* **5**, 14–22.

HERSKOVITZ, M. J. 1941 – *The Myth of the Negro Past*. New York: Harper.

HUNTER, M. 1932 – Results of culture contact on the Pondo and Xhosa family. *S. Afr. J. Sci.* **29**, 681–6.

KING, C. E. 1945 – The negro maternal family: a product of an economic and a cultural system. *Soc. Forces* **24**, 100–4.

KRIGE, E. J. 1936 – Changing conditions in marital relations and parental duties among urbanized natives. *Africa* **2**, 1–23.

KUNSTADTER, P. 1963 – A survey of the consanguine or matrifocal family. *Am. Anthrop.* **65**, 56–66.

LEVIN, R. 1947 – *Marriage in Langa Native Location*. Communications from the School of African Studies (New Series No. 17). Cape Town: Univ. of Cape Town.

MAASDORP, G. and A. S. P. HUMPHREYS 1975 – *From Shantytown to Township*. Durban: Juta.

MAIR, L. 1969 – *African Marriage and Social Change*. London: Frank Cass.

MAYER, P. 1963 – Preface in Pauw, B.A. *The Second Generation: A Study of the Family among Urbanized Bantu in East London*. Cape Town: Oxford Univ. Press.

PAUW, B.A. 1963 – *The Second Generation: A Study of the Family among Urbanized Bantu in East London*. Cape Town: Oxford Univ. Press.

PENDLETON, W. C. 1974 – *Katatura: A Place where We do not Stay*. San Diego: San Diego Univ. Press.

PRESTON-WHYTE, E. M. 1973 – The making of a townswoman: the process and dilemma of rural-urban migration amongst African women in Southern Natal. In *Sociology Southern African 1973*. Durban: Univ. of Natal.

PRESTON-WHYTE, E. M. and H. SIBISI. 1975 – Ethnographic oddity or ecological sense? Nyuswa-Zulu descent groups and land allocation. *Afr. Stud.* 34, 283–314.

RADCLIFFE-BROWN, A. R. 1950 – Introduction to *African Systems of Kinship and Marriage* (eds.) A. R. Radcliffe-Brown and D. Forde. London: Oxford Univ. Press.

RANDOLPH, P. R. 1964 – The 'matrifocal family' as a comparative category. *Am. Anthrop.* 66, 28–31.

READER, D. H. 1966 – *Zulu Tribe in Transition*. Manchester: Manchester Univ. Press.

SMITH, R. T. 1956 – *The Negro Family in British Guiana*. London: Routledge and Kegan Paul.

————— 1957 – The family in the Caribbean. In *Caribbean Studies: A Symposium*. Jamaica Institute of Social and Economic Research.

————— 1973 – The matrifocal family. In *Character of Kinship* (ed.) J. Goody. Cambridge: Cambridge Univ. Press.

SOLIEN, N. L. 1960 – Family and household in the Caribbean. *Soc. & Econ. Stud.* 9:101–106.

STACK, C. B. 1970 – The kindred of Viola Jackson: residence and family organization of an urban black American family. In *Afro-American Anthropology Contemporary Perspectives* (eds.) N. E. Whitten and J. F. Szwed. New York: The Free Press.

————— 1974 – Sex roles and survival strategies. In *Women, Culture and Society* (eds.) M. Z. Rosaldo and L. Lamphere. Stanford: Stanford Univ. Press.

VERSTER, J. 1965 – The trend and pattern of fertility in Soweto: an urban Bantu community. *Afr. Stud.* 24:3–4, 131–98 [470, 471].

WILSON, M. and A. MAFEJE 1963 – *Langa: A Study of Social Groups in an African Township*. Cape Town: Oxford Univ. Press.

WILSON, M. 1969 – Changes in social structure in Southern Africa: the relevance of kinship studies to the historian. In *African Societies in Southern Africa* (ed.) L. Thompson. London: Heinemann.

# COMPLEX HOUSEHOLDS AND JOINT FAMILIES AMONGST INDIANS IN DURBAN

## Sabita Jithoo

Although the existing literature on Indian South Africans contains some discussion of household and family structure amongst them (e.g. Kuper 1960:103–110; Meer 1969:64–72), it is couched in rather general terms and makes little reference to studies of other Indian communities. There is room therefore for a more intensive treatment with some comparative reference and this paper is a preliminary attempt to provide one. The material on which it is based formed part of a study initiated and largely supervised by Professor Eileen Krige whose student I was and whose advice and encouragement have meant a great deal to me.[1]

The fieldwork for the study was conducted part-time between 1964 and 1967, during which period 100 Indian households (in a sense to be defined below) were surveyed. Seventy-nine of these households were concentrated in three distinct Indian areas of the borough of Durban. One of these areas was Overport, just outside the old borough boundary, where Indians had long been resident and where 21 households were contacted; the second area was Asherville, further west of Durban, where 35 households were studied; the third area was 'Tintown', still further west, where, as its name implies, there was temporary housing for poor families who had been moved there from elsewhere and 23 of these were interviewed. To offset the predominantly low- to middle-income range of these 79 households, another 21 more prosperous families distributed all over Durban were chosen for interviewing, on the basis of their apparent wealth, judged in terms of property and income.

It must therefore be emphasized that the sample was not random, nor was it properly stratified, though it did cut across economic differences. It also included different patterns of residence, from the often long-established households of Overport to the much more recent, temporarily housed ones in Tintown. Even so, these different residential patterns did not include any examples of those obtaining in the very large, new Indian townships, such as Chatsworth with its 18 000 'dwelling units' most of which have been built according to a limited number of designs. Consequently the material presented in this article does not reveal anything about household composition in such townships which now contain a large proportion of the Durban Indian population.

On the other hand, the heads of the households studied have a wide range of occupations which may be divided into three categories. In the higher category which included 21 households, were doctors, lawyers and business men; in the middle category which included 56 households, were clerical, educational, service and commercial occupations; the lower category of 23 households were mainly semi-skilled and unskilled manual workers, ranging from handymen and small market gardeners to street-sweepers. Household incomes varied accordingly, from as little as R8 to as much as R2 000 per month.

The households were also differentiated on the basis of language, religion, caste, and descent from 'passenger' or 'indentured' immigrants.[2] I doubt, however, if the results of tabulations based on such criteria would be either statistically significant or analytically useful for my purposes. It is true, of course, that a 'high-caste', Gujerati-speaking, Muslim household of passenger origins differs from a 'low-caste', Tamil-speaking, Hindu household of indentured origins. But they do not *necessarily* differ in household composition. The Gujerati household is perhaps more likely to be, or to have been, 'complex' containing a 'joint' family, but it could be 'simple' with an 'elementary' family; the Tamil household may well be 'simple' and 'elementary', but it might be 'complex' and 'joint'. For this reason, rather than trying to correlate household composition with language, caste, religion and origins as has been attempted in some other studies (often with inconclusive results), I prefer to move directly to consideration of the households. In doing so, I have been guided by some of the more recent literature on other Indian communities, not all of which was available to me when my study was being made. My present use of that literature is therefore limited by the extent to which my data can be fitted into the categories deriving from it. Within those limitations, I have found the comparison enables me to bring out features of my material which were not always apparent to me when I was collecting it.

For a long time, discussions of household and family in Indian communities tended to revolve around the concept of the 'joint family'. This concept was, however, often used in varying and even conflicting ways by different writers, leading to confusion and making comparisons difficult if not impossible. More recently, attempts have

been made to reduce the confusion and foster comparisons by speci-
fying more precisely what is meant by 'joint family' (e.g. Madan
1963; Kolenda 1968; Shah 1964, 1974). Although no agreed, single
definition of the concept has resulted from these attempts, what has
emerged from them is that at least four aspects need to be distinguished. These are the genealogical, the coresidential, the commensal and
the coparcenary aspects.

The *genealogical* aspect has been succinctly stated by Shah (1974:
109; see also 1964): ' "Joint Family" means "two or more elementary
families joined together" '. This summary implies, of course, the
prior understanding that 'the generally acknowledged meaning of
"elementary family" is "a group composed of a man, his wife and
their children" ' (1974: 107). It also requires further definition of the
ways in which such 'elementary families' may be 'joined together'.
A comprehensive definition of these ways is not a straightforward
matter, but Shah states (1974:110) that the ' "Hindu or Indian joint
family" generally implies a patrilocal (or virilocal) patrilineal joint
family', which means that the elementary families are often 'joined
together' by patrilineal ties between the married males.

The reference to 'patrilocal (or virilocal)' introduces the second,
*coresidential* aspect of the joint family which is usually expressed
in such terms as 'occupying the same dwelling' or 'living under the
same roof'. These terms are more specific than 'patrilocal' and
'virilocal' which do not normally require that the unit to which
they apply should actually inhabit the same dwelling. But when they
are applied to the 'Indian joint family' they do often (though not
always) mean that a man after marriage continues to reside in the
same dwelling where his father (or other married male agnate) re-
sides.

The third, *commensal* aspect of the 'joint family' may be expressed
as eating food 'from the same kitchen' (Kolenda 1968:344) or
'cooked at one hearth' (Shah 1974:113). Such expressions imply
that the elementary families which compose the 'joint family' do not
cook and eat separately, but together. (They do not, however, pre-
clude segregation of the sexes in eating, so that all the men of the
'joint family' may eat in one group and the women and children in
another).

The term for the fourth aspect, *coparcenary*, was originally a
legal one referring to the implicit 'parts' or shares which certain
members (usually the males) of the family have in property that is

jointly owned, until it is eventually 'partitioned' between them. This aspect is therefore often summarized as 'holding property in common or jointly'.

The process of distinguishing and defining these four aspects shows that the overall concept of the 'joint family' is a compound and flexible one. It must always include the minimum genealogical specification of two or more related elementary families, but they can form a group that is coresidential, but not commensal, nor coparcenary; or a group that is coresidential and commensal, but not coparcenary; or a group that is coresidential and coparcenary, but not commensal; or even a dispersed group that is still coparcenary, but not coresidential and therefore not commensal.

This flexibility itself suggests that the 'joint family' is not a static 'type' but a dynamic 'process', as indeed many studies have shown it to be (even when they were not intending to do so). It is therefore ill-suited for classifying and comparing domestic groups within the same community, let alone between communities. For this reason, I do not use 'joint family' as the basic unit of description and analysis. Instead I follow the precedent that has become increasingly common in the literature and take the 'household' as my starting point. One advantage of doing so is that household can be initially defined by the single criterion of coresidence which is usually more straightforward than other criteria. Moreover, it is the criterion which presents itself most obviously in the early stages of fieldwork: what one usually finds, after knocking at the door, is a group of people living together. Whether and how they are related to each other, whether they are commensal and coparcenary are only discovered later, if at all. So, the 100 households which I investigated were such groups of coresidential people, though I must add the qualification that in some of these households the members were not all 'occupying the same dwelling' or 'living under the same roof'. Instead, some of them occupied out-buildings on the same premises as the main dwelling. For my purposes, such cases were still counted as 'coresidential'.

These 100 coresidential households may then be divided into two main types of 'simple' and 'complex' households. In making this division, I follow the example of Shah in his study of a village in Gujerat (1974). The division depends on adding genealogical criteria to the coresidential one. The particular ones used by Shah make more distinctions than I could conveniently apply to my smaller sample. Therefore for my purposes a household was defined as 'simple' if

it consisted of a husband and wife, living together with their unmarried children. It was also a simple household if it contained a
widow or (less likely) a widower, with such unmarried children.
Other possible forms of 'simple household', such as solitary persons
or two or more unmarried, adult siblings were not encountered in the
study. In effect, therefore, a simple household comprised the whole
or part of an elementary family, within the limits specified. Of
the 100 households, I classify 60 as simple, two of which were aug-
mented by other, single relatives; in one case a crippled cousin of the
husband and in the other, an elderly spinster sister of the wife. The
remaining 40 households I classify as 'complex'. This classification
again depends on the genealogical relationships obtaining between
the members within the households. These relationships can be summarized by saying that complex households contain the wholes or
parts of at least two related elementary families. This summary
covers, of course, a wide variety of different combinations which
can be used to form a number of sub-types of complex households,
as was done by Shah in his Gujerati study (1974).

If I were to follow his example closely, I should have only one
or two cases in each sub-type, which seems unrealistic. I therefore
prefer again to reduce drastically the number of sub-types of complex households to three. The first of these sub-types may be defined
in terms of the link between the elementary families being that of
parent and daughter. There were four such cases: in one of them the
parents' only child was their daughter and she and her husband were
living with them; in the second, a widower left with three school-
going children had his married daughter and her husband living with
him; the third comprised a deserted woman with three children, her
married daughter and the latter's husband; in the fourth case, a
particularly poor couple had their married daughter and her husband
living with them. In each of these four cases, then, there was some
special circumstance which prevailed against the usual view in the
Indian community that a married couple should not live with the
wife's parents. There was one other case that may be grouped with
these four, if only for the reason that it, too, was exceptional. In this
household, a couple with several young children had the wife's sister
and her husband and family living with them, apparently because
they could not get accommodation elsewhere. It is worth noting that
none of these cases could be described as 'joint families' in the sense
previously mentioned of a patrilocal (virilocal) and patrilineal group.

They are nevertheless still complex households, because they included the wholes or parts of at least two related elementary families.

The remaining 35 complex households can be distributed between two further sub-types resulting from the operation of a more usual organizing principle which Shah (1974:16) summarized as 'the principle of the residential unity of patrikin and their wives'. In one of these two sub-types, both spouses of an original married couple (or, sometimes, the surviving spouse of such a couple) were coresiding with at least one of their married sons. Where the father was still alive and present, this type of complex household contained what has been called for India the 'lineal joint family' (Kolenda 1968:347). In the second of these two sub-types, neither spouse of the original couple was present and the coresiding patrikin were then two or more married brothers. This sub-type of complex household therefore contained what has been called the 'fraternal' or 'collateral' joint family (Kolenda 1968:346). The specification of these two sub-types in terms of the link between parent(s) and married son(s) or between married brothers does not, of course, cover the full composition of the households which could contain up to three and even four generations of persons, adult and juvenile, single and married.[3] It does, however, emphasize the fundamental genealogical connections around which the households were organized.

Classifying according to these two types, there were 29 households that could be assigned to the first and six that belonged to the second. Since the two types are in fact usually successive phases of the developmental cycle, it seems that in Durban, as in other Indian communities, the complex household tends to break up after the death of the original male head. The actual proportion of households of the second type with coresiding brothers happens to be higher than, for example, in Shah's Gujerati village (1974:29–30), but it would be unsafe to draw from it any firm conclusions about the comparative strength of the fraternal tie amongst Indian South Africans.

Indeed, the relatively large number of the first type and the small number of the second type make it clear that many of the simple households must have emerged from previously complex ones, usually after the death of the husband of the original couple. Consequently, in Durban as elsewhere, one cannot assess the significance of either simple or complex households by merely counting the numbers of them which exist in those forms at any one time. One must allow for the likelihood that those found in simple households may once

have lived in complex ones. In fact, all of the 60 simple households
turned out to have experienced a previously complex phase. This re-
markably high proportion finds some confirmation in Kuper's report (1960:109) that all but three of 84 Indian men in one area of
Durban had spent at least some time living in their parental home
after their own marriages.

One must also allow for the expansionary phase in the developmental process by which currently simple households themselves
eventually develop into complex ones. It is, of course, impossible to
predict from past experience just what proportion of simple households will become complex. Those which do not produce any married
sons obviously cannot assume that form of complexity in which
married male agnates coreside. The declining birth-rate amongst
Indian South Africans may well contribute to a reduction in the in-
cidence of that form. On the other hand, some of the households
without sons could retain married daughters, as in the five cases already cited, and they would then be 'complex', if not 'joint'. Of those
simple households which do produce sons, it is possible that more will
lose them immediately after their marriages than has been the case
in the past. Nevertheless, the fact that 35 of my cases had retained
married sons, six of them even after the death of the fathers, strongly
suggests that a good many of the 60 simple households would eventually do the same.

It is therefore reasonable to claim that, in at least some sections
of the Durban Indian population, a substantial proportion will continue to have the experience of living in complex households for part
of their lives. However, the nature of that experience cannot be identical in every case. The relationships between the members of a complex household are affected by the extent to which the family they
compose is 'joint' in other aspects besides the genealogical one. I
have already noted that the coresidential aspect can itself vary. In
some cases, it means that the married couples live in one house within which only their sleeping accommodation is separate. In other
cases, both their living and sleeping space may be separated, but
still be contained under one roof. In yet other cases, there may be
several buildings on the same premises to accommodate the related,
elementary families. In some households, these different residential
arrangements may be successive phases in a developmental process,
the junior married couples being given increasingly distinct quarters
of their own, as their elementary families evolve.

Similar variations may occur with the commensal aspect. The preparation of food may mean cooking common meals at one stove which corresponds to the definition of commensality previously cited – 'cooked at one hearth'. But it may mean cooking separate meals at different stoves in the same kitchen. In some complex households, there are separate kitchens for component elementary families. Once again, these variations may be part of a developmental process, as each daughter-in-law is given progressively more independence in preparing meals for her own husband and children.

The flexibility of all these living and eating arrangements may depend partly on whether the house is rented or owned. If it is owned, it can be altered to suit changing requirements and, since it is a form of property, it makes the family to that extent 'joint' in the coparcenary sense, as well as in the other senses. The family is even more 'joint' in the coparcenary sense, if it also owns and operates a business. It is presumably rather less 'joint' in that sense, if the family depends instead for its livelihood on the wages of some of its members who may pool part or all of their earnings, though some authorities have treated such arrangements as virtually equivalent to running a joint business.

Jointness in these 'functional' aspects of living, eating and sharing property is therefore, as I indicated earlier, a matter of degree which fluctuates not only between families, but also often within one family according to its developmental phase and its changing material circumstances. This fluctuating 'jointness' can therefore be regarded as an index of adaptation to a variety of opportunities by families that differ in terms of demography, skills, enterprise and even luck. To grasp the adaptive value of the fluctuation it is best to present case studies rather than abstract summaries. I therefore give something of the history of two cases which I reconstructed from the memories of informants.

The first case was a family that initially had a very limited set of resources which the members together developed to a point where there was enough property for a formal division of it with adequate provision for each recipient. The founder of this family was a man I call Singh who came to Natal in 1886 under the indenture system to work for the Natal Railways for five years. After his time had expired, he did not renew his contract, as many other indentured labourers did; instead he started a small business catching and selling fish not far from the centre of Durban. At this time he married a local

Hindu woman by whom he eventually had three sons and two daughters. The sons received primary school education, but as they grew up, they joined their father in the fish business which flourished sufficiently to support them all and to allow for the extension of the family house, as more space was needed.

Adjoining this house were five acres of unused land which Singh simply took over at about the turn of the century and used for growing vegetables and other crops, particularly maize, thus providing both subsistence and further income for the family. Subsequently, the fish business was abandoned in favour of dairy farming which entailed a move further inland to what is now a suburb of Durban, but where land was then available for keeping cattle.

By this stage the household had become complex and the family a 'lineal' joint one, in that two of the sons were married and the eldest of them, Ramchund, had children of his own, as shown in Figure 1.

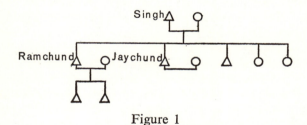

Figure 1

In 1920 Singh died, and for a while the sons continued to work the dairy farm with their widowed mother. Then the third son married a Coloured woman and went to live in Cape Town. This 'out-marriage' caused the family to sever its ties with him and he was disinherited from any share in the family business. He has never visited the family since then. Singh's two daughters also married and went to live with their husbands. At this stage, therefore, the household was still complex, but now comprised a 'fraternal' or 'collateral' joint family, as shown in Figure 2.

For some years, Ramchund and Jaychund worked the diary business together, but gradually disagreements between them began to multiply and eventually Jaychund wanted to have his share of the estate in money and take a job as a book-keeper elsewhere in Durban.

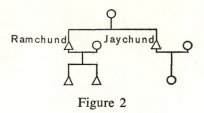

Figure 2

This dissension finally led to the separation of the brothers in 1930, with Jaychund being given his share, and the household was then reduced to its smallest extent – Singh's widow, who was by now old and infirm, Ramchund, his wife, and four children. At this stage, though the household was still complex, the family was no longer strictly 'joint'. However, a period of re-expansion then commenced, when Ramchund switched from the dairy business and invested in a shop, with which his three sons assisted as they grew up. Over the years, the business was so successful that other enterprises were added and ultimately included a supermarket, a grocery, a restaurant near the Indian market in Durban, a small cinema in central Durban, and another shop in a township south of Durban. As these enterprises were added, they were managed by the three sons, while Ramchund ran the original shop. The sons all married and they and their families lived with their parents in one large house, where, however, each of the daughters-in-law was eventually given her own kitchen. Ramchund's own daughters all married and moved out in the usual way. His mother died in the 1940s. In 1959, the composition of this complex household and lineally joint family reached the dimensions shown in Figure 3.

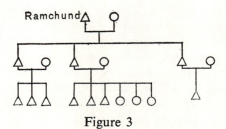

Figure 3

In the following year, Ramchund, who was then nearly seventy and had heart trouble, decided to divide the large estate equally amongst his three sons, because he foresaw that there might be friction between them after his death. He also provided a house for each of the first two sons and himself remained with the youngest son in the original family house. When Ramchund finally died in 1968, this household was reduced again to the minimal complexity of Figure 4.

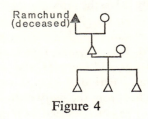

Figure 4

From this case, it can be seen how the 'joint family', at its various phases, repeatedly provided an 'estate' which sustained its members who, in turn, contributed their labour and skills to developing the estate to the point where it was possible to divide it into shares large enough for each 'coparcener' to make a living from his share. The case also indicates the extent to which both the cohesion of the household and the successful development of the estate depend upon the 'managerial' skills of the family head. These skills were exercised first by Singh who laid the foundation of the family business in foodstuffs, an avenue often followed by Indians in earlier decades, as Durban grew into a sizeable local market. While he was alive, he was able to keep his sons together as contributors to the estate and as beneficiaries of it. He was succeeded by Ramchund who, building on the foundations laid by his father, created a very successful commercial enterprise. He, too, kept his sons together for most of his life. It is noticeable, though, that the skills needed to keep the family together are more likely to be exercised effectively when the head is the father, than when he is the brother. Thus Ramchund's brothers did not stay with him and he anticipated conflict between his own sons after his death and divided both the household and the estate in order to prevent this. It seems that he, and his father before him, deployed essentially the same human and commercial skills within the constraints of the joint family structure, as did family heads in similar circumstances in East Africa and India (Benedict 1968; Owens 1971).

However, the urban setting creates other opportunities besides the formation of coparcenary commercial enterprises and among the most important of these is wage labour. A case in which the male members took advantage of this opportunity shows how complex households may be compatible with wage-earning. As in the previous case, the founder of the family was an indentured labourer, Naidoo, who came to South Africa in the 1860s and worked for five years. Like Singh, he then married a local Indian woman by whom he eventually had six sons and two daughters. He supported this large family by small-scale farming on leased plots near Durban. As the sons grew up, the land was not sufficient to provide them with a reasonable living, so they all went out to work and were employed as chefs in various hotels in Durban. By 1918 four of them were married and two lived with their families in the same dwelling as their parents. The other two occupied 'rooms' or outhouses in close proximity to their parents' home.

Naidoo then moved to a bigger, rented house in another part of Durban where he lived until his death a few years later. All of his married sons and one bachelor son apparently lived there too, with their own wives and children who, except for those of the third son, called Munsamy, all happened to be daughters. At this stage, therefore, the household was as shown in Figure 5.

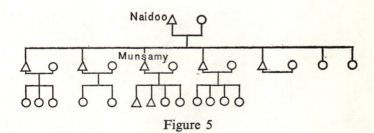

Figure 5

Since this stage occurred some fifty years before my fieldwork, I could not reconstruct with any confidence what the arrangements for cooking and eating were. But it is clear that there must have been contributions from the sons' wages towards such common expenses as the rent of the house. If, therefore, the family was not joint in the commensal and coparcenary senses, it was certainly more than a merely coresidential unit. Indeed, my informants from this family pointed out that living together provided all the members with security, particularly in times of unemployment, which implies that those who were earning were prepared to support the others who, at any one time, were not earning. The advantages of this arrangement were apparently sufficient to encourage the brothers to stay together after Naidoo died in the early 1920s and after the death of his wife a few years later. The fact that none of the brothers, except Munsamy, had sons who survived may have had something to do with their continuing coresidence, since it seems to be particularly the need to provide for sons which often leads to conflicting claims by brothers on the joint resources. Certainly, as the daughters married and moved out, there must have been less pressure on each brother to use his wages more in the interests of his own nuclear family.

As the brothers themselves died one by one during the next few decades, the continuity of the family depended on Munsamy and his sons. Up until his death in 1963, his eldest son and his youngest son, together with their respective families, lived in the same house, as had the middle son for the first five years after his marriage in 1935. By 1963, therefore, the composition of the household was as in Figure 6.

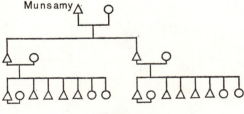

Figure 6

With the marriage of Munsamy's grandsons, pressures for division seem to have grown and certainly his two sons were not on very good terms. Even so, it was only after Munsamy's death and after the municipality had acquired for development purposes the land on which the house stood, that division did occur, each of the two sons finding accommodation for himself and his offspring elsewhere, and Munsamy's widow going with her eldest son.

The overall history of this family thus shows how dependence on wages earned in similar occupations and the sharing of rented accommodation can be just as compatible with a 'joint family' structure and developmental cycle, at least in the coresidential sense, as can common business interests and ownership of a house. It is true that families without a business and without fixed property lack the incentive of building up the profits of a common enterprise and are perhaps less able to adjust their accommodation to their changing needs. But, on the other hand, the pooling of wages to meet the expenses of a large household is efficient, relatively secure and, provided there is not too great a disparity of individual earnings, quite equitable.

These cases and the other material presented thus show yet again that the Indian 'joint family' has considerable adaptive value in a wide variety of situations. In South Africa, Indian people have had to cope with many disabilities, in addition to those normally confronting the poor when experiencing rapid industrialization and urbanization. The successes they have nevertheless achieved may in many cases be attributed at least partly to their modern versions of the ancient Indian institution of the joint family.

## NOTES

[1]The study was originally written up as an M.A. thesis in the Department of African Studies, University of Natal. I am very grateful to Professor John Argyle, the present Head of that Department, without whose help this paper could not have taken the form it has.

[2]The distinction between 'passengers' who came to South Africa at their own expense and 'indentured labourers' whose passages were provided, has been quite significant in the history of the Natal Indian community. Discussions of it, and of the other differentiating criteria, may be found in Kuper (1960) and Meer (1969).

[3]In four of the 35 households, there were additional members whose presence could not be accounted for in terms of the connections between male agnates. These were a divorced daughter and her children; a deceased daughter's orphan children; a married daughter and her husband; the child of a daughter who was temporarily overseas. As in the five cases of the first type of complex household, the link in these cases was from parent to daughter.

# REFERENCES

BENEDICT, B. 1968 – Family firms and economic development. *SWest. J. Anthrop.* **24,** 1–19.

KOLENDA, P. M. 1968 – Region, caste and family structure: a comparative study of the Indian 'joint' family. In *Structure and Change in Indian Society* (eds.) M. Singer and B. S. Cohn. Chicago: Aldine Publishing Co.

KUPER, H. 1960 – *Indian People in Natal.* Pietermaritzburg: Univ. of Natal Press.

MADAN, T. N. 1963 – The joint family: a terminological clarification. In *Family and Marriage* (ed.) J. Mogey. Leiden: E. J. Brill.

MEER, F. 1969 – *Portrait of Indian South Africans.* Durban: Avon House.

OWENS, R. 1971 – Industrialization and the Indian joint family. *Ethnology* **10,** 223–50.

SHAH, A. M. 1964 – Basic terms and concepts in the study of family in India. *Indian Econ. & Soc. Hist. Rev.* 2(3), 1–36.

————1974 – *The Household Dimension of the Family in India.* Berkeley: Univ. of California Press.

# USES OF THE KINSHIP IDIOM IN FRIENDSHIPS AT SOME VENDA AND ZULU SCHOOLS

*John Blacking*

In honouring a distinguished colleague and good friend, I have chosen to contribute briefly to what I consider to be the anthropologist's most lasting and fundamental task: the accumulation of detailed ethnographic data relating to the creation and use of cultural systems. Although ethnography is partly bound to culture and context by the subjective perceptions of observer, actors, and informants, it can transcend current anthropological fashions and theories, and, particularly in South Africa, it could be of some use to the descendants of the people studied, if only as a 'colonialist' viewpoint, when they have attained their political freedom and come to write their own social and cultural history.

I shall describe some aspects of an institution that I found in the northern Transvaal, in Johannesburg, and in north Natal, and which seemed to be commonly practised by girls in most modern schools for Africans in the 1950s and 1960s.

I encountered fictive kinship during fieldwork amongst the Venda in 1956–58, and I reported on its use by girls both at traditional 'puberty' and at modern primary and secondary schools (Blacking 1959). I had at first thought that the modern institutions, involving a complex of rights and obligations between a 'play mother' (*mme wa u tamba*) and her 'play child' (*ñwana wa u tamba*), was an adaptation of the traditional institution, in which a novice at the beginning of her formal education in the traditional *vhusha, tshikanda,* and *domba* schools, was given a 'mother' by the mistress of the novices (*Nematei*). The 'mother' and 'child' were called *mme* and *nwana wâ vhukomba* respectively (*vhukomba:* the state of being a nubile girl; the 'puberty' rites are often referred to as *khomba*). Venda informants drew my attention to the fact that the use of the possessive concord *wa* instead of the *a* that is appropriate for *mme* (e.g. *mme a ñwana*), indicates that the speaker is not referring to a real mother.

However, although the traditional and modern institutions do have much in common, particularly in their patterns of gift-giving, visiting, and of the dominance of the senior partner, there is no evidence of cultural continuity, except that similar social situations

101

may give rise to similar institutions. The origin of the use of fictive
kinship in schools can be traced to the late 1940s. It diffused to
Venda from the towns by way of the Lemana Teachers' Training
College near Louis Trichardt. In 1952, it was being 'played' in two
secondary schools, and by 1958 it had spread to several primary
schools. Further evidence of the separateness of the two institutions
is suggested by the behaviour of schoolgirls who had also attended
the traditional *vhusha*; they never pursued the relationship with the
'mother' chosen for them by the mistress of the novices. Moreover,
schoolgirls in general were far more enthusiastic about their 'play
mother/child' relationships than were uneducated girls about their
ritual companions.

I did not collect enough of the right kind of information to be
able to determine how far, if at all, this contrast in attitude was
generated by the importance attached to affection in relationships
and to individual choice in friendship, or by the need to establish
clearly the boundaries of the most valued social groups. Schoolgirls were fond of many of their kinsfolk, whether or not they
attended school, but they never chose kin as 'play children'. It
seemed important to disregard traditional distinctions of tribe,
clan, and social class: Venda, Lemba, Shangana-Tsonga, Sotho,
noble and commoner, all mixed freely in establishing fictive kin
bonds, and the disregard of real kin in the 'game', though not in
day-to-day relationships, reinforced their allegiance to a new way of
life, with corresponding new social groups similar to the 'School/
Red' contrast that Mayer reported amongst the Xhosa (Mayer 1971).
In this sense, the fictive kinship bond was equally symbolic of a
new status in both the modern school and the traditional *vhusha*
situations. But if the new social status *was* the prime factor in the
traditional fictive relationship, it was not correspondingly valued
by the uneducated girls. They could not choose their partners, and
they were rarely assigned real kin; but several said that they would
have been happier if the 'mother' chosen had been a relative. Were
they less interested than the schoolgirls in their fictive relationships
because they could not exercise individual choice and choose
friends (who might well be kin), or because the new, wider network
of social relationships established through *vhusha* was not as important as the network of ongoing relationships between families
which is confirmed and crystallized by marriage? Unfortunately,
my information on this is inconclusive.

I shall not consider further fictive kinship in the traditional Venda context, because there is no direct connection between it and the modern school institution which is the subject of this paper. Nor shall I discuss a special adaptation of the school kinship 'game' that was played in a girls' reformatory, since this will be the subject of a separate paper. I shall rather concentrate on the use of fictive kinship in boarding schools in north Natal, because its coexistence there with other kinds of association highlights those aspects that had seemed essential to the institution, judging from the way it was used in Venda day schools (Blacking 1959:156–7).

In the Venda day schools, which included Sotho and Shangana-Tsonga girls who were being educated in the same area, girls chose 'play children' and acted as their 'play mothers'. Through the initial relationship, some girls built up a network to include their 'mother's'* real siblings as 'mother's sister' and 'mother's brother', and their 'mother's' own 'mother' as 'grandmother'. In 1958, a few girls were taking girls as 'wives' and little boys as 'sons', but these elaborations were exceptional. During the same period, girls in some north Natal boarding schools were including boyfriends as 'husbands', 'fathers', or 'brothers', and the practice of taking other girls as 'husbands' or 'wives' was firmly established. A further relationship at boarding schools was that between 'eat-mates', who shared food, money, soap, and other goods. 'Mothers' and 'daughters' at boarding school seemed to lose contact more easily than those at day school, chiefly because their homes were often separated by great distances, often because the friendship cooled off, and sometimes because of certain restrictions on contact in the boarding school situation. The girls from Venda schools more frequently continued their fictive relationships into later life, selecting their 'children' (or 'mothers', if the 'child' married first) as bridesmaids, exchanging gifts, and so on, even after they had children of their own.

A comparison of the institution in Venda day schools (Blacking 1959) with that in Natal boarding schools, as described below, convinces me that the essential contrasts between the two are to be explained chiefly by the differences in the constitution of day schools

---

*In order to avoid constant repetition of the epithet 'play', all fictive relationships will be given in inverted commas, to distinguish them from actual relationships.

and boarding schools, and the longer history of the 'game' in the latter. I am convinced that the differences, at least in 1959, could not be usefully accounted for in terms of any significant cultural differences between Venda and Zulu. We are dealing with an institution that has been diffused from a single unknown source, or perhaps invented more than once, but one that is part of a common Black South African culture and is associated with modern school education. I do not know to what extent it was peculiar to women's culture, but I am sure that it had no significance in the maintenance of ethnic boundaries. I hope that someone may care to investigate the history of the institution further, while there is still a chance of discovering its origin and possibly its earliest uses.

## FORMAL AND INFORMAL RELATIONSHIPS IN A NORTH NATAL BOARDING SCHOOL

The context of the 'game' can best be illustrated by its practice in one particular school in northern Natal. This was a Catholic secondary school covering education between Standard VI (Higher Primary) and Matriculation (pre-University). It was a boarding school for girls, but some local youths attended as day boys.

Though primarily for Catholics, there were several who belonged to the Methodists or other denominations. Many of the parents had made great sacrifices to send their children to this school.[1]

Within the boarding school, there were different categories of person with whom girls had special relations, other than with the fictive kin that are my chief concern: new-comers, old-comers, bed-mates, class-mates, table-mates, eat-mates, gangs, and friends. Not everyone used the terms 'bed-mate' and 'table-mate', but the relationships were generally recognized.

*New-comers* (*msila*) were distinguished from old-comers, regardless of age, size, and stage at which they entered the school, though the status was most emphasized in the higher primary grades. Although dormitories were recruited on the basis of forms, the Sisters separated new-comers from the others, so that they should not be ill-treated at night. Most of the initiation of new-comers consisted of minor impositions, such as demands for pieces of chicken at meal-times by old-comers who were only one year senior. Failure to conform was noted and eventually punished at the Freshers' concert, which was referred to as 'the cutting of the tails'. If new-comers failed to do what was required of them at this concert, at which they were publicly pilloried, they were beaten by old-comers.

As far as I could find out, the term *'old-comer'* was used primarily to refer to girls in their second year at the school. Another of their functions was to organize the 'mother' – 'child' and 'husband' – 'wife' relationships of the new-comers. For the latter, they set up a 'court' and a 'priest' to conduct the 'marriage' ceremony after the new-comers had chosen their 'husbands'. Then, at the end of the first quarter, they set up a 'divorce' court, so that new-comers who had made a wrong choice, could have their 'marriages' dissolved. One group of old-comers in 1951 demanded payment of twenty fat-cakes for a 'divorce', and insisted that new-comers should carry out their obligations to their 'husbands' until they could pay.

The allocation of beds in the dormitories was arranged at the beginning of each year by the Sister in charge. But if a girl came early, she could choose her own bed, and so avoid an undesirable position, such as near the night bucket in the Upper Primary dormitories, or by the passage to the lavatory in the Standard VII dormitory. Furthermore, a girl could select her bed-mates, those who slept next to her. Talking in dormitories at any time was officially forbidden, except on Saturday mornings. On Saturday the girls rose at 0700 hours instead of 0500 hours, there was no Mass, and breakfast was at 0730 hours instead of 0700 hours. However, it was possible for a girl to talk quietly to her bed-mates, and when it was cold in winter, bed-mates sometimes shared their blankets and slept together, hoping that they would not be discovered by the Sister-in-charge. When bed-mates slept together, it was to keep warm, and girls insisted that there was none of the sexual contact that was associated with 'husbands' and 'wives'. Thus, whether or not girls who shared a bed actually kissed or petted each other, their behaviour was conceived of in two different ways, depending on whether they were bed-mates or 'spouses'.

Although the interaction of *class-mates* was broadly determined by their academic position in the school, girls brought to the classroom situation relationships that had been forged in other contexts, such as membership of a gang. If their interaction in the classroom interfered too much with the teaching, they would be separated, and particularly 'naughty' girls would be made to sit in the front row.

Just as the recruitment of dormitories was based on membership of the same form, or class, so girls were allocated to places at table on the basis of membership of the same form. I do not know what the rationale of the Sisters' allocations was, apart from the fact that senior matric girls were placed at the head of the junior form tables, to maintain good order. I had hoped that I might be able to detect the influence of groups of *table-mates*, whose positions are assigned, on patterns of friendship, and I was particularly interested in who sat opposite, and who sat beside, a particular person. I did not gather sufficient data on table-mates, but that which I had showed no special connection between a girl's position at table and her selection of other kinds of associate. Perhaps it is significant that informants had the most difficulty in remembering their table-mates, whereas their memory for 'mothers', 'children', 'husbands', 'wives', friends and eat-mates was generally very good.

The food at the school was considered to be very bad, but when complaints were made, the Sisters explained that the girls were not paying sufficient money for good food. In 1950 breakfast consisted of a plate of European-type porridge, with sugar but no milk, and a piece of brown bread. On Sunday they had, in addition, jam with the bread and a mug of cocoa. Lunch consisted of maize meal porridge with vegetables, but three times a week meat was added. Supper was porridge and a small slice of bread. The food improved in 1951, and in 1952 peanut butter was added to the bread at supper.

I have described the food in detail, because it may be a significant factor in the importance attached to *eat-mates*. The eat-mates relationship was concerned with the distribution of extra food, and although much of this was eaten outside the dining-room, the relationship impinged on that of table-mates: girls felt obliged to give to their nearest neighbours at table a little of the food that they had received from their eat-mates.

Eat-mates also shared money and soap, and did each other's laundry, especially when one of the group was taking matric and needed extra study-time. The importance of reciprocity and sharing was emphasized more strongly in this relationship than in any other. One girl was expelled from a group of eat-mates for 'swallowing' their money; another for not sharing her own money; and another for gossiping about the meanness of her less wealthy fellow eat-mates. If a girl was sick, one of her eat-mates had to write and tell her parents. Similarly, nobody talked about power or authority in the eat-mate relationship, as they frequently did vis-à-vis 'husbands' and 'wives', although older eat-mates were inclined to verbalize their relationship to younger eat-mates in terms of protection.

Eat-mates were not commonly found in day schools, because children ate at home. However, there were groups of eat-mates in one day school where the lunch break was too short for girls to go home and they had 'found it embarrassing to eat alone'. The obligation to share food is deeply rooted in all Black societies in South Africa.

Most informants were agreed that the eat-mates relationship was the most permanent of all those I have mentioned, with the possible exception of that of friends. It was considered a 'much higher and stronger relationship', than that between 'husband' and 'wife'. Eat-mates were not necessarily recruited from the same dormitories or classrooms, but all eat-mates that I investigated were either 'home-girls' or kin, or both, or the established eat-mates of an eat-mate, and almost all of them had been known or met *before* arriving at the school. If it was sometimes described as 'strong as a blood relationship', it may have been because it most frequently was a blood relationship. At one extreme were eat-mates who had been introduced by a relative, at the other were girls from the same place who had met in the train. They had found they were going to the same school, had shared their travel food, and had promptly struck up a relationship. Thus, the eat-mate relationship was, neither in the first place, nor when it continued after school, based on food, though a gift of food might be given as a symbolic expression. For instance, a good friend of one of my informants, who was a nurse in Johannesburg, suddenly gave her four bottles of peanut butter and said she still cherished the good relationship they had had at school.

I have little information on *gangs* in girls' schools. In the particular boarding school I have been describing, there was a gang of oldcomers who threw their weight around, particularly in their second year. Most of them came from Johannesburg. There was a belief that Johannesburg children had a better knowledge of 'civilization' than those from Natal, and this was generally upheld in a number of Natal schools by this solidarity and arrogance of groups of boys and girls who came from Igoli, the City of Gold. The association of these informal gangs with modernity was further indicated by the name of an obstreperous group that called itself the Hot Trio.

The original topic of my investigation was *friendship*, which I thought might be influenced by the restrictions on interaction and the chance associations (such as table-mates, bed-mates) imposed by the institutions of the school. By investigating friendship in the context of schools, I was also introducing an additional limitation: the minority position of educated Black women in South Africa restricted their range of choice of friends, because they felt compelled to stick together as educated, modern young women.

Taking into account all the different kinds of associations of one girl over a period of ten years, from Higher Primary School to University, I found that the four friendships which she described as true and enduring emerged during her last three years at boarding school, when she was 'growing out of' the kinship games. The importance of these four friends, in contrast to other companions, was reflected in her photograph albums, in which they all feature prominently, whilst only three out of six 'husbands', one out of six 'mothers', two out of seven 'children', and one of the Hot Trio, are represented. A common interest in educational success was an important feature of the friendships, but they were also based on affection and mutual attraction, which rendered any of the more formal relationships unnecessary: 'because I felt close to these girls, I didn't have to fish out friendship with them. I was sure of their friendship'.

## THE 'MOTHER' – 'CHILD' GAME

The rules of the game in north Natal boarding schools were basically the same as those described for the Venda. The relationship was asymmetrical, and the 'child' had to show respect to her 'mother'. In most schools, physical age and size were important criteria of selection, so that a 'mother' could have a 'daughter' in a higher academic class. In only one school known to me were girls' positions in class regarded as the crucial factors in selection. 'Mothers' liked to protect their 'children', give them presents and extra food (especially when they were prefects and had privileged access), offer advice and settle quarrels. In general, 'mothers' chose 'children', but some girls offered to fag for a 'mother' and become her 'baby', and, as indicated above, a group of girls could instruct new-comers to choose their 'mothers'.

There seemed to be two significant differences between the practice of the game in day and boarding schools. Firstly, in boarding schools the relationships generally ceased after only one or two years, often because one of the partners left the school, and in any case, they were very rarely pursued in later life, as they were, for example, amongst the Venda. Secondly, the rule that a 'baby' could not have two 'mothers' was observed in boarding schools but frequently broken in day schools, so that some 'children' had as many as four 'mothers'. An explanation given was that in day schools the game was not taken as seriously. 'Besides, it is easier to check who has more than one mother in a boarding school. A girl who was found to have multiple 'mothers', or 'husbands', was punished. When they found out, her 'mothers' and/or 'husbands' beat her and ordered her to choose single partners and 'forget all about' the others.

### THE 'HUSBAND' – 'WIFE' GAME

The relationships were asymmetrical, and the rules were similar to those for the 'mother' – 'child' partnership. One aspect of the relationship was the exchange of gifts, Christmas cards, presents of photo albums, handkerchiefs, etc., but the most important feature was that which aroused ambivalent feelings amongst the girls themselves, and also provoked criticism and banning by school authorities: a good 'husband' was expected to call 'his' 'wife' to 'his' bed and tell her stories – especially about 'his' experiences with boyfriends. When a 'man' asked a 'wife' to come to 'his' bed, he was said to have dished her up (*phaka*).

When girls first came to school or were asked to be 'wives', they were often shy about kissing and petting and pretending to be lovers. This reticence generally passed with time, especially if they became deeply attached to another girl and found that they enjoyed intimate physical contact. Though the game was never regarded as a substitute for real relationships with boyfriends, it was practised even in co-educational schools; and though some girls used an improvized dildo, the sexual play was not considered as important as the status derived from being a 'husband' and having the authority to 'command my "wives" and order them about', or the pleasure of listening to a 'husband's' experiences in love with boyfriends.

The objections of Europeans were rarely effective, because girls noted that they did not apply the same rules to their own kind. 'Why do churches condemn in Africans what they condone in Whites?

Is it because they have a greater protective feeling for Africans?'
'The Chaplain at a conference in Cape Town allowed European
boys to go into the European girls' rooms, but he forbade African
boys to enter African girls' rooms.' 'Why are White students allowed by the Church to kiss in public, but Black students are forbidden?'

The language of the game was commonly Sotho or Zulu, but
*tsotsi-taal* (an urban dialect) was favoured in the 'husband' –
'wife' relationship. Writing letters was an important part of the
relationship, and they always had to be in English. 'At this stage,
we used to spend Saturday afternoons writing gorgeous letters to
our "boy-friends". We used all the beautiful words we had heard
or read about.'

## THE USES OF FICTIVE KINSHIP IN BOARDING SCHOOLS

As a general rule, girls progressed from being 'daughter', 'mother',
and 'wife', to being 'mother' and 'husband' only. Girls began to
choose 'daughters' before they chose 'wives', and when they became 'husbands' they gave up having 'mothers'. Thus, D chose her
first 'daughter' when she was fifteen and in Standard VII. When
she was eighteen, she chose her first 'husband' and ceased being
a 'child' to anyone.

Since fictive kin relationships were asymmetrical, the choice of
'child' or 'wife', as with the choice of eat-mates, but for different
reasons, generally transcended class and dormitory boundaries.
Reasons given for the choice of particular people varied considerably,
as did explanations of the significance of the relationship. Without
implying any hierarchy, the following factors were considered relevant:

a. *Conformity* to the system. It was because of this that a number
of girls distinguished between 'free, spontaneous' friendship and
the formal requirements of fictive kinship. Thus, when 'V became
so friendly to me that she was more of a friend than a "mother",
and I could not give her the respect due to a "mother" ', V's 'child'
decided to call V 'husband', 'in order to escape being proposed to
by other girls'. Because V had become a friend, she could pretend to
be a 'husband'.

Resistance to conformity was very rare. Thus one of the few who
would have nothing to do with the 'husband' – 'wife' game at

the north Natal school had a particularly strong personality and was the daughter of a Zulu *nduna*, and her mother was a diviner (*isangoma*). She had confidence from the beginning, was popular and a prefect, and needed none of the protection that comes from being a 'wife'. Another non-conformist flatly refused to be a 'child' or a 'wife', but she accepted being a 'mother' and a 'husband'.

A common observation was that 'the big girls wanted *everyone* to take part in the "husband–wife" game'. Some girls became so engrossed in their role as 'wife', that they forgot their 'husbands' were really girls and could not bring themselves to eat with them. And so important was conformity that having more than one 'mother' or 'husband' was never condoned, even though it might be attempted.

b. The desire for *authority* or the exercise of *protection*, together with their counterparts of *submission* and *security*, were often given as explanations of the emergence of particular 'husband' – 'wife' and 'mother' – 'daughter' relationships. In some cases, senior girls simply wanted a fag, or junior girls wanted a patron. It was often argued that the 'mother' – 'child' relationship helped new girls to adjust to the strange environment and to avoid loneliness.

c. A concern for *expanding social relationships* was commonly expressed in three ways, two of which were contained within the system:

(i) *Discussions about girls' relationships* within the system were accompanied by attempts to connect 'families' into larger networks. Girls did not necessarily share the knowledge of all the ongoing relationships of their 'kin', so that in the course of such discussions they often discovered new 'relatives' e.g. M discovered that her 'husband' had a 'child', who then claimed her as 'mother'.

(ii) The offer to *'bring you into a family'* was attractive to many: on becoming the child of a 'married woman', D 'welcomed the prospect of joining a big family'.

The process of expansion was not automatically accepted by all concerned, and this was one reason why some were secretive about certain 'kin'. When A wanted to have as a 'child' a girl who happened to be her 'mother's' eat-mate, it was important that A's 'husband' approved, and it was an added advantage that her 'mother' also liked 'her son-in-law', who would become the 'father' of the 'mother's' eat-mate.

(iii) *Bringing real brothers and boyfriends into the system* was a common practice, and it was often allied to match-making. For instance, J liked P very much, asked her to be her 'wife', introduced her to her brother and started arranging their (real) marriage. They were subsequently engaged, but they eventually broke it off at University.

When boyfriends were introduced into the system, it did not conflict with the rule that a girl could not have two 'fathers' or 'mothers'. For instance, when a 'mother' introduced her 'child' to her real boyfriend, he could become her 'father'. If the 'mother' later married, her husband could also be a 'father' to her 'child'. There was no linguistic distinction between internal and external 'father'.

d. The most striking and common explanation of behaviour, apart from the general agreement to conform, was the desire to consolidate an unexplained but clearly stated *attraction* for another person. At the general level of rationalization one informant said, typically, 'the reason one chooses a child is that one admires someone very much and seeks a way of coming close. One would like to have a child like that'.

More specifically, D chose J as a 'child' because she was 'good-looking'; another was chosen because she was 'attractive', and another because she was 'a nice little girl'. The definition of 'nice' was in some cases accompanied by the attribute of obedience, but since this was an automatic feature of the 'mother' – 'child' relationship it was not as significant a quality as the 'niceness'.

When I began to investigate the game and pattern of friendship, I anticipated that the explanation of affection might be a rationalization of other, perhaps more basic bonds. Indeed, there were cases where a girl chosen was already known (J's aunt had taught with D's mother; L chose D as her 'wife' through V, who was her home-girl; one 'mother' – 'child' relationship was revived after a lapse of two years, because in the meantime the 'mother' had become interested in her 'child's' real brother, who was a student at Fort Hare University College), and more than once a girl confessed that she remained loyal to an 'unattractive' 'mother' because she had money.

But again and again, the reasons given for inaugurating or breaking a relationship were affective. If relationships were not dropped because a partner left the school, it was because they lost interest in each other, or one partner simply could not bring herself to like the other, even though the other wanted to continue. For example, a break of relationship in one girl's second year seemed at first to be the result of her moving into a different class from her 'mother' with whom she had shared a desk; but the relationship invariably transcended classroom bonds in any case, and closer examination of this case revealed that they had had a quarrel and their mutual affection had waned. Even so, they later became eat-mates and continued with a different kind of relationship.

This emphasizes apparent contradictions between the actors' behaviour and their rationalizations of it: their formal relationships tended to be more permanent and they dramatized some strongly affective relationships in terms of the formal language of kinship, and yet they considered mutual attraction to be the sole ground for a really good relationship and spoke of bonds with kin in a matter-of-fact way. There is one possible explanation which rests on psychological assumptions that are beyond the scope of this paper and the range of my data, but it should be mentioned: the actor's comment that she did not need to formalize relationships with others when she 'was sure of their friendship'; the fact that those deeper, lasting friendships developed towards the end of her school career; and the generally held view that passionate, romantic relationships cannot last, which for most of my informants had been reinforced both at home and at school. All these suggest that an important use of the kinship 'game' was to provide emotional stability during a period of physiological change and fleeting fancies, or even a substitute for more regular relations with boys. There was, however, no correlation between, say, a girl's lack of boyfriends and a greater interest in fictive kinship: in fact, I often found that girls who used fictive kinship enthusiastically were extrovert and friendly, and that their network served as a base for discussing their boyfriends. Moreover, fictive relationships were taken very seriously and seemed to be more lasting in Venda day schools, where girls had every opportunity to meet their boyfriends regularly. In the Venda case, I still hold to my original explanation of the behaviour, seeing the fictive kinbonds as a means of reinforcing the solidarity of girls in a social environment where educated women were very much a minority group (Blacking 1959:158). In the north Natal schools, women's education seemed to have been more common and more generally accepted. Here, although anyone who was able to attend a secondary school was clearly exceptional in relation to the total population, I have no verbal statements and behavioural data to suggest that the girls saw themselves as a minority group or fictive kinship as a means of social support. It might also be argued that fictive kinship served as a substitute for family life in the event of its breakdown, and, indeed, three of the most enthusiastic 'kin' operators in one Natal school happened to come from broken homes and had strong views on the kind of relationships they hoped to have with their husbands; but these same three girls, like many others, maintained good relationships with family and kin, which were reflected in their recruitment of and comments on their eat-mates.

The apparent contradictions between the Zulu girls' behaviour and their rationalizations, between relationships that were affection-ate and lasting, affectionate but transitory, prescribed, formal, or informal, and their expression in the idioms of kinship and friend-ship, begin to disappear when one considers the range of sentiments that were subsumed under the same kinship categories. Although behaviour between kin may have been formal and obligatory, it could also be intimate and affectionate, and in either case the genealo-gical closeness of the relationship was not necessarily the crucial criterion. Closeness and continuity of residence seemed to be more important, so that the order of precedence in affection tended to be (1) genealogically close kin who were regularly visited, such as parents' siblings, cousins, and grandparents; (2) neighbouring kinsfolk, regardless of genealogical closeness; (3) neighbours; (4) genealogically close kin who were rarely visited, spatially distant kin, and distant friends. Friends might be placed at any point, but I do not think that any fictive kin were placed above (3). In the con-text of the boarding school, (2) and (3) were referred to as 'home-girls' and often with equal affection, and it was considered appro-priate to express this affection in the kinship idiom, as I pointed out earlier. Thus, the formal language of kinship could be used with complete consistency to refer both to the quality of a relationship, as an ideal of affection, and to the status of a relationship, which might be formal and not particularly affectionate. When the same girl said that she liked one girl so much that she wanted her to be her 'child', and another so much that it was not necessary to establish a fictive kin relationship, she was neither expressing confusion and ambivalence about the meaning of kinship, nor being insincere about fictive kinship; she was adjusting her use of the kinship idiom to different social situations. The kinship idiom provides a way of expressing and crystallizing affection, just as much as it can refer to a formal, permanent relationship which may rarely be invoked and probably involves no special feelings of affection.

When I began to extend my study of fictive kinship after leaving Venda, I was interested in finding out to what extent the growth of friendship and affection might be influenced by external conditions and constraints imposed upon the actors, and it seemed to me that the relatively restricted environment of boarding schools provided particularly suitable cases for study. I was not denying the possibility of free choice in friendship, but I sought to eliminate as far as possible all psychological considerations, and look for the kinds of situation that made it more likely that particular girls should become friends – such as being placed together at table or in the classroom, or in dormitory beds that allowed talking after lights out. For the estimates of the quality of friendship I relied on the girls' accounts and their decisions to crystallize certain relationships in the form of eat-mates, fictive kin and so on.

As I gathered more data, so the picture of patterns of interaction and explanations of behaviour became less clear. For a number of reasons, I was not able to collect the additional data that might have restored the clear vision that I had at the beginning of my study, though it would have been a rather different picture. Although my account is inevitably incomplete and inconclusive, two facts emerge very clearly from the Venda and Zulu behaviour relating to fictive kinship and friendship. Firstly, there were no significant ethnic culture differences between the systems of relationships, either in observed behaviour or in actors' perceptions of situations: both belonged to a common Black South African culture. Secondly, a common denominator in the creation and evaluation of relationships was mutual affection, which often emerged as a spontaneous surge of fellow-feeling and, if it developed into a lasting relationship, was the most valued aspect of the bond. Girls did not seem to make much effort to maintain a relationship unless they *felt* good with each other.

In recent years, anthropologists have begun to turn their attention to friendship and affection in relationships. These factors become increasingly important as studies of social organization focus on patterns of recruitment and group interaction, rather than the structures of the categories that are invoked. The connections between fictive kinship and real kinship in the school situations that I have described, cannot be properly understood unless it is appreciated that the fictive is no more or less real than the real: both fictive kinship and real kinship are uses of the kinship idiom that cover a broad range of behaviour and values, depending on their situational context; and amongst the important variables are spatial proximity and quantity of encounters, but most particularly the quality of interaction. It is not enough to refer to the quality of interaction as 'warm' or 'close-knit', particularly when such observations are based on purely quantitative data: we have to devise some way of measuring and evaluating compassion and affection, for it is ultimately these qualities that most deeply affect decision-making processes, and hence the use of cultural knowledge in social interaction and the distillation of social experience in cultural tradition.

## NOTE

[1] One example will illustrate the aspirations and disappointments that afflict families who seek to improve the chances of their children. The parents of E were working in Johannesburg, to provide for their family, while she lived at home in Natal with her father's sister, who wanted her to marry. As a result of the persuasion and financial assistance of a friend of her mother, E came to the boarding school in 1955 and completed her studies during the following three years. Then, in quick succession, she suffered the loss of her father's brother, who was stabbed in Johannesburg; her father's sister, who died in a train accident; and her father's father, who died in 1959. Shortly after this, she herself died of tuberculosis in Natal. Though there were no suggestions of witchcraft in the deaths that preceded E's, people said that she had been bewitched by the wife of another brother of her father when she was staying with them in Orlando, Johannesburg. They did not go to a diviner, but the explanation of misfortune emphasizes the kind of anxiety that prompts people to send their children away from the big cities to boarding schools.

## ACKNOWLEDGEMENT

I would like to thank many African informants who helped me in the collection of data. I have not been able to contact them personally, and so I am unwilling to cite them individually without their permission.

## REFERENCES

BLACKING, J. 1959 – Fictitious kinship amongst girls of the Venda of the Northern Transvaal, *Man* **59**; 155–8.

MAYER, P. 1971 – *Townsmen or Tribesmen*, (second edn.) Cape Town: Oxford Univ. Press.

# BOND FRIENDSHIP AMONG AFRICAN FARMERS IN RHODESIA*

## Angela P. Cheater

In the past, social anthropologists tended to concentrate their analytical attention on involuntary, ascribed relationships located within the jural domain of kinship. More recently, however, there has been an increasing tendency to focus on voluntary, achieved relationships of various kinds. In this paper, therefore, I wish to examine the particular type of extra-kin relationship, known among Shona-speakers as *usahwira*[1], which I translate as bond friendship.

Bond friendship is, of course, widely known throughout the world, in the South Pacific (Firth 1936), North America, Australia, Asia (Okada 1957), Europe (Hamilton-Grierson 1909) and Africa, where it is particularly widespread. This type of extra-kin relationship is generally regarded as falling outside the jural domain of legally enforceable rights and obligations (cf. Pitt-Rivers 1973), but it is nevertheless essentially contractual in nature. This contractual aspect, based on promise and reinforced only within the moral domain, specifies commitments which are formally and publicly assumed. While these obligations are freely chosen and rely mainly on honour for fulfilment, they nevertheless remain close to the jural domain. Indeed, where bond friendship is heritable and becomes ascribed, in second and subsequent generations, it might well be regarded as part of the jural domain, despite the absence of legal mechanisms to enforce these publicly-assumed commitments.

### DEFINING BOND FRIENDSHIP

The confusion over whether bond friendship is or is not 'jural' in nature, is reflected in the plethora of English terms used to describe relationships which, in their essentials, do not appear to differ significantly. Artificial brotherhood, fictitious brotherhood, pact bro-

*I am deeply indebted to Eileen Krige for inspiring in me, as an under-graduate student, an abiding interest in and love for her academic discipline. This essay is a small gesture of gratitude. I should also like to thank John Argyle, Don Baker, Michael Bourdillon, Gordon Chavunduka, Graham Cheater and Desmond Reader for their comments on earlier drafts of this paper.

therhood, ritual brotherhood, sworn brotherhood, blood brotherhood, the blood pact and the blood covenant have variously been
used by those writers seeking to locate this relationship within the
jural domain of pseudo-kinship. In contrast, ritual friendship, funeral
friendship, bond friendship and even, on occasion, 'joking relationship', emphasize non-jural definitions. Possibly because of this difficulty in defining the nature of the relationship in question, only a
few limited attempts at cross-cultural comparison have been made
for African societies: by Moreau (1943) for a number of Tanzanian
tribes; by Tew (1951) for those Central African societies in which
'funeral friendship' is found; and by Beidelman (1963) for the Kaguru
and Azande. No-one has yet attempted to examine systematically the
common components of this type of relationship for all African
societies in which it occurs: Tegnaeus (1952) restricts his consideration only to those societies reported to exhibit some form of 'blood
brotherhood', although his coverage does remain the most extensive.
It is, of course, beyond the compass of this paper to attempt such
broad comparisons in detail, but it is necessary to isolate the features
common to bond friendship in its various forms in all the African
societies for which there is published information, before consider-
ing the Shona material.

CONTRACT

Firstly, then, bond friendship links people who are not kinsmen in
a voluntary relationship based on promise. The commitments of the
partners are specified, at least minimally, when the relationship is
formally established and publicly ratified: they entail mutual assistance in social, economic and sometimes political fields. A recurrent
theme, particularly in East and Central Africa, is the obligation to
protect bond friends from potential hostility: thus, in precolonial
times, this relationship frequently linked trading partners belonging
to different tribes, guaranteeing their security when travelling. A
somewhat different type of protection operated among the Gurage
of Ethiopia, where this bond ensured that a man had allies against
his own brothers when inheritance disputes occurred (Shack 1963).
Among the Nyoro, the *mukama* (king) was reputed to have entered
into bond friendship with his personal attendants and cooks, to safe-
guard his life and health (Hamilton-Grierson 1909; Tegnaeus 1952;
Beattie 1958).

The contractual aspect of bond friendship is clearly apparent from the public specification of commitments at the time the relationship is established. In many cases, these commitments are supported by supernatural sanctions, which are, of course, moral and not legal and which are believed to operate automatically against partners guilty of breaching the relationship, in thought or deed. In some cases, these supernatural sanctions may stem from the ingestion of the bond friend's blood[2] when the relationship is established. However, even where such ingestion is *not* a diacritical feature of the establishment of the bond (as among the Shona, for example), the fact of having made a public promise to fulfil certain commitments to one's partner, creates moral sanctions of a diffuse nature, which in practice may prove quite as effective as legal mechanisms of enforcement. That supernatural and moral sanctions are not complemented by legal backing does not necessarily negate the contractual aspect of bond friendship: a promise remains binding, partly because it is useful.

EQUALITY

The second common feature of bond friendship is that it usually links people in a relationship of equality, which is reflected in familiarity and intimacy between partners. Such familiarity may develop into the 'ritualised aggression' (Beidelman 1963) of a fully established joking relationship.[3] The egalitarian nature of contractual bond friendship usually contrasts quite markedly with the hierarchical nature of jural kinship relations in African societies. The only exceptions to the rule of equality between bond friends that I have been able to find in the African literature, concern the bonds established between *mukama* and servants, and between Bito and non-Bito, in the stratified society of Bunyoro (Beattie 1958); and perhaps those bonds linking the Swazi king to his *tinsila* (Kuper 1947).

Because bond friendship is contracted between social equals, and also because the functions of bond friendship fall largely within the domain of male behaviour, it is hardly surprising that this relationship usually links men. In rare cases (as among the Ambo, Azande and Ndembu, for example), women may also contract bond friendship with other women, but it is very unusual indeed for women to become the bond friends of men, perhaps because relationships linking men and women generally fall within the jural domain of kinship. Only the Kaguru and Luguru seem to have permitted intersexual bonds freely, although among the Azande, Ganda and Shona, spouses are (or were) more or less automatically drawn into the bond friendships of their marital partners. In such cases, it is the individual families, rather than the actual spouses, who are deemed 'equal' within the relationship.

EXTENSION

Thirdly, in most African societies bond friendship is contracted between individuals for whom the contractual obligations of this relationship are personally binding. Nevertheless, it is possible for the contractual relationship to be extended, in 'treaty' form, to include the elementary family, lineage, clan or even tribe. The further such extension ramifies, the more likely it is that the relationship will be nominal rather than effective. Among the Shona, for example, where wives are drawn into their husbands' bond friendships, they are recessive participants, the main link being between the men. It is possible that some of the clan and tribal joking relationships reported in Central African societies (cf. Moreau 1943; Stefaniszyn 1950) arose through this mechanism of extension, particularly following the establishment of bond friendship between chiefs as a means of making peace (cf. Weeks 1914; Tegnaeus 1952). For example, joking relationships link the Nguni to those tribes they could not defeat in war (their military equals), and it is most probable that such joking relations represent an extension of treaty bonds between chiefs suing for peace (Tegnaeus 1952).

FUNCTIONS

So we come to the fourth feature of bond friendship in African societies: its common functions. I have already touched upon its uses when noting earlier that bond friends were obliged to protect one another from potential or actual harm. Frequently, then, by linking unrelated people in contractual relationships, bond friendship was concerned with extra-group relations, 'foreign relations' on a small scale. Trade and travel, feud and warfare, recur time and again as the contexts within which bond friendship was established, particularly in precolonial times. With pacification and incorporation into wider territorial units under colonial administrations, the need for bond friendship to protect people in foreign territories largely fell away.

As a result, the institution itself died out in societies such as the
Kaguru (Beidelman 1963) and Nyoro (Beattie 1958); and in others,
such as the Azande (Evans-Pritchard 1933), it assumed purely social
significance, indicating an unusual degree of intimacy in friendship
without the specific commitments attaching to the traditional institution.[4] If the environment within which bond friendship once
flourished has changed so radically as to cause it to die out in some
societies, one should ask why it has persisted in others. Among
Shona-speakers, for example, *usahwira* may still be found in contexts
very different from those of precolonial society.

BOND FRIENDSHIP AMONG SHONA-SPEAKERS

Although the *usahwira* relationship among Northern Shona tribes
dates from precolonial times, it is not mentioned by the early standard authors (Bullock 1928; Posselt 1927, 1935); and with the exception of his note that *usavira* pacts used to be important among the
Budjga, incorporating 'unlimited hospitality and assistance in times
of emergency' together with undertaking services (1953:viii), Holleman (1952, 1958) also ignores bond friendship. Bourdillon (1972,
1976), however, in keeping with the formal translation of *sahwira*
as 'ritual friend' (Hannan 1968:556), describes in some detail the
ritual functions of bond friends among the Korekore. But no systematic attempt has yet been made to examine *usahwira* bonds in their
contemporary social context, nor, indeed, to examine the recognized
commitments, other than ritual obligations, of this relationship.

My concern in this paper, then, is to fill at least part of this gap in
our knowledge of bond friendship in Rhodesia. My data on *usahwira*
bonds were gathered during 1973–4 in an African freehold farming
area in Central Mashonaland, some 100 kilometres west of the capital, Salisbury. Farmers from different tribal backgrounds began buying farms in Msengezi some forty years ago and have since established
a polyethnic community[5] which differs considerably, in social and
political organization as well as economic pursuits, both from precolonial Shona societies and from contemporary 'tribal' areas in
which the traditional basis of society, while undoubtedly modified
in many important respects, is nonetheless still detectable. Each of
the 300-odd farmers in this area was asked about *usahwira* bonds,
particularly with other farmers in the area: fifty-four claimed to have
such ties, usually with neighbours on adjacent farms. Over half of

these ties supposedly linked men of different ethnic identities. Yet, on analysis of the data, only fourteen of these claims were found to be reciprocal, eight involving men of the same tribal category. Non-Shona immigrants, especially Mfengu and Tonga, most frequently claimed involvement in *usahwira* bonds which were not reciprocated: I shall consider the possible reasons for such non-reciprocation later.

Since this material was collected in a new society, in which Zezuru 'owners of the land' comprised only two-fifths of all farmers, its reliability and representativeness may certainly be questioned in the wider Shona context. But since this information pertains to a commercial farming area in which considerable cultural interchange has occurred, it is particularly interesting to note the persistence of *usahwira* bonding in such a new environment and to consider its contemporary significance. I shall discuss *usahwira* in Msengezi following the four broad areas of common characteristics identified earlier: contract, equality, extension, and functions.

## CONTRACT AND COMMITMENT

*Usahwira* is institutionalized among Shona-speakers through a clearly-defined mode of establishment which, in turn, implies recognized commitments. People believe that the relationship grows over time and the point at which simple friendship (*ushamwari*) becomes bond friendship (*usahwira*) should be a public affirmation at which first one partner and then the other brews beer, slaughters a beast and publicly acknowledges the formal relationship at an open neighbourhood feast. It is this public affirmation of *usahwira* rather than the ingestion of blood (which is, apparently, unknown among Shona peoples), which establishes the contractual obligation of mutual assistance. Such assistance may be economic (for example, the loan of oxen for ploughing); or social (such as arbitration in domestic disputes between husband and wife, or between parents and children); or educational (in the absence of a suitable *vatete* [father's sister], for example, an adolescent girl may be sent to a female *sahwira* for instruction on sexual and marital matters[6]). The diacritical obligation, however, is the responsibility to 'organize everything for the home' when the bond friend (or a member of his family) dies, to make sure that the mourners are fed, and especially to receive the coffin in the grave. In Msengezi, however, this organizational responsibility did *not* include the personal obligation to wash and enshroud the corpse and carry it to the grave, nor to dig the grave itself, as occurs among the Korekore (Bourdillon 1972) and many Malawian tribes (cf. Fraser 1914; Stannus 1922; Mitchell 1951). In addition, the importance of the *sahwira* is recognized in the obligation to send to him or her the 'best part' (the rump and tail) of each and every beast that is slaughtered, for whatever reason (cf. Bourdillon 1972). Sending parts of publicly slaughtered animals to the *sahwira* may reflect repeated affirmation of the original contract, or at least a continued willingness to abide by promises made at the time the bond was established.

Apart from these clearly defined commitments, the nature of the *usahwira* bond makes the *sahwira* the most appropriate person to perform other duties within his partner's family, such as acting as marriage negotiator (*munyai*) and ensuring that people are fed at any wedding. These duties, however, are optional rather than obligatory.

In real life, of course, both the manner of establishing bond friendship and the performance of partners in meeting their commitments may leave something to be desired when set against the ideals that people hold. For example, in 1967 two Msengezi farmers contracted *usahwira* in the local pub: they had frequently drunk together in the past and simply bonded their friendship by the exchange of half-a-crown and an extra quart of 'Chibuku'. Despite this unusual manner of establishing the relationship both men nevertheless regarded it as binding perhaps because it was contracted in public.

Regarding the type of relationship established, and notwithstanding Bourdillon's (1976:80) assertion that *usahwira* is a 'quasi-kinship' bond, there is no suggestion among Shona-speakers that *usahwira* converts the partners to kin of any kind. 'You may have brothers and other relatives, but generally the one close to your heart is the *sahwira*' was the way in which one farmer expressed his conception of this relationship, implying a distinct contrast between kin and bond friends. Other factors also make this distinction plain: in normal circumstances, a kinsman should not act as marriage negotiator, whereas the *sahwira* is preferred in this role; kin should not interfere in marital disputes, whereas the *sahwira*, having licence as an equal to say exactly what he thinks, is thought to be most suitable for domestic arbitration and most likely, as an 'outsider', to have his judgement accepted. Finally, there is a weak but explicit preference for a later marriage tie between the families linked in *usahwira*: 'Now

out of *usahwira*, eventually the children of the two families will encourage intermarriage between the two families'.[7]

## EQUALITY AND ASYMMETRY

This clear distinction between kin and bond friends reflects the difference between the egalitarian nature of bond friendship and the hierarchical nature of kin relationships. As in other African societies, the
egalitarian element of *usahwira* is shown in reciprocal joking and
'borrowing' of property: '. . . you can say anything to a *sahwira* and
he will accept . . .'; '. . . he is free to ask for food, not like other
visitors . . .'; '. . . he is free to borrow anything from you that you
have . . .'; '. . . there is no paying back for a *sahwira* . . .'; '. . . he's
entitled to challenge you that you are wrong, if you have family
trouble, or if you have been misbehaving . . .'

Such joking is particularly important at funerals: 'They say all
silly things, like he is not dead, and they are going to have a big feast.
They tie all the relatives up [with *tambo*, pieces of thong or tree bark;
alternatively relatives may be adorned with disused saucepans or
other household items] and you can only remove it when you have
paid them. When I was young [the speaker was nearing seventy],
that custom was not common. It comes from the fact that this is a
world of money and a *sahwira* can do anything – even prevent the
coffin from being lowered – to get some money. I saw this for the
first time at Kwenda Mission, some thirty years ago. Quite a lot of
new inventions are coming in! In the old days, such joking at funerals
was not done. This is a new thing.'

Yet although this particular form of joking is apparently new in
Shona areas, other forms of funeral joking have been widely reported
among Malawian tribes, both in modern times (cf. Fraser 1914;
Stannus 1922; Mitchell 1951) and in the distant past (Gamitto 1960).
It is unlikely, then, that no form of funeral joking existed among
Shona tribes in the past, though it may well have been less visible
and overt than in its newer forms.

Specifically in the context of funerals, of course, this joking is
asymmetrical: members of the deceased's family do not retaliate
against their *sahwira's* taunts. People explained this asymmetry,
which is not normally characteristic of this egalitarian relationship,
in terms of the *sahwira's* specific function to relieve the atmosphere
of mourning. One clear example of this function occurred during my

fieldwork: the officiating priest had already agreed to marry a couple on the Saturday on which an old lady was to be buried. As a result, he did not arrive until nearly three o'clock in the afternoon. The mourners, on the other hand, had begun arriving at nine o'clock in the morning. During the intervening hours, the tedium of waiting was relieved at frequent intervals by the buffoonery of the *sahwira*. The spectacle of the well-dressed graduate teacher, for example, pleading for minutes on end with the *sahwira* to accept his fine and untie the dirty, old, holed frying pan which was hanging down his back and half-choking him, while the *sahwira* purported to believe that he didn't exist, had people rolling with laughter.

There is another reason for the asymmetry in funeral joking, however, which relates to the temporary removal of social equality from those linked by the *usahwira* bond when one partner dies. Those who contract bond friendship are equals, but wives and children are no longer equals with the remaining partner when the husband and father dies. In the context of the funeral, then, the *sahwira* becomes primarily a man (thus not the social equal of the widow, a woman) of the adjacent generation (thus in an hierarchical relationship to the children of his deceased partner). He also has the authority of the person who controls the funeral proceedings. It is only later, therefore, that a strictly egalitarian relationship can be resumed between the children of both partners, because the original equality in the relationship is the prerogative of the main, contracting participants. Even though the bond is extended to include wives and children (or, in the case of bond friendship between women, their husbands), their participation is limited. 'The husband starts the relationship and the wife falls into it . . .'; '. . . a husband's *sahwira* is automatically the wife's . . . if a woman has her own *sahwira*, then the husband automatically accepts him or her, though somewhat at the back, of course'.

EXTENSION: INHERITANCE AND METAPHOR

Such extension of *usahwira* to include elementary family members is normal among Shona-speakers, as Bourdillon's (1976:80–81) short exposition indicates. Further extensions are possible, but these depend heavily on individual inclinations and social circumstances. Basically, there are two means by which the *usahwira* bond may be extended: through inheritance and through metaphor.

Theoretically, when two *sahwira* die, the bond is inherited by their children and remains binding. In practice, however, not all children are involved equally and the relationship rarely remains as strong or as binding on subsequent generations as it did upon the original partners: an explicit distinction is drawn between 'own' *sahwira* and 'inherited' *sahwira*, which may be illustrated by the example of the man who failed to invite his recognized *sahwira* to his wedding.

The man getting married was a widower of approximately fifty, the younger of two sons of a polygynist who had died many years before and who had contracted *usahwira* with another man decades before his death. Indeed, it is possible that the relationship had been established still earlier, by the grandfathers of those involved: none of the present generation knew exactly when the relationship had been started. This particular bond had thus been inherited at least once and possibly twice and, for that reason, the man marrying did not consider that he personally was bound by the commitments of bond friendship to people with whom he rarely interacted. While disapproving of this rather cavalier attitude to an old-established bond, the man's elder half-brother admitted that there was some justification for it, since only eldest sons, in his opinion, were strictly bound by the contractual obligations of inherited bonds, even though all family members acknowledged such relationships. Inheritance thus converts achieved relationships into ascribed roles, the obligations of which may be evaded because they become nominal rather than contractual.

The gradual elimination of individuals from inherited bond friendships is also seen, in slightly different form, in another case in which only one of the original partners had died. His two sons, particularly the younger, were meticulous in maintaining the *usahwira* bond with their deceased father's partner, yet neither was on intimate terms with this man's sons, with whom they will, theoretically, resume egalitarian relations when the remaining original partner dies. It is likely, in this instance, that both families will continue to acknowledge the bond verbally for some years after this man's death, but in action the bond will gradually lapse until it will cease to be remembered at all.

From these examples, therefore, it would seem that bond friendship cannot be extended beyond the original partners without undergoing some considerable degree of dilution, formal rules notwithstanding, because the original, highly personalized reasons for contracting the bond no longer obtain. Yet these formal rules requiring transmission of the *usahwira* bond through inheritance may sometimes be useful, as a third case indicates.

Two men had contracted bond friendship some decades previously and one had died nearly twenty years ago. The dead man's son, working in Salisbury, had inherited the bond and maintained it. However, because his deceased father's *sahwira* died on a Wednesday and was buried on the Friday, the son was not able to travel to the funeral 'to organize everything for the home' in the manner strictly required. His father's younger brother, who owned the adjoining farm, was on hand and waited in vain for the special messenger to arrive with the formal news of his family *sahwira*'s death. Eventually he arrived at the funeral without the obligatory special invitation and fined the family fifteen cents for their breach of etiquette. The master of ceremonies made a point of announcing publicly to the family that the brother of their deceased *sahwira* was their *sahwira* and that they should regard him as such. Yet, despite his earlier concern and attendance at the funeral this proxy *sahwira* one week later no longer acknowledged the *usahwira* bond he had assumed so publicly! Quite apart from any mercenary calculations of individual entitlement, this unusual case does show how the formal rules governing extension of *usahwira* bonds may be used to bridge a temporary gap in the continuity of commitments. Once such need has passed, however, the individuals concerned may continue to allow the bond to fade.

The metaphorical extension of *usahwira* is perhaps more interesting than extension through inheritance, for in such instances one sees the idiom of bond friendship being applied on a categorical basis. Of a sardonic article on literary pretensions among those who regard themselves as 'educated', for example, a university colleague recently noted that he was writing 'in the *sahwira* style' ('. . . you can say anything to a *sahwira* and he will accept . . .'). The most interesting example of such metaphorical extension which occurred during my fieldwork concerned the competitive relationship between two of the four Intensive Conservation Areas in Msengezi and their relative performance at the Salisbury Show. One of these two ICAs had just won the annual Inter-ICA competition for the third successive year and was holding a celebration of this achievement. The chairmen of the successful and unsuccessful ICAs orated at length on their respective areas' achievements and potential, in stylized and

semi-insulting boasting, in the course of which the unsuccessful
chairman (Karanga) referred to his successful counterpart (Mfengu)
as *sahwira*. His rival promptly denied that such a relationship could
obtain, since his ICA was so much more successful than the other,
while he himself was so much worse a farmer than his rival chairman:
the conditions for equality between *sahwira*, he alleged amid much
laughter, were definitely not present! Yet both men were using the
*sahwira* idiom to contain a public joking relationship between defined groups on a categorical basis. In this aspect of extra-group relations, then, this example of metaphorical extension is perhaps comparable to the precolonial concern with 'foreign relations'. Such
metaphorical extension of elements of bond friendship might indeed have been another means by which joking relationships between lineages, clans and even tribes arose in precolonial times.

## FUNCTIONS: ADAPTATION AND BEYOND

The functions of bond friendship in precolonial times no longer
apply in the present: commercial farmers in Msengezi, for example,
do not require protection from hostile strangers. Yet *usahwira* bonds
persist in this area, even though an increasing number appear to be
in the process of repudiation or natural elimination, being recognized by only one party to the purported bond. This somewhat unexpected pattern of contemporary recognition may perhaps be explained in terms of the past uses of *usahwira* bonds, together with
their increasing incompatibility with changing production modes in
the present.

To begin with, I would suggest that in the past in Msengezi, bond
friendship has acted as an important mechanism for adjusting behavioural expectations among neighbours from different cultural
backgrounds, by creating (or helping to create) expanded social networks in which commitments between contracting parties were
clearly defined. One area in which such ties used to be of considerable
importance was labour co-operation in crop production. Not only
the traditional type of work party (*nhimbe*) but also, more important-
ly, new forms of more efficient labour co-operation used to involve
bond friends and, to a very limited extent, still do. In a resettled community, composed of people from many different cultural backgrounds, the standardized form of bond friendship undoubtedly provided a clearly-defined basis for such co-operation. Indeed, one

would imagine that similar considerations of certainty and reliability were present in the historical links between bond friends of different ethnic identities who were traders, for specified commitments are more reassuring, when behaviour patterns are vague or potentially conflicting, than are generalized expectations of 'friendship'. In the past, then, economic considerations may have prompted farmers to contract bond friendship with their neighbours.

However, the traditional obligations of *usahwira* have little to do with modern production methods and it is perhaps for this reason, together with emerging socio-economic stratification in this area (Cheater 1974), that so many bond claims were not bilaterally recognized. Bond friendship may ensure adequate labour when required, but for the relatively prosperous farmer, the obligations of *usahwira* present a problem. The *sahwira* 'is free to borrow anything from you that you have' and 'there is no paying back for a *sahwira*'. Demands for seed, fertilizer and the use of mechanized equipment, in terms of these rights, could prove financially embarrassing to successful producers, especially to those who, having mechanized production, no longer need labour on a large scale. However, as one farmer pointed out, such 'borrowing' would not necessarily present a problem, because 'you can say anything to a *sahwira* and he will accept. You'd tell him he was exploiting you and refuse to give it! Oh yes!' But even though such a refusal to give or to share can thus be justified, ultimately it is incompatible with the expectations of bond friendship. Economic inequality thus militates against bond friendship.

This incompatibility between expectations and economics, together with the dilution of the *usahwira* contract which follows inheritance of this bond, perhaps explain why so few farmers were involved in reciprocal *usahwira* relationships; and why the social functions of *usahwira* were, by 1974, dominant in this community. In practice, economic reciprocity was very rare, even in relationships acknowledged by both partners. Moreover, even the social functions were restricted to a small proportion of the total population.


CONCLUSIONS

It is probable that bond friendship in most African societies involved only a limited proportion of the total population and it must, therefore, be seen as an alternative solution to the performance of certain functions in these societies. For example, when only one-sixth of all

Msengezi farmers claimed to have contracted *usahwira* bonds, funeral arrangements among the remaining five-sixths had to be made by people standing in other relationships to these families, even though customary ideology requires that one be buried by a *sahwira*. Unfortunately, we do not know enough about extra-kin relationships to identify the conditions under which people may opt for bond friendship, as opposed to other possible relationships, to meet their particular needs. Yet bond friendship is so widespread that it must be especially useful, under widely different conditions.

Thus we are left with one concluding question: why, given its otherwise widespread distribution in Africa, did bond friendship not exist in Southern Bantu societies? Or were the common elements of this relationship, identified in the first part of this paper, indeed present, remaining unrecognized or unreported because they were not characterized by the blood covenant as a means of establishing the contract?

## NOTES

[1] *Usahwira* is the Zezuru (and now standard Shona) form; in the Korekore dialect the relationship is known as *husahira* (Bourdillon 1972) and in chiBudjga, *usavira* (Holleman 1953). The semantic relationship of these terms to *sabuhira* among the ancient Marave (Gamitto [1960]) is obvious.

[2] It is from the ingestion of the partner's blood, of course, that the term 'blood brotherhood' derives. Nevertheless, many African ethnographers make quite explicit that the establishment of such a bond does not make the partners kinsmen of any description.

[3] This common element of licensed familiarity may permit bond friendship to be compared with relationships of quite a different nature in any given society. For example, Bourdillon (personal communication) suggests that *usahwira* could be compared to the relationship between *sekuru* and *muzukuru* (mother's brother and sister's son; alternately grandfather and grandchild) among Shona-speakers, since both are 'joking relationships'.

[4] That a similar process of natural death may have occurred among certain Shona sub-tribes is suggested by Holleman (1953:22, footnote 44), when he states that 'the term *savira* is commonly used in Budja, but conveys the same meaning as the ordinary term for a friend, *shamwari*, used elsewhere': the special term may be retained long after it has lost its specific meaning.

[5] The tribal classification of farmers in Msengezi was as follows: Zezuru 42 per cent; Karanga 21 per cent; other Shona 8 per cent; Ndebele 8 per cent; Mfengu 6 per cent; Shangane 3 per cent; Sotho/Tswana 3 per cent; other 9 per cent.

[6] I am grateful to Mrs Jane Mutambirwa for this information.

[7]Although Holleman's (1952) analysis of Shona marriage shows a markedly inegalitarian *status* relationship between *tezwara* (wife-givers) and *vakuwasha* (wife-receivers) – which Holleman himself warns against over-emphasizing – in practice this differential means very little. In any case, specifically in respect of their functions at funerals, bond friends and affines may be interchangeable (cf. Holleman 1953:22ff). Hence the contradiction between the equality of bond friendship and affinal asymmetry, which might be thought to militate against inter-marriage between families linked by *usahwira* bonds, may be more apparent than real.

## REFERENCES

BEATTIE, J. M. 1958 – The blood pact in Bunyoro. *Afr.Stud.* **17**, 198–203.

BEIDELMAN, T. O. 1963 – The blood covenant and the concept of blood in Ukaguru. *Africa* **33**, 321–42.

BOURDILLON, M. F. C. 1972 – Some aspects of the religion of the Eastern Korekore. D.Phil. thesis, University of Oxford.

————1976 – *The Shona Peoples*. Gwelo: Mambo Press.

BULLOCK, C. [1928] – *The MaShona*. Cape Town: Juta.

CHEATER, A. P. 1974 – Aspects of status and mobility among farmers and their families in Msengezi African purchase land. *Zambezia* **3**, 51–9.

CHRISTENSEN, J. B. 1963 – *Utani:* joking, sexual licence and social obligations among the Luguru. *Am.Anthrop.* **65**, 1314–27.

EVANS-PRITCHARD, E. E. 1933 – Zande blood brotherhood. *Africa* **6**, 369–401.

FIRTH, R. 1936 – Bond friendship. In Dudley-Buxton, L. H. (ed.), *Custom is King*. London: Hutchinson.

FRASER, D. 1914 – *Winning a Primitive People*. London: Seeley, Service.

GAMITTO, A. C. P. [1960] – *King Kazembe and the Marave, Cheva, Bisa, Bemba, Lunda and Other Peoples of Southern Africa* (Trans. I. Cunnison). Lisbon.

HAMILTON-GRIERSON, P. J. 1909 – Brotherhood (Artificial). *Encyclopaedia of Religion and Ethics* **2**, 857–71. Edinburgh: T. Clark.

HANNAN, M. J. 1968 – *Standard Shona Dictionary*. London: MacMillan.

HOLLEMAN, J. F. 1952 – *Shona Customary Law*. Cape Town: Oxford Univ. Press.

————1953 – *Accommodating the Spirit amongst some North-Eastern Shona Tribes*. Rhodes-Livingstone Paper No. 22. Cape Town: Oxford Univ. Press.

————1958 – *African Interlude*. Cape Town: Nasionale Boekhandel.

KUPER, H. 1947 – *An African Aristocracy*. London: Oxford Univ. Press.

MAIR, L. P. 1934 – *An African People in the Twentieth Century*. London: Routledge.

MITCHELL, J. C. 1951 – The Yao of Southern Nyasaland. In Colson, E. and Gluckman, M. (eds.) *Seven Tribes of British Central Africa*. London: Oxford Univ. Press.

MOREAU, R. E. 1943 – Joking relationships in Tanganyika. *Africa* **14**, 386–400.

OKADA, F. E. 1957 – Ritual brotherhood: a cohesive factor in Nepalese society. *S. West. J. Anthrop.* **13**, 212–22.

PITT-RIVERS, J. 1973 – The kith and the kin. In Goody, J. (ed.) *The Character of Kinship*. Cambridge: Cambridge Univ. Press.

POSSELT, F. W. T. 1927 – *A Survey of the Native Tribes of Southern Rhodesia* Salisbury : Govt. of S. Rhodesia.

——————1935 – *Fact and Fiction*. Bulawayo.

SHACK, W. A. 1963 – Religious ideas and social action in Gurage bond friendship. *Africa* 33, 198–208.

STANNUS, H. S. 1922 – The WaYao of Nyasaland, *Harvard African Studies* 3, 229–372.

STEFANISZYN, B. 1950 – Funeral friendship in Central Africa. *Africa* 20, 290–306.

TEGNAEUS, H. 1952 – *Blood-brothers: An Ethno-sociological Study of the Institution of Blood-brotherhood with Special Reference to Africa*. Stockholm: Ethnographical Museum of Sweden.

TEW, M. 1951 – A further note on funeral friendship. *Africa* 21, 122–4.

TURNER, V. W. 1957 – *Schism and Continuity in an African Society*. Manchester: Manchester Univ. Press.

WEEKS, J. H. 1914 – *Among the Primitive BaKongo*. London: Seeley, Service.

# DO THE SOUTH-EASTERN BANTU WORSHIP THEIR ANCESTORS?

*W. D. Hammond-Tooke*

This paper, dedicated with respect and affection to Professor Eileen Krige, was prompted by an increasing dissatisfaction with a trend in African ethnography to deny that the term 'worship' is adequate for describing the ritual acts (and the accompanying states of mind) directed by participants in the so-called ancestor cult. The term 'cult' itself seems to pass muster (West 1975:186) but a number of scholars (Kenyatta 1938; Kopytoff 1971; Brain 1973:126; West 1975) have come to the considered opinion that the term 'worship' is inappropriate. Kopytoff quotes Kenyatta (1938:265-8) that the relationship between the Kikuyu and their ancestors was, rather, one of 'communion'. West (1975:187) states that 'propitiation and conciliation, however, do not necessarily imply worship' and Mbiti (1969:8-9) agrees with him: 'it is wrong to interpret traditional religions simply in terms of "worshipping the ancestors" . . . Libation and the giving of food to the departed are tokens of fellowship, hospitality and respect . . . "Worship" is the wrong word to apply in this situation . . . It is almost blasphemous, therefore, to describe these acts of family relationships as "worship".' Other, earlier writers who reject the term worship are Driberg (1936) and Young (1947).

There is apparent backing for these views in the ethnographies. The Kriges, for instance, in their study of the Lobedu (Krige and Krige 1943:239-40), state: 'we must not expect a behaviour pattern of humble worshipper to omnipotent god . . . People pray to their ancestors as man to man, scolding them or reminding them of their duties to their children . . . As the gods have human attributes, "worship" is not characterized by humility or formality'. Junod (1927 II:425) says of the Tsonga: 'the attitude of the worshippers . . . the freedom they show in insulting their gods, indicates that they consider them as exactly on the same level as themselves', and Pedi rituals are explicitly stated to be aimed at preventing the ancestors from interfering in the lives of their descendants (Mönnig 1967:60). Berglund, in his recent book on Zulu symbolism, states 'there is in Zulu society no worship of the shades, if by worship we understand a veneration of them . . . There is, on the other hand, a fairly complex

ritual of communion with them in which the shades and the sur-
vivors commune with each other in the widest and most intimate
sense of the term' (Berglund 1976:198).

Yet, despite this mass of evidence, the denial of the term *worship*
seems to me counterintuitive. At the lowest level there is the problem
of what other term to use. There is, of course, 'veneration', but
what exactly does this mean? Are we to resort to Catholic theological
terms such as *dulia, hyperdulia* and *latria?* And there seems to be
something ethnocentric in West's otherwise useful analysis. He refers
(1975:187) to the 'commonly accepted' definition of worship and
states that, in his view, worship 'implies elements of adoration, devotion and supplication of a superior power'. Leaving aside the
question of 'supplication', which surely *is* present in the ancestor
cult, the problem seems to lie in the semantic area 'adoration' and
'devotion', both heavily loaded with Judaeo-Christian theological
presuppositions. Are we not in danger of importing our own ideas of
what worship should be into what is surely an analytically useful concept, almost indispensable for discussing 'religion' cross-culturally?

Moving from the known to the unknown, one should not be too
naïve even about the Christian Church's attitude to worship. No
church, denomination or sect can be certain of the state of mind of
its worshippers, even in the 'enthusiastic' or 'pentecostal' groups
which stress so strongly a personal relationship with the Godhead.
The majestic cadences of the Roman or Anglican liturgy, as also the
simpler 'Protestant' forms, are designed as *corporate* actions, the
verbal formulae of which are designed to express the ideal, 'as if',
state of mind that a really committed worshipper *should* experience,
well knowing that this is, more often than not, a device of perfection.
If this is so in Christianity, with its emphasis on individualism, how
much more is it true of traditional, 'structural' religions, in which
individualism is repressed in the interests of the group as a whole?
The point here is that it is methodologically unsound to use as a
touchstone of 'worship' (as in the case of the literature cited above)
the apparent feeling states of the 'worshippers'. The true emotions of
the participants in a ritual are opaque to satisfactory observation
and, especially in cross-cultural contexts, it is dangerous to infer
attitudes from behaviour that we would consider disrespectful. To an
Anglican or Roman Catholic, especially, brought up to believe that
worship should be performed decently and in order, the relaxed behaviour in *schul* comes as something of a surprise. Surely this is not

*worship?* Where is the reverence, the sense of awe? It would seem that 'worship' is more often in the eye of the worshipper than in that of the beholder!

Then, too, there is the well-authenticated phenomenon of the railing against the saints in Mediterranean and South American catholicism. The saints are holy, they are *venerated* (to be discussed below), but this does not mean that extra-liturgical behaviour towards them is not sometimes markedly lacking in respect and reverence. So the first point I want to make is that overt behaviour can be difficult to interpret, and in any event is not diacritical in solving the problem of ancestor worship. Structure and sentiment do not always coincide.

An obvious alternative approach is to attempt to define the concept 'worship' more clearly. Here we are up against the problem of ethnocentrism again, for the theology of the concept finds its most self-conscious development in the Western mind, whether Christian or Jewish. Obviously definitions (as in the quotation from West) will be strongly influenced by the concept of a supreme Godhead – but let us see how far we can get.

Perhaps the most sophisticated definition of worship is that put forward by Professor Ninian Smart, of the University of Lancaster, whose summary (1972:26–7, 44) of the elements of worship can be quoted in full:

> First, worship is a relational activity: one cannot worship oneself. Second, the ritual of worship expresses the superiority of the Focus [of worship] to the worshipper(s). Third, the ritual also performatively sustains or is part of the power of the Focus. Fourth, the experience which worship expresses is that of the numinous, and the object of worship is thus perceived as awe-inspiring... Fifth, the Focus of worship is unseen, i.e. transcends any particular manifestations of it that there may be. Sixth, the superiority of the Focus gives it greater power than the worshipper, and this gap is infinite in the case of an undoubtedly supreme Being [but *only*, presumably, for such a Being], so that the worshipper has no relevant merit, except in so far as this may be conferred on him by the supreme Being.

Smart himself does not think that the ancestor cult corresponds in all respects to this paradigm. He says (p.45): 'the ancestor-cult fulfils very nearly the criteria we have listed above – with one major exception, however, and possibly two. First, the ancestors are not thought of as superior . . . Second, ancestors are not especially numinous', and here he distinguishes between the numinous and the uncanny. Let us look at the evidence more closely.

Smart's first criterion (relationship) is self-evident. The cult is an explicit attempt to influence the ancestors through prayer and ritual action – and here, with Brain (1973), one must reject Kopytoff's contention that African ancestors are merely the dead elders. Certainly in southern Africa the class of ancestors is clearly marked off from the living (apart from a few cases when old people are, perhaps metaphorically, referred to as 'ancestor') and forms an essentially undifferentiated category of beings. Among both Nguni (Hammond-Tooke 1968:40–1) and South Sotho (Murray 1975:68 fn.) the term for ancestral shade is never used in the singular and the conceptualization is one of a collectivity. In addition (and this is an important factor, unaccountably neglected by commentators), the ancestral shades are *invisible* (Smart's fifth criterion), which clearly marks them off from elderly people who may be referred to as *an* ancestor. This invisibility, and the ability to be in a number of places at once, feeds power into the state of ancestorhood. It is not just that the ancestors can cause illness and misfortune through their displeasure (as can the slighted elder), but that they are (continually) aware of one.[1] There also seems no doubt that the ancestors are conceived to be 'superior' to their worshippers in an absolute sense. Apart from their invisibility and transcendence, they are *genealogically* superior in that, with few exceptions, they belong to ascending generations, and respect for all seniors is a basic value in Southern Bantu ethical systems (Hammond-Tooke 1974:360).

The one criterion on which they appear to fail is numinousness. As is well known, this concept derives from Rudolph Otto, who defines the essence of the 'religious' as the emotion of awe before the *mysterium tremendum et fascinans* (Otto 1959). Is it possible that Smart is right: that the ancestors, at least among the Southern Bantu, are not awe-inspiring in this sense?

But how necessary is this idea to the concept of worship? It would seem unlikely, on the face of it, for the idea of the ineffably holy, with all its implications of power and majesty, to be *necessarily* part of all religious concepts, especially in relatively egalitarian societies. It is undoubtedly part of the so-called World Religions, on which Otto bases his analysis. Smart acknowledges the difficulty in distinguishing the numinous from the uncanny (as he says: are not the dead uncanny and a ghost eminently awe-inspiring?), but he does not, to my mind, satisfactorily solve the problem. Also, a reading of Otto shows that the idea of the numinous is more closely associated with the mystical experience and what Lewis (1971) calls 'ecstatic religion'. It is not so evident in the 'mainline' central cults of the Southern Bantu: if the numinous is experienced here it is more likely to be by the diviners, who have a special association with the shades.

How far will a reclassification of the attitudes in the ancestor cult in terms of *veneration* get us? Again Smart (1972:48) poses the question: 'What *is* the supposed difference between worship and veneration, so that one could differentiate attitudes and intentions? Saints are holy, superior to the cultist, numinous in their miracle-working, invisible' – in short, they have all the hallmarks of gods. And yet it would be blasphemous to accord them 'worship' (*latria*). Smart finds a possible clue in the fact that the holiness of saints is derivative. It is God who sanctifies (op. cit. 48); the holiness of saints is not intrinsic to them.

Does this help us? Should we say that the ancestors are 'venerated'? But, if so, whence do they derive their holiness? Certainly not from the Supreme Being for, as it is well documented, the creator among all the South African peoples was a *deus otiosus* to whom no rituals were directed and no prayers offered (Hammond-Tooke 1974: 319). And the oft-repeated statement that the ancestors stand in a hierarchical relationship to the Supreme Being and mediate between him and man, is not part of any indigenous world-view. Where such an idea has been recorded it is almost certainly due to missionary influence. There is nothing in indigenous concepts to indicate such a relationship. So veneration, as a substitute for 'worship', just will not do. If, then, both terms are inadequate to describe the behaviour in 'religious' contexts, what are we to do? It is the burden of this paper that the term 'worship' should be retained.

Goody seems to have felt this intuitively. Instead of jettisoning the concept, he stoutly maintains that he intends to use Frazer's definition, viz., 'a propitiation or conciliation of powers superior to man which are believed to direct or control the course and nature of human life' (Goody 1962:379). A number of other writers also use the term without embarrassment and Edwin Smith, although he was never absolutely certain on the subject, on balance achieved a 'hesitant affirmation of the validity of the term "ancestor worship" ' (McVeigh 1974:103). As Smith (1950; 26) writes:

we may accept the caveat by T. Cullen Young and J. H. Driberg;

but only on a narrow definition of religion can the ancestral cult be dismissed as "purely secular". If the essence of religion is the sense of dependence upon supersensible powers who are able and willing to help, then we are in the presence of religion when Africans commune with their kinsmen in the unseen world, who have enhanced powers associated with their new status and particularly as mediators between man and God, although, as indicated above, the final point is not true for the traditional Southern Bantu form of the cult.

Worship is analytically both a formal series of actions and a state of mind. I have indicated the dangers in placing too much weight on the latter criterion. The ethnographers of the Tsonga, Lobedu and Pedi have shown that day-to-day relationship tends to be informal, and among both Lobedu and Venda there is occasionally an attempt to deceive the ancestors by substituting water for beer in the *phasa* libation rite (Stayt 1931:257[2]; Krige and Krige 1943:240). But this is after all, the sphere of practical, everyday religion and not the more formal ritual sphere. It may be that the attitudes and behaviour of participants in worship, especially those peripheral to the main ritual action, give little evidence of a sense of the numinous, but this is a commonplace in religious behaviour – and who will deny that *individuals*, as often as not in solitude, experience their ancestors as a numinous presence? I suggest that, to determine whether the term 'worship' is appropriate, the formal ritual statements (analogous to 'liturgy') must be examined.

The first point to make is that the communication is as much through ritual acts as through verbal formulae. The very act of stabbing a beast in the cattle byre, as among the Nguni, or the pouring of a libation of millet beer on a shrine, as among Venda and North Sotho, is a symbolic expression of dependence on the ancestors, and Radcliffe-Brown (1952:157), among others, has stressed the critical element of dependence. There are also, especially among Nguni, non-verbal elements that are associated with 'ritual' killings. Thus there is the use of a special spear, certain medicines associated with the home are poured onto the dung of the byre after the immolation is completed, a special part of the victim (*intsonyama, imbethu*) is tasted by the one for whom the ritual is performed, gall may be smeared and gall bladders attached to the head, and so on. But acts are usually also accompanied by statements, and it is in these (presumably) that clues may be found as to states of mind and attitudes to worship. And here, because of exigencies of space, I wish to concentrate on Nguni material.

Perhaps the most authentic evidence, in that it was recorded in the nineteenth century, is that of Callaway (1870). A close reading of his verbatim record of informants' statements reveals that three separate terms are translated by him as 'worship'. These are *bonga*, *khuleka* and *phatha*. Not long afterwards, Bryant (1905) rendered the first two of these terms as follows:

> *bonga* — 'praise, extol, a person or thing . . . hence, worship, offer sacrifice to, pray to, as to the *ama-Dhlozi* or ancestral spirits'.

> *khuleka* — 'salute a person from respect . . . adore, as in adoring God; humbly or respectfully request or beg a thing of a person; hence, pray, utter a petition (for which it is the best word)'. It can also mean to tie up an animal by the leg with a grass rope or 'keep or hold fast a person to his word when he wants to get free from it or deny it'.

The term *phatha* presents problems as the dictionaries of both Bryant (1905) and Doke & Vilakazi (1948) give it as 'touch', 'hold', 'handle', or 'to have to do with'. It is probably the latter sense which is meant. Callaway in a footnote (1870:10) says that *bonga* is equivalent to *phatha* 'which is used for all and every kind of adoration and worship'.

Berglund (1976:198) and others also give the word *thetha*, glossed by Bryant as 'speak the praises, etc., of the *ama-Dhlozi* or ancestral spirits at the sacrifice of a beast, or of a brave when he displays his feats at a dance'. But *thetha*, in Zulu, can also mean 'scold, find fault noisily, as a scolding woman or fault-finding man' (Bryant 1905). It is this alternative meaning that is partly responsible for the idea that the Zulu scold their ancestors – another bit of evidence against the worship concept. Berglund, however, feels that this emphasis is incorrect and that Bryant's first meaning is the only appropriate translation of *thetha* when used in connection with the ancestors. 'Asked whether it is possible to scold a shade [using the more specific form, *thethisa*], Zulu have been most emphatic that this connot be done. "Who are we to scold our seniors (*abadala bethu*)?" But they readily agree that *ukuthetha idlozi* is a correct expression and implies something quite different from *ukuthethisa idlozi*' (Berglund 1976:198, 220). Despite this Berglund still insists that 'there is in Zulu society no worship of the shades, if by worship we understand a veneration of them' (1976:198): enough has been said to indicate the essential obscurity of such a statement.

And here, in parenthesis, it may be said that it is straining facts to deny that, even in more 'advanced' religions, what Smart calls the Focus is immune from criticism. The Israelites were particularly prone to 'murmur', and even Moses was constrained to say 'wherefore hast thou afflicted thy servant? and wherefore have I not found favour in thy sight, that thou layest the burden of all this people upon me . . .' (Nu. 11.11–15). Callaway's informant stigmatized the shades as 'jealous' (*umona*) (Callaway 1870:75): but Yahweh was also a jealous God.

Among the Cape Nguni there does not appear to be the same proliferation of terms. In Xhosa the word *nqula* is used for calling on the ancestors (Kropf 1899). *Thetha* is the common word for 'to speak' (cf. Zulu, *khuluma*). Sometimes *bonga* (praise) is also used in connection with the shades.

I am not suggesting that recourse to dictionary definitions is a decisive argument. Dictionary makers do their best, but concepts are elusive. Even so, I think the definitions serve to expose in Berglund's work a paradoxical tension between denial of 'worship' and descriptions which belie this denial. There is the distinct impression of the numinousness of the shades in such comments as: 'A worthy invocation presupposes dignified language . . . much care is given to the choice of words, expressions and gestures . . . Very poetic and extremely beautiful Zulu is often heard at the invocation of the shades' (Berglund 1976:230). 'The atmosphere in the hut was one of supreme reverence and dignified quiet' at a ritual killing he attended, although people outside were talking and shouting (1976:217), and, when the officiant cut strips of the *insonyama* and gave it to his sick son to eat, we get the following graphic account, pregnant with reverence (and the numinous?):

> When smoke rose from the strips on the coal, the officiant instructed his son to cross his arms, cut the strips in half, placed a piece of each strip into each hand and told him (the patient) in a whispering voice to eat them. He himself ate the remaining two bits and prior to putting the meat into his mouth said, whispering, yet fully audibly: "*Makhosi!*" ["Chiefs!"]. Both re-

mained seated until they had completed eating the meat when the host, on his knees, fetched the vessel containing beer which had been placed on the skin by his sister. He handed it to his son who took a mouthful. Thereafter he took a mouthful himself, repeating: "*Makhosi !*" The vessel was returned to its place (1976: 218).

It is true that this account refers to a ritual performed at a time of serious illness and thus invested with a highly-charged emotional element. Perhaps not all 'ritual' is performed with such concentrated attention and piety. And here the ethnography of Southern Bantu (or at least Nguni) religious behaviour presents another problem which is difficult to resolve: are *all* killings to be classed as rituals? There is no problem in the case of sacrifices made in time of sickness and diagnosed as 'sent' by the ancestors, but what of the many other killings that occur? The ethnographic literature is full of examples: what follows, though not exhaustive, gives some idea of the range that exists.

Among the Bhaca, some of the killings made, involving either a goat or an ox, are: if a birth is delayed; a few days after the mother comes out of seclusion (*imbeleko*); at the commencement of a girl's initiation (*umhlonyane*) and at the end (*udlisw' intusi*); at marriage (a number) and at funerals. In some cases, perhaps the majority, the gall bladder of the victim is emptied and is fastened to the head of the person for whom the killing is performed (Hammond-Tooke 1962: 74, 75, 84, 86, 105, 106). A similar situation is found among the Mpondomise, and Professor Wilson's study of the Mpondo (Hunter 1936) has particularly full details. But when it comes to the question of actual *invocation* of the shades the matter is not so clear – frequently from neglect to record the crucial details. However, Hunter states quite unequivocally for the Mpondo: 'At no ritual killing other than *idini* [piacular sacrifice] is there any calling on the ancestors, unless there has been sickness and the *iyeza lasekhaya* [medicines of the home] have been used' (Hunter 1936:248).

One complication is that the actual invocation may apparently be omitted and Wilson and her associates comment for the people of Keiskammahoek: 'The position of the slaughtered animal, lying on its right side with its head pointing towards the gate of the byre, marks the occasion as a sacred one on which the ancestors are not necessarily invoked aloud, "they know the meat is for them"' (Wilson *et al.* 1952:195). Mpondomise informants maintained that merely addressing the assembled lineage members (*imilowo*) had the effect of informing the ancestors. The presence of ancestors and living members is believed to 'bless' (*sikelela*) the performance of the custom 'When the *imilowo* come, I tell them that the child is sick and I wish to *lungisa* his health. They must be present so as to bless the occasion. Both dead and living are listening when I speak these words'. Pauw, writing of the Cape Nguni generally, states that 'there is evidence that most of these rituals traditionally also have the significance of *invocations* performed to ensure that the ancestors remain benevolent' (Pauw 1975:174).

Information collected from Xhosa, Thembu, Mpondomise and Bomvana areas shows considerable uniformity (with slight differences in detail): the following table gives a rough classification of the most important 'killings':

A. PIACULAR

|  |  |  |  |
|---|---|---|---|
|  | *idini* | ox or goat | propitiation in time of sickness. |

B. LIFE CYCLE

|  |  |  |  |
|---|---|---|---|
| birth | *bingelelo or mbeleko* | goat | to end seclusion period after birth of child. |
| initiation (male) | *ngcamisa* | goat | on day before circumcision to ensure healing of wounds |
|  | *ojiswa* | goat | to end 8-day period of strict food taboos. |
| initiation (female) | *mhlonyane* | goat |  |
| marriage | *dlisw' amasi* | goat | to permit bride to drink sour milk of husband's lineage. |
| mortuary | *khapha* | ox | to 'accompany' the deceased after burial. |
|  | *guqula or buyisa* | ox | to 'bring back' the deceased as an incorporated shade. |

C. CONTINGENT

| | | |
|---|---|---|
| *ukupha* | ox | as 'gift' to named ancestor. |
| *ukuvula umzi* | goat | to inaugurate a newly-built homestead. |
| *bulela* | goat | thanksgiving for a safe return. |

Of these the *idini* is quite clearly a ritual killing directed to the ancestors. All the formal elements of sacrifice are present – the stabbing with a ritual spear; dancing (*xhentsa*) and the singing of clan songs; the tasting (*shwama*) of the *intsonyama* (piece of meat from top of right foreleg) not only by the sufferer but by all the lineage members who are present; the drinking of beer especially brewed for the ancestors; the use of special medicines of the home; the placing of the sacrifical meat on the branches of special trees, and the burning of the bones of the victim on the third day. Informants stress the importance of *shwama:* 'Even those who do not eat meat or drink beer must, on this day, at least taste a little bit. This is to show that they are doing this with a single heart'. The *intsonyama* is tasted only at an *idini*, and at no other ritual. At all other killings the person for whom they are made *shwama*'s the *inguba* (*isiphika*), a much smaller piece from the neck and covering the scapula. It is found below the cartilage of the *intsonyama* proper.

It is at an *idini* that the ritual calling on the ancestors takes place. The word used for this is *nqula* and it refers to the reciting of the most important clan names of the sufferer, interspersed with certain verbal formulae. Here are some examples[3]:

1. '*Camagu!* (Blessings!) Friends of Sonkila, of Kasangane, of Mphankomo'.
2. 'Ndosi, Hairy-penis-sheath; Mtikiti; Shoot-the-cowards; Friend of Lamyeni'.
3. '*Camagu!* Cattle of Mondinga; Beast-does-not-give-birth: it-gives-birth-only-by-being-made-to; Friends of Mgcwima'.
4. '*Camagu!* Sarelebha, Mdzobha, Masikane, Magqagqana; The-water-is-coagulated-blood; But go!'
5. '*Camagu!* Cattle of Nxuba, of Mduma, of Lushoda; Of-the-one-who-counts-stars-whilst-other-men-count-cattle; of Ngole-ka'.

6. '*Camagu!* Friend of Jali, of Shiyelwayo, of Kakane'.
7. '*Camagu!* Cattle of Gebe, of Ngobe, of Mduduma, of Galeka, of Ndlozi, of Ngcangcashe; Yellow testicles'.
8. '*Taruni*! (Pardon!) Cattle of Mbhodi, of Dala, of Mbese, of Nongwangwa; Of-the-grey-heads; Ngokude'.
9. 'Miya, Gcwanini, Mja, Sibewu, Bincelehlezeni; One-who-refuses-to-be-followed-by-a-girl-saying-marry-me; Vezi, Rengqwa'.

It should be noted that these are all clan names. Not even the names of lineage dead are included, except that the invocation might end with the name of the apical lineage founder, usually in the form 'And you, people of So-and-So'. But even though not all are called by name, all the lineage dead are believed to be included in the invocation (Hammond-Tooke 1968:40–1). The invocation might be preceded by *bika*, a report to the gathered assembly (and, by implication, the shades), of the nature of the illness and the identity of the sufferer (cf. Berglund 1976:231).

Finally, if the ritual does not achieve its purpose, *ngxola* (*shwabula, lila*) might be tried. *Ngxola* can be translated as 'to make a noise', 'to utter words angrily', 'to utter a curse ("but not really so")', or to speak with deep feeling. The form '*lila*' means 'to cry'. *Ngxola* is performed by a senior man of the homestead, or by the lineage head, for a person who has failed to respond to treatment or ritual. The officiant makes two stations, in the cattle byre and in the space between it and the huts of the homestead (*inkundla*), and finally enters the hut in which the sick person lies. He *ngxola*'s as follows: 'What can it be? Is it that this homestead has no people of its own (i.e. shades)? How can it be that I am in difficulty when they are here?', or, 'Here is something, people of So-and-So, here is something we don't understand in our homestead. Do thou reveal it'. If the ancestors hear, the beast they want becomes restive and drops soft dung. *Ngxola* is obviously similar to the Zulu *thethisa*, and here again 'scolding' is not a happy translation. It is rather, like Moses's remonstrance to the Lord, a gentle chiding.

The *idini* stands alone. As one informant put it, it is the only killing at which there is true prayer (*isicamagushiso*) (see Pauw 1975:173 for a discussion of *Camagu* and its cognates). It also conforms to the Durkheimian (and theological) principle of *corporate* worship. As we shall see, at other killings it is only the person for whom the kill-

ing is made who *shwama*'s the sacrificial piece: at an *idini* the unity
of the lineage is symbolically underlined by the participation of all
in a very real communion service, which also involves a show of
lineage solidarity through the dance, 'hymn' singing (cf. Zulu *ihubo*,
Berglund 1976:198), and the necessity for ritual purity on the part of
the officiant. If this is not 'worship' one wonders what is!

The problem of worship is not so easily solved when we come to
the other killings. Informants state quite unequivocally that these
killings are not for the *izinyanya* (ancestors) and point out that only
the person for whom the killing is made *shwama*'s the *ingaba*, (but
not the *intsonyama*). They also mention the absence of *umthathi*
(the special leaves used to asperse the victim), the 'beer of the ancestors' and, of course, *nqula*. These killings are referred to as 'merely customs' (*amasiko*). At all such killings a knife is typically used
instead of the ritual spear (*umkhonto wekhaya*).[4] It is used to cut the
throat of goats and to sever the spinal cord of the *khapha* mortuary
ox. All the meat at a *khapha* killing must be eaten on the day it takes
place: 'Its purpose is to drive away a thing that is bad'. 'The *umkhonto wekhaya* is not used because it is a beast of misfortune
(*yelisha*)'. Not even ordinary beer may be made. Informants notice
the special, instrumental, nature of *khapha*, with its total lack of communication with the shades: 'It is like administering medicines to the
people of the home'.

Nevertheless at all the *amasiko* killings there is always some form of
words, addressed ostensibly to the subject of the ritual, or to those
present, but intended for the ears of the *izinyanya*. A child at *bingelelo*
will be told, 'Here is your blanket'. At a *khapha* ceremony among the
Ndlambe, the officiant said: 'Today, my people, here at the home of
the Vulanes, we accompany Lungi, son of Manukwana', and, at a
*buyisa*: 'AmaBamba, the thing I am doing here, I am bringing back
Mlamli with this red ox. Therefore, I say, may I remove the burden
by bringing him back'. There may even be a more specific allusion
to the shades, as in this statement at a *bingelelo* birth ceremony:
'Today we are here at the home of Mpokonxa. We are taking out a
suckling mother from the house. With this white goat I say to the
Ciras, our old people of this home, long life to this child of ours'
and, again, at a girls' initiation (*intonjane*): 'Today we are taking out
these girls of the Zangwes, so that they will be healthy. We are ful-
filling the custom so that they do not worry us in the future. You all
know that by custom we are supposed to slaughter two oxen, but the

Zangwes (i.e. the ancestors) see we have nothing on account of the drought. They will excuse us.'

This last reveals the importance of the *amasiko* killings for the ancestor cult. Although they themselves are not specifically directed to the ancestors in the form of prayer or praise, their neglect can have grave consequences by incurring ancestral wrath, which will have to be assuaged by an *idini* ritual at some later date. They are thus rites of rogation, involving gestural symbolism, and the frequent use of gall as an unction expresses the solemnity of the occasion. Up till now, in this discussion, we have not called them 'ritual' killings. However, there does not seem to be any reason to deny them this status.

This paper has addressed itself to the question: can the South-eastern Bantu, especially Zulu and Cape Nguni, be said to worship their ancestors? I conclude that they can. To suggest otherwise would seem to border on ethnocentrism, if not cultural arrogance. Examination of the invocations and their accompanying ritual acts has brought out an important aspect of the worship. In all there is a formal distancing of the shades from living men. The effect of the invocations, with the repetition of the form *'Camagu!'* (sometimes *Taru*, 'Pardon'), as an almost invariable preface, is to separate the two, formally and cognitively, preparatory to a mediation through the ritual itself. And here we come to the heart of the matter. Objects of religious ritual are *set apart*, consecrated, and to achieve this they have to be created or constructed for the purpose of the ritual. The shades are always there, invisible and immanent in the background of the life-world: what is needed is a *focusing* of the interactional situation that brings them into the foreground, as it were, so that they can be confronted and influenced. Focusing involves the disengaging (setting apart) of the situation from its profane background and the construction of it as a sacred one. This is done spatially, by locating the killing in the byre, but also verbally, through the mechanism of a special language form, the *nqula* invocation.

## NOTES

[1]Philip Mayer records the Xhosa as saying 'the spirits of your father and grandfather are wherever you are yourself'; 'There is absolutely nowhere the spirits cannot reach, if the one they love is there' (Mayer 1961: 151),

[2]On this point, Dr N. J. van Warmelo informs me that in fact water is the essential element in the *phasa* rite, directed at 'cooling' the ancestors, with beer a possible substitute on the analogy of gift-giving.
[3]These texts were collected by one of my former students, Mr E. Bigalke, among the Ndlambe of East London.
[4]Hunter records that in Mpondo killings the victim is stabbed over the aorta muscle with the spear of the *umzi* (Hunter 1936: 171, 193, 195, 201), but all my informants denied this for the groups mentioned.

## REFERENCES

BERGLUND, A. I. 1976 – *Zulu Thought-Patterns and Symbolism.* Uppsala: Alinqvist and Wiksell.
BRAIN, J. 1973 – Ancestors as elders in Africa: further thoughts. *Africa* **43**, 122–33.
BRYANT, A. T. 1905 – *A Zulu-English Dictionary.* Pinetown: Mariannhill Mission Press.
CALLAWAY, H. 1870 – *The Religious System of the Amazulu.* Springvale: John A. Blair.
DOKE, C. M. & VILAKAZI, B. W. 1948 – *Zulu-English Dictionary.* Johannesburg: Witwatersrand Univ. Press.
DRIBERG, J. H. 1936 – The secular aspect of ancestor worship. In supplement to *J. Roy. African Soc* **25**, no. 138.
GOODY, J. 1962 – *Death, Property and the Ancestors.* London: Tavistock.
HAMMOND-TOOKE, W. D. 1962 – *Bhaca Society.* Cape Town: Oxford Univ. Press.
————————— 1968 – The morphology of Mpondomise descent groups. *Africa* **38**, 26–45.
————————— (ed.) 1974 – *The Bantu-Speaking Peoples of Southern Africa.* London: Routledge and Kegan Paul.
HUNTER, M. 1936 – *Reaction to Conquest.* London: Oxford Univ. Press.
JUNOD, H.–A. 1927 – *The Life of a South African Tribe.* London: Macmillan.
KENYATTA, J. 1938 – *Facing Mount Kenya.* London: Martin Secker and Warburg.
KOPYTOFF, I. 1971 – Ancestors as elders in Africa. *Africa* **41**, 129–41.
KRIGE, J. D. & KRIGE, E. J. 1943 – *The Realm of a Rain Queen.* London: Oxford Univ. Press.
KROPF, A. 1899 – *A Kaffir-English Dictionary.* Lovedale: The Mission Press.
LEWIS, I. M. 1971 – *Ecstatic Religion: An Anthropological Study of Spirit Possession and Shamanism.* Harmondsworth: Penguin Books.
MAYER, P. 1961 – *Townsmen or Tribesmen.* Cape Town: Oxford Univ. Press.
MBITI, J. 1969 – *African Religions and Philosophy.* London: Heinemann.
MCVEIGH, M. J. 1974 – *God in Africa.* Cape Cod: Claude Stark Inc.
MÖNNIG, H. O. 1967 – *The Pedi.* Pretoria: Van Schaik.
MURRAY, C. 1975 – Sex, smoking and the shades. In M. G. Whisson & M. West (eds.) *Religion and Social Change in Southern Africa.* Cape Town: David Philip.
OTTO, R. 1959 – *The Idea of the Holy.* Harmondsworth: Penguin Books.

PAUW, B. A. 1975 – *Christianity and Xhosa Tradition.* Cape Town: Oxford Univ. Press.

RADCLIFFE-BROWN, A. R. 1952 – *Structure and Function in Primitive Society.* London: Cohen and West.

SMART, N. 1972 – *The Concept of Worship.* London: Macmillan.

SMITH, E. W. 1950 – *African Ideas of God: A Symposium.* London: Edinburgh House Press.

STAYT, H. 1931 – *The BaVenda.* London: Oxford Univ. Press.

WEST, M. 1975 – The shades come to town. In M. G. Whisson & M. West (eds.) *Religion and Social Change in Southern Africa.* Cape Town: David Philip.

WILSON, M., S. KAPLAN, E. M. WALTON & T. MAKI. 1952 – *Social Structure* Vol. 3, Pietermaritzburg: Keiskammahoek Rural Survey.

YOUNG, T. C. 1947 – *Contemporary Ancestors: A Beginner's Anthropology for District Officers and Missionaries in Africa.* London: Butterworth.

# RITUAL: RESILIENCE AND OBLITERATION

*Monica Wilson*

In the large literature on ritual produced during the past twenty years there has been little discussion of which rituals survive, which disappear and why, nor has there been systematic comparison of the occasions on which ritual of some sort persists.

Eileen Krige, in a model study of 'Divine Kingship, Change and Development' shows how divine kingship among the Lovedu has changed through time (over nearly 400 years), but continues. 'Many features of the divine kingship of the Lovedu remain unchanged' (Krige 1975:66). Since Professor Krige's main preoccupation, other than chieftainship or kingship, has been with kinship, a consideration of change in kinship ritual is not inappropriate as an offering to her. It joins on to her own illuminating work on changing kinship bonds.

This paper is concerned with the obliteration of certain rituals and the resilience of others in kinship contexts particularly with the extinction of twin rituals, once widespread in Africa.[1] Twin rituals, once elaborate, public, and held to be important, not only change but disappear altogether (unless protective medicines are drunk in secret) in communities in which other rituals at birth, puberty, marriage, and death continue to flourish and draw large congregations. This I have observed directly among peoples as far apart as Xhosa-speakers of the Cape and Nyakyusa-Ngonde of Tanzania and Malawi, and it seems to have happened elsewhere. Moreover, in the African Independent Churches of Southern Africa, where traditional rites are so commonly transformed and celebrated, no celebration of twin rituals is described (Sundkler 1948; Haselbrecht 1966; West 1975a, 1975b; Pauw 1975; Berglund 1976). So the question arises: why do rituals at twin birth disappear when other rituals persist in some form? Before this can be answered two further questions must be considered: what did twin rituals say? And was there any consistency in explicit intention in these rituals down Africa?

Detailed studies of symbolism based on associations made by participants in rituals and those relating to myths or folk-tales, show a marked consistency, combined with a detailed variation, in symbolic associations through Bantu-speaking Africa (Wilson, G. 1939;

Wilson, M. 1954, 1957, 1959; Douglas 1954, 1957; Richards 1956, 1960, 1961; Beidelman 1961a, 1961b; Turner 1961, 1962, 1967, 1968, 1969; West 1975b; Berglund 1975, 1976). Many of these extend to another language family in the Sudan (Evans-Pritchard 1956; Lienhardt 1961)[2] but differ from the symbolism of Europe.

One persistent image was that earth and sky were twins. Twins were 'of the sky', so twins were sought to drive off hail and lightning among some Xhosa and Zulu speakers. They might become 'heaven herds', lightning doctors, or diviners: they were 'lucky' as well as feared, dangerous but powerful and that power might be useful (Cook n.d.:97–105; Hunter 1936:299; Berglund 1975, 1976:34, 62ff., 148). The sky was the dwelling-place of God, and twins were associated with God. The evidence of this association among the Nuer and Dinka is well known (Evans-Pritchard 1956; Lienhardt 1961; Levi-Strauss 1962; Beidelman 1966; Firth 1966; Willis 1975). Among the Nyakyusa, too, twins were associated with God (Wilson 1957: 164, 166–70); and it is surely no accident that the word in Xhosa and Zulu for twins, *amawele*, is so close to the word *Wele*, meaning God, further north (Wagner 1949:99, 168, 175–6).

The association of twins with God, with the sky, seems to be a dominant one from the Sudan to the Transkei, but there is another widespread association, not felt to be contradictory, between twins and the shades 'beneath' who are of the earth (Wilson 1957:166). There is abundant evidence that among peoples who speak Bantu languages the shades are thought to control conception and be present in *coitus* and they were therefore involved in the conception of twins (Wilson 1957:126–9, 1959:108–10; Berglund 1976:253–5 *et passim*).

Among the Mpondo, twins were offered white beads by those who came to drink beer brewed at their birth when euphorbia trees were planted. The guests blessed them with the formal exclamation: *Cos!*, equivalent of *Camagu!* Be appeased! (Kropf 1899; Hunter 1931, 1932) and each guest presented each twin with three or four white beads. These the twins wore round neck, wrist, and ankle, just as a novice or diviner wore the beads presented to her with the same blessing (Hunter 1936:328); the twins themselves offered white beads to the sea when they first visited it – some said on each visit– for twins came from the sea which, in various contexts, is associated with the shades (Hunter 1931, 1932; Wilson: forthcoming). None would mention the death of a twin: of a boy it was said, 'he has

gone to the gold mines'; of a girl, 'she has gone to be married'.None
might mention that a twin was ailing: it was said, 'he is pretending'.[3]
None might mourn at the death of a twin: 'the mother just mourns
secretly in her heart'. This, too, was almost certainly because twins
were already so close to the shades.

Twins were *both* blessing and misfortune (Turner 1969:45) and
this was felt no more contradictory than the idea that they were both
of God above and the shades beneath, or the idea that they were both
a power for good and polluting, that is, they were *sacer* in the sense
so brilliantly analyzed by Otto (1926). The Nyakyusa twin ritual was
directed both to 'driving off Kyala (God)' with spear and shield,
separating men from too close association with God, and purifying
twins and their parents so that they could be incorporated into the
kinship group. The parent of twins was fearful (*umwipasya*), more
fearful than a twin himself; the parent was marked for life, 'no one
makes him move aside'; but the ritual made it tolerable for others
to mingle with him. This fear and reverence of the parent of twins
was evident also in Ndembu ritual and elsewhere, and in everyday life
men were aware of parents of twins for very often they were identified
by status names. Both twins were also so identified, and sometimes
even the next child born.

Twins were not quite human. In KiNyakyusa *ulupasa* meant not
only twin birth but included any multiple birth or breech presenta-
tion, and it is therefore most accurately translated as 'abnormal
birth'. Among some other African peoples children born with teeth,
or those whose top teeth erupted before the bottom teeth, were also
classed with twins as 'abnormal' (Stayt 1931:93–4; Krige & Krige
1943:218–9). The abnormality was thought of as inhuman, revolt-
ing, animal-like (Douglas 1957:50; Wilson 1957:168). The distinction between human and animal was fundamental, constantly reflected in Bantu noun classes, and for Nyakyusa and Xhosa-speakers
it represented the distinction between good and evil, between civilized
and barbarian. *Ubuntu*, meaning human quality which is *humaneness*
in Xhosa, was a dominant value for both Xhosa and Nyakyusa.
Man was not an animal; he lived in community and observed certain customs. In the Nyakyusa ritual cycle what was repeatedly
stressed was the fear of departure from human behaviour: naked-
ness, absence of restraint, a breach of civilized manners, madness
(Wilson 1957, 1959 *passim*). The raw and the cooked, the omnivorous
and those who respected taboos, the uncircumcised and the cir-

cumcised, the bush and the village: these distinctions kept recurring from the Nile to the Kei. Villagers were preoccupied with training children to behave like human beings.

Jeffreys (1953, 1963) criticized the view that twin rituals were celebrated because twin birth was abnormal, citing evidence to show that the rate was probably higher in Africa than in Europe and America, but Jeffreys missed the point: though twin birth was not very infrequent it was *felt to be abnormal*, animal-like. Even death before old age was felt to be 'abnormal' by Xhosa-speakers who held that unless a witch or sorcerer intervened men and women lived to grow old (Hunter 1936:272–5, 318–9; Moodie 1960 I:427). One must distinguish between fears which commonly beset men on similar occasions and the cultural interpretation of these fears.

Traditionally, the mystical fear of multiple birth was associated with a strong disapproval of too close spacing of children. In Bu-Nyakyusa I heard certain European families which had produced a child each year criticized as 'animal-like'; Nyakyusa women were deeply shocked by such unrestrained behaviour. In Bantu Africa generally, it was considered proper that children should be spaced at least two and sometimes four years apart. In Nyakyusa theory the elder child 'must be able to run' before the younger was born because no woman could flee carrying two children and a raid might occur any time. The spacing was for the welfare of the children, and parents who transgressed were said to be 'killing' the elder child. Emphatically, Nyakyusa women did not wish to bear twins, hence the thicket of taboos against contact with pairs, such as eating twin bananas. The rule against close spacing which was of practical advantage was reinforced by the symbolic association between unrestrained fertility and animal-like behaviour. Among Xhosa-speakers the insistence on spacing was recorded as early as 1688 (Moodie 1960 I:427) and was still constantly stressed in Pondoland in 1932 (Hunter 1936:159).

The fearfulness of twins and their parents (or any birth classed as abnormal) and the danger of pollution or infection spreading from them were adduced as the reasons for obligatory killing of twins (and sometimes other children) among a number of peoples in Africa. The fear of pollution spreading to kin, neighbours, stock, field, the heavens themselves with life-giving rain, drove parents, kin, or neighbours to smother infants or to leave them to starve. Eileen and J. D. Krige recorded convictions for twin killing among the Lovedu in

1923 and noted that in 1938, despite South African law, twins were
'still generally killed' (Krige & Krige 1943:218, 241, 321). At that
time the attitude towards twin births was one of the basic conflicts
between conservative Lovedu who were pagans and those who were
Christians. Schapera referred to the tradition of twin killing among
the Tswana (1938:26) as had Brown earlier (1926:64–5). Junod referred to it among the Tsonga (1927 I:41, II: 319, 357), and Stayt to
the continuing practice among the Venda in 1930 (1931:91–3, 310).
Among the Zulu it was once feared that the father of twins would die
if both twins lived and Bryant and Dudley Kidd suggested that
smothering of twins at birth had once occurred, but Bryant noted
that the practice had become 'practically extinct' *before* colonial
rule was established (Kidd 1904:202; 1906:14, 45–8; Bryant 1929:
641). Gusinde (1954) argued that it was not extinct in Zululand in
1935–53 but his assertion is questionable. Certainly the practice of
killing twins was not general among Nguni people since twins occur
in Xhosa folk tales, proverbs, royal genealogies, and a famous court
case. This is clear evidence of their acceptance and survival as far as
Xhosa tradition stretches back, long before colonial rule (Mqhayi
1914: *passim*; Hunter 1931, 1932; Jordan 1973a:193–216; 1973b:10,
30). Furthermore, there is no hint in early documents that twin killing ever occurred (Alberti 1807; Maclean 1866; *Report on Native
Laws and Customs* 1883).

But whether killed or not, twins were fearful and rituals were celebrated for them and their parents, and (among the Nyakyusa at
least) all the kin of both parents, their village neighbours, and even
the cattle of the village. The parents of twins lived segregated in
a little hut built for them until they had been purified (Wilson 1957:
152–171).

The killing of twins had two roots: practical and symbolic. Gusinde
(1954) reported that a hunting people with whom he spent eleven
months in the Kalahari, always left twins in the sand to die in order
to save the life of the mother. In a hunting band, constantly on the
move, it is impossible for a woman to suckle and carry two children
and keep up with the band. Among pastoralists and cultivators (still
further with modern food and medicine) the chances of survival for
twins and mother increase, but Mpondo and Bomvana (who kept
cattle and cultivated) remarked that a mother rarely succeeded in
rearing both twins (Cook n.d. 103; Hunter 1932), and though Mpondo said they rejoiced when twins were born the problem of suckling

two children and carrying them about pressed on she who bore them. Indeed, anxiety lest the mother be unable to nurse both children was probably reflected in the Xhosa, Mpondo, and Bomvana ritual of planting an *mhlontlo* tree (*Euphorbia grandidens*)[3] for each twin behind the hut in which they were born. These euphorbias exude a milky sap and are vigorous, resistant to drought, and long-lived. Although no explicit interpretation of milky sap was given by my friends who planted such trees, one may *guess* that there was some association between mother's milk and euphorbia sap. Aloes planted at the same time were called *izincelana*, 'little suck-drys'. The health of each twin was explicitly believed to be bound up with the growth of his tree, i.e. a poetic association was taken as practically efficient (Cook n.d.:97–105; Soga n.d.:292; Hunter 1931, 1932). The father-of-twins planted the euphorbias (common in the bush) and the aloes if he could find them (for they were rare and much less important than the euphorbias) and the twin babies were washed beside their trees, each with water in which was placed a sprig of his own tree. Throughout life twins, or one surviving twin, returned, sometimes from a long distance, to wash beside his tree if he were ill or celebrating some ritual. In 1931, near Ntibane in Pondoland, a twin, Paya, made an offering of beer in thanksgiving to his shades for safe return from gaol, and he was washed beside his *mhlontlo* tree. If the trees had died or the old homestead had been ploughed over, twins celebrated where their trees had been: this was also observed in 1931. The importance of the trees in ritual thus continued long after twins were weaned, but it is suggested that the primary association of the trees was with mother's milk.

Ambivalence regarding twins was a dominant theme down Africa: twins were polluting but powerful for good, dangerous but lucky, driven off but domesticated, abnormal but repeatedly recurring. Fecundity was valued but men sought to tame and consecrate it. They also acknowledged and minimized duality. They made an unfamiliar duality tolerable by admitting it and playing it down, treating twins as one in ritual situations. Among Xhosa-speakers twins were invariably treated together and 'they had a great love for each other. If one were beaten the other cried'. If one were ill and was scarified the other was scarified also; they washed together with medicines beside their trees; their hair-cutting was done together; they shared the ritual portion of an animal offered to the shades for one. Twins of opposite sex also shared the ritual portion when the girl was initiated, and she was treated as if she were to join the lodge when her brother went to be circumcised (Soga n.d.:296). Twin sisters were invariably married together and before marriage they exchanged clothes. Should one twin die the other exchanged blankets and ornaments with him and lay down in the grave until earth was sprinkled over him. Nyakyusa friends described the complications of wooing a twin for one of a pair could only marry at the same time as the other, and at death, among Nyakyusa as among Mpondo, a surviving twin lay down in the grave of one who had died. The confusion engendered by what was felt should be a single identity being two was minimized by treating twins as one.

But the ritual actions had a further dimension. It has been argued, very persuasively, that what twin rituals represented to the Nuer was duality, the duality between men and God, earth and heaven, lineage and lineage (Evans-Pritchard 1956; Beidelman 1966:453ff; Willis 1975:114ff).[5] It has been shown that similar ideas of duality pervaded Zulu thought about sky and earth, rain and soil, husband and wife (Berglund 1976:34, 62–3). Twin birth, the duality about which men were ambivalent, was thus linked to dualities which were acceptable, part of the order of the cosmos.[6]

If one of the functions of ritual is to resolve emotional conflict, to teach people what it is proper to feel when they are distraught (Wilson 1957:222–33), then rituals which admit and minimize duality in twins and link them to acceptable dualities provide a guideline to reintegration for those shocked by duality where they have learnt to expect and value individuality.

Certain ideas about twins have been shown to be widespread in Africa: their association both with God and the shades; their 'abnormality' and animal-like quality; and the fact that they are polluting, sometimes so polluting that they must be killed. Ambivalence of attitudes towards them; the sense that they are numinous; and their intolerable duality have also been shown. We turn now to our original question: why have twin rituals disappeared when other rituals continued? For this no complete answer has been found but some indications are offered.

The sense of the numinous is visibly diminishing in Africa and men do not fear either twin birth or death as once they did. In isolated societies in Africa fear of the numinous was most conspicuous at death, twin birth, and when lightning had struck. The depth of the fear was apparent at Nyakyusa funerals when men and women bound their bellies because they 'trembled' (Wilson, G. 1939); it was apparent at twin birth; and it was apparent among Mpondo after lightning had struck. I would have found it difficult to grasp the depth of fear had I not witnessed it in BuNyakyusa, though I had heard it described by others as it had formerly existed among Mpondo and Xhosa after a death, particularly the death of a chief. Early mission records are full of references to 'releasing people from their fears'. The Xhosa were so fearful of a corpse that they did not even bury a commoner until the early nineteenth century: it was Makanda, the prophet, who taught that all should be buried (Theal 1908 I:270). Both Xhosa and Nyakyusa-speaking Christians commented on the fact that pagans in their respective communities no longer feared death as once they had done (Hunter 1936:231; Wilson 1959:174, 177–9).

The reality of fear of twin birth was most apparent in conservative parts of the Rungwe valley in 1934–8, but already Nyakyusa Christians had ceased to celebrate any twin ritual and certain modern-minded men, though avowedly pagan, were ignoring it. Their comment was: 'we see that nothing happen when it is not celebrated'. In 1932, in conservative Pondoland, twin rituals were widely celebrated by pagans, and pairs of small euphorbia trees behind huts – evidence of such celebration – were common. But travelling in Pondoland or other parts of the Transkei or Ciskei in 1976 it is evident that euphorbia trees standing conspicuously in pairs are all of a past generation, th rty years old or more. One cannot doubt that the old ritual has been dropped. Why then do both Nyakyusa and Mpondo continue to celebrate elaborate funerals?

The sense of need for some celebration at death, birth, maturity, and marriage persists: celebrations on these occasions seem to be all but universal (Bocock 1974; Pickering 1974), and though some rituals are transformed and reappear as ceremonial in secular societies (Wilson 1957:9; 1971:3, 62, 133ff) funerals are the last to be so transformed. One reason may be that it is easier to secularize a birth than a death: there is no body to dispose of, there is no overwhelming grief. In Western Europe and North America families are slow to forgo some ritual at death but a twin birth is met with secular aid. The feeling that it is *not right* that an individual, particularly a spouse, should have a double is widespread, as jokes about twins and the comments of mothers fearing lest they bear twins reflect. Ambivalent feelings are expressed in the convention of dressing twins alike and criticism of this. Multiple birth is recognized to be an occasion of emotional tension for parents: a Californian paediatrician remarked that in his practice there had been no case of twin birth in which the parents had not had some difficulty in reconciling themselves to the event. In conversation Western mothers (non-anthropologists) have stressed two points: the practical difficulties for a mother of coping with more than one child, and the emotional difficulties of duplication of what is felt *should* be a single identity. No ritual specific to multiple birth is celebrated in Western society but the press publicity and subscription lists mobilize public sympathy and support for the parents and may be interpreted as a secular ceremonial, repeated on the birthdays of 'quads' or 'quins', which makes the mother feel she has achieved something noteworthy for which gifts are showered on her, and so also provides emotional and practical support. In South Africa there is some evidence that a shift to such secular ceremonial at multiple birth is taking place among Africans.

A second possible reason for the dropping of twin rituals is that they involved the use of medicines rather than a communion feast in which living and dead kinsmen participated. Where the rituals involved the smothering of one or both twins they necessarily changed as colonial law was effectively established but, even where there is no tradition of killing, rituals varied. As early as 1927 (or thereabouts) P. A. W. Cook noted in Bomvanaland (then as now the most conservative part of the Xhosa-speaking area): 'twin customs . . . are subject to extreme variation . . . Variations occur not only in the larger groups, e.g. in the clans, but also within small family units. Neighbours of the same *siduko* [*sic*] will practise slightly different customs' (Cook n.d.:96). Among Xhosa-speakers generally, enormous stress was laid on following traditional custom in every detail in rituals directed to the shades. Variations between lineages were acknowledged (and sometimes the charter for them given) but the efficacy of the ritual was held to depend upon following precisely the traditional form, for the shades themselves watched over and prized traditional custom. The liturgy of rituals celebrated for the shades – 'the living dead' – tends to persist, for the details of action are held to be practically efficient (Hunter 1936:235–64; Wilson 1959:202).

Medicines, that is material substances in which power was thought to reside, were different in this regard. Everywhere new medicines were readily accepted. They were introduced by diviners and doctors and the foreign doctor, with new medicines, was commonly the most highly regarded. In the most isolated societies medicines were, indeed, among the few things traded from afar. New substances are 'seen' (still in 1976) by diviners in dreams – waking or sleeping – and no one queries the right of doctor or diviner to innovate in this matter (Hunter 1936:322, 454–8; Wilson 1959:51–3).

For the Nyakyusa-Ngonde twin rituals were purifications from contamination of abnormal birth and the *dominant* feature was the medicines used. Among them twin rituals were comparable to rituals for purification celebrated after blood had been shed or lightning had struck, rather than to the rituals of birth, puberty, marriage, and death which involved a communion with the dead. In their prolonged and elaborate twin ritual there was no invocation of the shades or communion meal (such as occurred at ordinary birth, marriage, and death) until the husband who had begotten twins returned to sleep with his wife, the mother of twins. One contributory reason for the disappearance of the Nyakyusa-Ngonde twin ritual, where other rituals of kinship survive, may therefore be that twin rituals turned on medicines, but other rituals on communion feasts with prayers to the shades. The cleavage is not absolute for medicines were used in Nyakyusa rituals, the *ikipiki* representing 'the blood of the lineage' just as the *iyeza lasekhaya* (with which twins like other people were washed) represented the lineage among Xhosa-speakers. But a distinction can be drawn between rituals directed to the shades and the cleansing after misfortune. However, the argument that twin rituals generally turned on medicines rather than on offerings to the shades, is tentative and requires further examination on a cross-cultural basis, since those who cleansed themselves with medicines did in fact link twins with shades, as has been shown.

A more profitable line of enquiry might be to compare the patchy distribution of twin rituals with another patchy distribution, that of the ritual of god-parents, which is exceedingly persistent in some areas, even reappearing in secular form, whereas elsewhere no trace of it is found. Why god-parents disappeared at the Reformation in Scotland but continued in England merits a study in itself. Half a century ago F. C. Barlett (1928:42, 149; 1946) raised the question of selective conservatism and selective borrowing but little work has been done on these problems by anthropologists who have been fearful of intruding into the field of psychology. At many points anthropologists have, in fact, so intruded, unawares or unadmitted, and it seems pusillanimous to ignore a large and important field on account of Durkheimian inhibitions. At least the forms of selection taking place in changing societies may be analysed and questions posed.

One test case of selection in survival is that of boys' circumcision and girls' initiation rituals. Circumcision rituals have been dropped within historical times by Zulu and retained by Xhosa. Why? And why, among most Xhosa-speakers should the initiation ritual for young men be retained and that for girls dropped?

According to Bryant (1929:99), who in this case names his authority, circumcision was dropped among the Mthethwa (who later formed part of the Zulu kingdom) in the time of Jobe, father of Dingiswayo. Kay, writing in 1833, remarked that it did not obtain among Mfengu refugees from Natal (1833:406), though later these refugees conformed to Xhosa custom, some claiming a tradition of circumcision. Certainly circumcision diminished during the period in which a Zulu kingdom was formed and age regiments incorporating contemporaries from all over the kingdom replaced local circumcision lodges, such as still obtain among Xhosa, Mpondomise, Bomvana, and Thembu (Wilson and Thompson 1969 I:124–5, 341). Among the Mpondo it was dropped in the time of Faku (who died in 1867) and his heir, Mqikela, born in 1831 (Steedman 1835 II:288), was not circumcised (*Report on Native Laws and Customs* 1883: Minutes of Evidence, 17). During the period of resistance to Zulu raids and fighting with Bhaca refugees and Xesibe, Faku had extended his area of rule and developed a measure of centralized government (Ndamase n.d.:14–17); the abandonment of circumcision coincided with increase in his power, probably before Mqikela grew up. In Pondoland it was the chiefs who stopped circumcision and those who organized lodges were fined. Circumcision only began to creep back into Pondoland with Mfengu settlers coming from Xhosa country about 1931, when the lodges they organized for themselves were winked at by Mpondo chiefs. According to assessors in an Appeal Court case, the reason for dropping circumcision in Pondoland was that Mqikela himself was deformed, and the reason given to me in 1931 was that a number of boys had died after circumcision, but these reasons alone are hardly adequate for so fundamental a change (Hunter 1936:165). The Bhaca dropped circumcision in the time of their chief Madzikane, when they were fighting Mpondo and others for living space and independence south of the Mtamvuna river (Hammond-Tooke 1962:80–2). One common reason that covers Zulu, Mpondo, and Bhaca is that abandonment of circumcision coincided with a marked growth in the power of *one* chief, as well as a period of warfare in which young men learnt in their regiments (though these were not necessarily based on age) many of the virtues inculcated in circumcision lodges. Since 1935 circumcision has again become widespread among both Mpondo and Bhaca.

Girls' initiation (*intonjane*), still generally practised in Pondoland in 1932, has largely been dropped by Xhosa-speakers, and it has recently been argued, very cogently (Whooley 1975:257–80), that the time of transformation for a girl was not the weeks of seclusion at initiation, but the year or more spent as a bride working under the supervision of her mother-in-law, and this living with her husband's parents survives as an obligatory introduction to married life.

Reasons for the resilience and obliteration of ritual are complex and detailed analysis of each particular case is necessary before wide generalization is acceptable. This paper is intended to raise questions and suggest possible lines of investigation.

## NOTES

[1] I am indebted to Professor Philip Tobias for a number of references on twins and reprints of papers; to Mr. William Beinart for drawing my attention to the date of Mqikela's death; and to the Botanical Survey, Albany Museum, for identifying Euphorbias.

[2] There are also similarities with West Africa not here pursued.

[3] Bantu languages are not hampered by sex differences in pronouns, distinctions being made on other grounds, and the 'him' used here and elsewhere implies male or female.

[4] Or *Euphorbia tetragona* or *E.triangularis*. *Umhlonhlo* (without a 't') is used in Zulu for *E. ingens* and *E. Cooperi* (cf. Palmer and Pittman 1961:237–9).

[5] Insistence on duality as the key to cosmological thought is perhaps a reflection of the present preoccupation of intellectuals with opposition, particularly class conflict.

[6] Tolerable duality was magnificently expressed by the Hebrew poet, the writer of the Song of Songs:

'Thy teeth are like a flock of sheep . . . whereof every one bear twins . . .

Thy two breasts are like two young roes that are twins, which feed among the lilies . . .'

*The Song of Solomon* 4:2, 5.

162                                    MONICA WILSON

## REFERENCES

ALBERTI, L. 1807[1968] – *Alberti's Account of the Xhosa* (English translation, W. Fehr). Cape Town: Balkema.

BARTLETT, F. C. 1928 – *Psychology and Primitive Culture*. Cambridge: Cambridge Univ. Press.

————1946 – Psychological methods for the study of 'hard' and 'soft' features of culture. *Africa* **16**, 145–55.

BEIDELMAN, T. O. 1961a – Hyena and rabbit. *Africa* **31**, 61–74.

————1961b – Right and left hand among the Kaguru. *Africa* **31**, 250–57.

————1966 – The ox in Nuer sacrifice. *Man* I, 453–67.

BERGLUND, A–I. 1975 – Heaven-Herds: a study in Zulu symbolism. In *Religion and Social Change in Southern Africa* (eds.) M. Whisson and M. West. Cape Town: David Philip.

————1976 – *Zulu Thought-Patterns and Symbolism*. Uppsala, Swedish Institute of Missionary Research; Cape Town: David Philip.

BOCOCK, R. 1974 – *Ritual in Industrial Society*. London: Allen & Unwin.

BROWN, T. 1926 – *Among the Bantu Nomads*. London: Seeley, Service.

BRYANT, A. T. 1929 – *Olden Times in Zululand and Natal*. London: Longmans, Green.

COOK, P. A. W. n.d. [*c.* 1929] – *Social Organization and Ceremonial Institutions of the Bomvana*. Cape Town: Juta.

DOUGLAS, M. 1954 – The Lele of Kasai. In *African Worlds* (ed.) D. Forde. London: Oxford Univ. Press.

————1957 – Animals in Lele religious symbolism. *Africa* **27**, 46–58.

EVANS-PRITCHARD, E. E. 1956 – *Nuer Religion*. Oxford: Clarendon Press.

FIRTH, R. 1966 – Twins, birds and vegetables. *Man* I, 1–17.

GUSINDE, M. 1954 – Twins in South Africa. *Anthropos* **49**, 685–7.

HAMMOND-TOOKE, W. D. 1962 – *Bhaca Society*. Cape Town: Oxford Univ. Press.

————1975 – Symbolic structure of Cape Nguni cosmology. In *Religion and Social Change* (eds.) M. Whisson and M. West. Cape Town: David Philip.

HASELBRECHT, H. 1966 – 'Why seek ye the living among the dead?' *Ministry*.

HUNTER, M. 1931, 1932 – Unpublished field notes on twin rituals in Pondoland.

————1936 – *Reaction to Conquest*. London: Oxford Univ. Press.

JEFFREYS, M. D. W. 1953 – Twin births among Africans. *S.Afr.J.Sci.* **49**, 89–93.

————1963 – The cult of twins among some African tribes. *S.Afr.J.Sci.* **59**, 97–104.

JORDAN A. C. 1973a – *Tales from Southern Africa*. Berkeley: Univ. of California Press.

————1973b – *Towards an African Literature*. Berkeley: Univ. of California Press.

JUNOD, H. A. 1927 – *The Life of a South African Tribe* (second edn.). London: Macmillan.

KAY, S. 1833 – *Travels and Researches in Caffraria*. London: Mason.

KIDD, D. 1904 – *The Essential Kafir*. London: Black.

————1906 – *Savage Childhood*. London: Black.

KRIGE, E. J. and KRIGE, J. D. 1943 – *The Realm of a Rain Queen*. London: Oxford Univ. Press.
KRIGE, E. J. 1975 – Divine kingship, change and development. In *African Social Anthropology* (eds.) M. Fortes and S. Paterson. London: Academica Press.
KROPF, A. 1899 – *A Kaffir-English Dictionary*. Lovedale: Lovedale Press.
LAGERCRANTZ, S. 1941 – *Über Willkommene und Unwillkommen Zwillinge in Africa*. Goteberg: Etnografiska Museet.
LEVI-STRAUSS, C. 1962 – *Totemism* (English translation, R. Needham). London: Merlin Press.
LIENHARDT, G. 1961 – *Divinity and Experience*. Oxford: Clarendon Press.
MACLEAN, COLONEL 1866 – *Compendium of Kafir Laws and Customs*. Cape Town: Saul Solomon.
MOODIE, D. 1960 [1838–41] – *The Record: Official Papers relative to . . . the Native Tribes of South Africa*. Cape Town: Balkema.
MQHAYI, S. K. R. 1914 – *Ityala lamaWele*. Lovedale: Lovedale Press.
NDAMASE, V. P. n.d. [*c.* 1929] – *Ama-Mpondo Ibali ne-Ntlalo*. Lovedale: Lovedale Press.
OTTO, R. 1926 – *The Idea of the Holy* (English translation J. W. Harvey). London: Oxford Univ. Press.
PALMER, E. and PITMAN, N. 1961 – *Trees of Southern Africa*. Cape Town: Balkema.
PAUW, B. A. 1975 – *Christianity and Xhosa Tradition*. Cape Town: Oxford Univ. Press.
PICKERING, W. S. F. 1974 – The persistence of rites of passage: towards an explanation. *Br.J.Sociol.* **25**, 63–78.
*Report on Native Laws and Customs*. 1883 – *Report of the Government Commission on Native Laws and Customs*. Cape Town: Government Printer.
RICHARDS, A. I. 1956 – *Chisungu: A Girl's Initiation Ceremony among the Bemba of Northern Rhodesia*. London: Faber and Faber.
————1960 – Social mechanisms for the transfer of political rights in some African tribes. *Jl R.Anthrop.Inst.* **90**, 175–90.
————1961 – African kings and their royal relatives. *Jl R.Anthrop. Inst.* **91**, 135–50.
SCHAPERA, I. 1927 – Customs relating to twins in South Africa. *Jl R. Afr. Soc.* **26**, 117–37.
————1938 – *A Handbook of Tswana Law and Custom*. London: Oxford Univ. Press.
SHAW, W. 1972 – *Journal of William Shaw* (ed. W. D. Hammond-Tooke). Cape Town: Balkema.
SOGA, J. H. n.d. [*c.* 1931] – *The Ama-Xhosa: Life and Customs*. Lovedale: Lovedale Press; London: Kegan Paul.
STAYT, H. A. 1931 – *The Bavenda*. London: Oxford Univ. Press.
STEEDMAN, A. 1835 – *Wanderings and Adventures in the Interior of Southern Africa*. 2 vols. London: Longman.
SUNDKLER, B. G. M. 1948 – *Bantu Prophets*. London: Lutterworth Press.
THEAL, G. M. 1908 – *History of South Africa since 1795*. 5 vols. London: Swan, Sonnenschein.

TURNER, V. W. 1961 – *Ndembu Divination: Its Symbolism and Techniques* (Rhodes-Livingstone Pap. **31**). Manchester: Manchester Univ. Press.

————1962 – *Ch hamba, the White Spirit* (Rhodes-Livingstone Pap. **33**). Manchester: Manchester Univ. Press.

————1967 – *The Forest of Symbols*. Ithaca: Cornell Univ. Press.

————1968 – *The Drums of Affliction*. Oxford: Clarendon Press.

————1969 – *The Ritual Process*. Chicago: Aldine.

WAGNER, G. 1949, 1956 – *The Bantu of North Kavirondo*. 2 vols. London: Oxford Univ. Press.

WEST, M. 1975a – *Bishops and Prophets in a Black City*. Cape Town: David Philip.

————1975b – The shades come to town. In *Religion and Social Change in Southern Africa* (eds.) M. G. Whisson and M. West. Cape Town: David Philip.

WHISSON, M. G. and WEST, M. (eds.). 1975 – *Religion and Social Change in Southern Africa*. Cape Town: David Philip.

WHOOLEY, P. 1975 – Marriage in Africa: a study in the Ciskei. In *Church and Marriage in Modern Africa* (ed.) T. D. Verryn. Groenkloof: Ecumenical Research Unit.

WILLIS, R. 1975 – *Man and Beast*. London: Paladin.

WILSON, G. 1939 – Nyakyusa conventions of burial. *Bantu Studies* **13**, 1–31.

WILSON, M. 1954 – Nyakyusa ritual and symbolism. *Am. Anthrop.* **56**, 228–41.

————1957 – *Rituals of Kinship among the Nyakyusa*. London: Oxford Univ. Press.

————1959 – *Communal Rituals of the Nyakyusa*. London: Oxford Univ. Press.

————1971 – *Religion and the Transformation of Society*. Cambridge: Cambridge Univ. Press.

————forthcoming – *Mhlakaza*. Paris: Jeune Afrique.

WILSON, M. and THOMPSON, L. (eds.). 1969, 1971 – *The Oxford History of South Africa*. 2 vols. Oxford: Clarendon Press.

# SOME KGATLA THEORIES OF PROCREATION

*I. Schapera*

The material presented below was obtained in the course of field-work carried on intermittently during the years 1929–35 among the Kgatla (Bakgatla-bagaKgafela) of Botswana. As I do not know if all or even some of the beliefs recorded then are still current among the people, I have used the past tense throughout, to indicate that what is said here relates to a period of more than forty years ago.

Much of this material has already been summarized in previous publications (notably Schapera 1933 and 1940), but the present paper gives considerably more detail and also includes some new information. By its very nature such material could only be obtained by talking to people, and not by 'participant observation' or similar techniques. The reader is therefore entitled to ask how many informants were used, who they were, and what each of them said. In the following list, which answers the first two questions, principal informants are identified by means of asterisks after their names. The others contributed isolated or scrappy details only, generally mentioned casually while we were discussing some other topic. The names of males are printed in small capitals, those of females in lower case. All quotations are free translations of the original Kgatla version. Where relevant I have also added the date of the interview.

*Dingaka* ('doctors'): MAGOLENG LEFI, NATALE MOREMA*, RAKGOMO SEGALE, RAPEDI LETSEBE*, SEBAITSENG MODISE, SEPHARE SEPHARE. (RAKGOMO was elderly, the others all middle-aged.)

Elderly persons: Mmampotele Modikwe*, Mmasenwelo Tladi, MORUE MODIBEDI*.

Middle-aged: (Ex-chief) ISANG PILANE, Mathee Ramatlai*, Mmapoonyane Ramodisa, Mmatsholofelo Ratsatsi, Mosalakwe Tshwene.

Young: (married) Manyama Mosaate*, Ntebeng Molefe*; (unmarried) LESAANE MAKGOTSO*, MAGANELO PILANE, Marutshwi Mpane, MOLEFE SEGOGWANE*, Motlhodi Kedisang, Seanokeng Motoma, SEIKANELO LEBOTSE, SOFONIA POONYANE*, Tsholofelo Ratsatsi*.

The list, it may be claimed, is reasonably representative of both sexes and various age-groups. But I cannot maintain that what my informants said is necessarily valid for the Kgatla as a whole (except perhaps when their statements were confirmed independently by others). For this reason I have entitled the paper 'Some Kgatla Theories . . .' and not simply 'Kgatla Theories . . .'.

CAUSES OF CONCEPTION

Kgatla theories of conception were summarized as follows (11.2.1930) by MOLEFE SEGOGWANE, an unmarried youth (age-set Chama created in 1928), who had been to school abroad:

> Children are told by the women that an old woman goes to a pool and from its side gets some fine stones (so that the child may be fine), which she throws into the water. She has a wooden spoon, with which she stirs the water near her. While doing so she sings: *Noga leledu, noga leledu, tswa metseng, tswa metseng, regobone*, 'Bearded snake, bearded snake, come from the water, come from the water, that we may see you.' Then, they say, a snake will bring out a child to her. She takes the child up to a cave in the hills and leaves it lying there, wrapped in blankets. Then she comes at night to fetch it, and brings it to its mother.

> Adults believe that children are produced by copulation, from a mixture of the man's semen (*marere*) with the blood inside the woman's womb (menstrual blood, *mosese*). The semen goes into the womb (*tsala*) and rests there until, after the fourth time or so of intercourse, it is sufficient in quantity. Then a mixture takes place. This mixture is not formed at the first coition, but after several; and when it has occurred, the woman ceases to menstruate. . . . She dates her pregnancy from the cessation of her menses, and starts counting the new moons; and when eight months have passed, she knows that she will bear her child in the ninth.

The first part of this statement was confirmed independently by two other unmarried members of the Chama age-set:

> (SOFONIA, 25.6.1931): When small children ask where a baby comes from, they are told that it comes from a well. They often ask each other, 'When is mother going to take a baby from the well', and also, 'From which well did your mother take it?' Then the bigger children tell them, 'No, a baby comes from its mother's stomach.'

> (LESAANE, 25.12.1933): When children ask where a baby comes from, they are told that it comes from deep waters. You will

hear one child say to another, 'My mother says that my little brother came from the well'.

All adult informants agreed that conception resulted from the passage of semen into the womb; this belief was in fact reflected in various contraceptive practices (see below, p. 178). As shown by the following simple statements (others are quoted later), they generally also agreed that children are formed by a mixture of semen and menstrual blood, i.e. of the man's 'blood' (see p. 168) and the woman's:

'A man sleeps with his wife in order to make a child, and if their bloods agree the woman will become pregnant and stop menstruating' (LESAANE);

'When a boy and a girl copulate their bloods coalesce into a big lump (*letlhole*), and this will grow until it becomes a child' (Tsholofelo).

According to some informants a single act of coitus was enough to cause pregnancy, 'if there is nothing wrong with husband and wife' (NATALE) or 'if their bloods agree' (LESAANE, Tsholofelo). But most of them said, like SEGOGWANE, that repeated coition was necessary, say 'for at least three successive nights' (SOFONIA) or 'for three or four nights running' (RAPEDI), in order that enough semen could accumulate in the womb. This particular belief was expressed as follows by two unmarried young women:

(Motlhodi, 5.3.1934): When I slept with a boy for the first time, . . . before he put in his 'thing' (*selo sagagwe*) I was afraid and said, 'Won't you make me pregnant?' He replied, 'No; a person impregnates someone (*motho akgorisa motho*) only after sleeping with her three or five times (*gararo kampo gatlhano*).'

(Marutshwi, 15.9.1934): I believe that the first discharge [ejaculation] can never make one pregnant, even if the boy's blood is very 'sharp'. But if he sleeps with you three nights in succession, then he has filled your womb and you will become pregnant.

Kgatla apparently did not have one specific name for semen. Because it comes out through the urethra it was sometimes called by the same terms as urine (*moroto, motlhapo*), and because of its texture it was sometimes called 'mucus, slime' (*marere, marerenyana, maregerege*). Other names, each mentioned by single though different informants, were *mothunyo* (discharge, lit. shot); *bothata* (strength); *bonna* (manhood); and *letshekgetshekge* ('slimy stuff'). Many people also referred to it as *madi*, 'blood'. This does not mean that they identified it with ordinary blood. Manyama said the name was used 'just to distinguish it from urine'; Motlhodi referred to it more precisely as *madi amasweu*, 'white blood'; MORUE similarly distinguished it as *madi amagola*, 'the blood of growth', i.e. the blood that forms a person; RAPEDI spoke of it in one context as 'porridge' (*bogobe*) stored in the womb after coition; and Mmampotele said that a child's flesh was made by its father 'because of the heavy lumps he puts into his wife'.

The only information given to me about its source is contained in the following statements: 'Semen (*moroto*) is blood (*madi*) that comes from the veins all over the body and takes a line going straight to the penis' (SOFONIA); 'It is prepared by the testicles and stored in the scrotal sac, but I don't know how' (LESAANE); 'It comes from the waist and hips' (Manyama). SOFONIA said also that during coition 'the girl's blood goes into your body to call your blood; then if you don't drop it out [by coitus interruptus] it all goes into the girl's body to make a child.' The belief that the woman's blood enters the man's body and 'calls' his blood was confirmed by several other informants (e.g. RAPEDI, Mmapoonyane, and LESAANE).

People were usually definite about the role of menstrual blood in conception. They said, firstly, that a woman stops menstruating on becoming pregnant, and in fact realizes or suspects her condition because of that. Thus, according to Manyama (25.8.1934):

A woman knows she is pregnant when she misses her period. If she ordinarily misses a period, it may be just because she is sick and her blood is no good; but then she will get well again. But if she has recently met a man, then she knows she is pregnant, because she used to get her periods regularly.

Similar statements were made by others, including for instance SEGOGWANE, SOFONIA, RAPEDI, SEPHARE, and the two quoted in the following paragraph (LESAANE and Tsholofelo).

Secondly, as SEGOGWANE said (see p. 166), it was believed also that menstruation stops after conception because the woman's blood helps to make the child. The following are other statements to the same effect:

(LESAANE, 13.1.1934): When a child is born we know that its father and mother both contribute to its physique. Its flesh comes from the father, and its blood from the mother. We say that the woman forms the blood because before she conceives

she menstruates regularly, and that is nothing but blood; but
after she is pregnant her menses stop and the child starts to be
formed. It is therefore obvious that she sacrifices her blood for
the child.

(Tsholofelo, 22.1.1934): When a girl sleeps with a boy,
nothing comes out of her [similar to ejaculated semen]. This is
because the blood she normally sheds while menstruating is that
which forms the child when it meets the blood of the boy.

Menstrual blood was usually spoken of by the same term as
ordinary blood, viz. *madi*. 'There is no difference between the two,
they are just the same, for they come from one body' (Manyama).
It was occasionally also termed *motlhapo* (flux, urine) or *moroto*
(urine). All three terms, as we have seen, were likewise used for
semen. (The last two are derived respectively from -*tlhapa*, wash, and
-*rota*, urinate.) Menstruation itself was sometimes referred to as
*gotlhapa metse*, lit. 'to wash water'; *gobona mosese*, 'to see the
skirt'; or simply *mosese*, 'skirt'. But the most common terms were
*bolwetse bakgwedi*, 'sickness of the moon' (or 'monthly sickness'),
and *gobona kgwedi*, 'to see the moon'; and when a woman had her
periods people often said of her, *oile kgweding*, 'she has gone to the
moon'.

As this indicates, menstruation was known to have a lunar cycle.
The following is the only explanation given to me: The blood passes
into the womb *momaleng*, 'from the intestines' (Manyama) or
*moditshekeng*, 'from the veins' (Seanokeng), and accumulates there
every month to form a clot (*lehuto*, knot), which then breaks up and
flows away (except after conception and recent childbirth). 'People
say that a woman is full of blood and if she does not menstruate regularly she will probably die; her blood must therefore be diminished
so that she can live' (SEGOGWANE). This particular statement lacks
confirmation. The term *lehuto*, incidentally, was sometimes also used
for menstrual blood 'while it is still in the womb'.

The relationship between childbirth and menstruation was reflected in several additional beliefs. Informants said that a woman
cannot bear children unless she menstruates, and barrenness in
young or middle-aged women was sometimes held to be due to
menstrual irregularities (see p. 173). They said also that women past
the menopause can no longer have children. For instance:

(SOFONIA, 16.4.1931): If a woman does not menstruate she
won't bear children. They say it prepares the womb. But if she

is an old woman who no longer menstruates, they say of her
*ofeletswe keletsalo*, 'she has finished with child-bearing'.

(Manyama, 11.6.1931): Menstruation is due to God, so that
you can get a child. If you don't menstruate you can't have
a child. If you have been bearing children and then afterwards
you don't menstruate any more, you know that you have finished
with children, you won't bear any more.

(LESAANE, 15.1.1934): When women get old they stop menstruating. This shows they will no longer bear children. We don't
know why it happens. It is just according to the will of God.

(Mmampotele, 30.1.1934): There are some women who have
never menstruated since they were born. We call such a woman
*mosadi sekamonna*, 'a man-like woman'. She will never bear a
child; she is no good.

It was likewise held that a girl cannot conceive until she has started
to menstruate. This explains the tolerance shown by some adults for
the sexual play of children, which often included attempts at copulation.

(LESAANE, 20.12.1933): Love among children is treated very
lightly, and so is *thobalo* (sexual intercourse, lit. 'sleeping,
sleep') . . . Because they are still young, adults say nothing, even
though aware of what is going on. There will be no consequence,
because the children are still immature. Their genitals are still
*kwasefalaneng* ('in the granary'); the girl has not yet menstruated, nor does the boy have any semen.

(Tsholofelo, 22.8.1934): Even if children copulate like adults
nothing can go wrong, for at this time the girls are still called
*basimane* (boys), because they do not yet menstruate. So it
doesn't matter how they sleep, there can be no trouble.

(Manyama, 25.8.1934): A girl can't have children before she
menstruates. That is the work of God. Until then she can sleep
with boys as often as she likes, but it makes no difference.

But when a girl's breasts began to swell, and especially when she
menstruated for the first time, she was generally warned about the
dangers of sexual intercourse:

(SOFONIA, 18.1.1934): As girls grow, their mothers say to
them, 'The day you menstruate you must know that you can
now conceive; before this you can't.'

(Tsholofelo, 19.1.1934): We know that when a girl's breasts
grow big she will soon menstruate. Now she must be careful

of boys; she is a complete woman, for if she sleeps with a boy she can conceive.

(Mosalakwe, 24.8.1934): As soon as girls get their periods they must no longer sleep with boys. This is a proper *moila* (taboo). Older girls warn them that as soon as they get that flow they must not again meet boys: 'If you dare to sleep with them you will become pregnant, and then get into trouble.'

There were apparently no similarly distinctive criteria by which people knew when a boy was old enough to beget. The following are the only statements I have about this:

(Manyama, 25.8.1934): Small boys can't make children. They can ejaculate, but very little. Small boys don't have semen, they get it as they grow older.

(SOFONIA, 6.9.1934): Boys at cattleposts sometimes play about in each other's presence with their penises. They roll back their foreskins, and in some cases they find white stuff round the glans. They say that shows *bonna* (manhood), and each comments about the other's. They know that when they have this they can *kgorisa* (impregnate), but not before. If one hasn't got it his mates laugh at him and call him *mosimanyana* (little boy).

(MORUE, 11.9.1934): We don't see by any signs that a boy is capable of begetting, except when he has grown big. We just guess that he is big enough to make a child. It is not as with girls, whom we see menstruate. When a boy is still small he can't make a child, perhaps because he has not got enough *madi* (blood, viz. semen).

It was recognized also that old men could sometimes no longer 'make' children. It was even usual for such a man to let a younger relative or friend have access to his wife in order to 'raise seed' for him. But I received no special explanation for this loss of potency, apart from what informants said about impotence in general (see p. 177).

## BARRENNESS

Kgatla theories of procreation were further reflected in various beliefs and practices relating to barrenness (*boopa*). All married people were said to want children, and a wife was expected to bear as many as she could, provided only that she did not become pregnant while still suckling an infant. A young bride when taken to her husband's home on the first afternoon of the wedding ceremonies was given a young baby to hold as she entered his hut. This rite, performed 'so that she too must get a child' (SOFONIA), symbolized the hopes now centred on her. It was her husband's duty to sleep with her regularly, and if he stayed away too long from her, for instance at work abroad, public opinion did not usually condemn her for taking a lover by whom she could continue to bear.

A woman with many children was highly honoured. If she had none at all she was an object of pity, often tempered with scorn; her husband's relatives, in particular, would sometimes reproach her openly and treat her unkindly. In the old days there was apparently even a special mode of burying such a woman when she died: 'they used to bind her right arm on her back, as if it was her child' (SOFONIA); 'she was buried with her hands at her back' (Mmatsholofelo).

The term for a barren person, *moopa*, was not applied to anybody either too young to have children or too old to have any more. It was normally restricted to those, whether men or women, who after several years of marriage had not yet produced any at all. Such people were not very numerous. Genealogical data I collected in 1931–2 showed that, of 462 married women then alive, 47 (10 per cent) were barren at the time of investigation. But these included many who, judged solely by their ages, could possibly still conceive. Of the 184 women past the menopause, only seven (4 per cent) had never been mothers.

If after a year or two of marriage a woman had not yet become pregnant, her husband usually called in a 'doctor' (*ngaka*, professional magician) who knew how to deal with such cases. The doctor ascertained the cause of the trouble by divination. Occasionally he found nothing wrong with either husband or wife except that 'their bloods do not agree'. He would then perform the rite of *gokopanya madi*, 'uniting the bloods': he cut each on the mons pubis and then, with his finger, transferred blood from the woman's wounds on to the man's, and vice versa. 'When the cuts heal, the couple sleep together, and they will have a child later on' (Mathee). But apparently not always: 'sometimes he cannot manage to make their bloods like each other, and so they will remain without children' (Tsholofelo).

Most commonly, however, the divination indicated that the fault lay with the wife. The causes usually mentioned were summarized as follows by Ntebeng (29.12.1933):

If a woman does not bear children, it may be that while still unmarried she had many lovers; the bloods of all these men coming into her disagree (*gaadumellane*), and so her womb becomes spoiled (*tsala yagagwe easenyega*). Or she may have spoiled it herself, if she became pregnant, by drinking medicines *gontsha mpa* (to take out her belly, i.e. to induce an abortion).

Her barrenness is sometimes due to the fact that her womb is withered (*eswabile*): it is narrow and its mouth is small, so that it does not open wide [to receive the semen]. Or on the other hand it does not close after she has slept with a man, but remains wide open; it is then said to have been worn smooth (*gatwe gogotlhilwe*), so that the semen all flows out of it, and this prevents her from conceiving.

Sometimes she may have been bewitched by an enemy who got hold of the rags she wears [as pads] when menstruating.

Her husband calls a doctor, who will say what is wrong. He gives them medicines and then, if God wills, she will get a child.

As this summary indicates, a woman's barrenness could be attributed to purely biological factors. She might never have menstruated at all (SOFONIA, Manyama, Mmapoonyane) or 'her blood may have gone bad' so that she menstruated excessively (MAGOLENG). Or, as mentioned by Ntebeng, something might be wrong with her womb. This was confirmed by other informants. For instance, Chief ISANG said (31.12.1933):

It is believed that there is in the womb a sort of snake (*noga*), which either bites or spits out the blood of the man and prevents it from coming inside. They speak of it as being there only when the woman is barren. The doctor then says he will have to kill it by medicine.

Sometimes the semen is rejected when the womb is 'sick' inside: it may be twisted, so that the semen is blocked from passing into the interior and is thrown back again; or it may have pimples or sores, which make the woman unable to hold the man's semen.

Mathee, whom I questioned on the point (12.1.1934), did not know of the belief about the 'snake'; and NATALE, himself a doctor, said in this connexion (22.1.1934), 'There is nothing like a snake in the womb; "snake" is only a nickname given to it because it spits out the man's blood'.

There was widespread agreement that this rejection of semen by the womb was perhaps the most common cause of barrenness in women. The phenomenon was termed *pusa*, repulsion (from *-busa*, send back, cause to return). It was variously described as follows:

(MAGANELO, 22.8.1932): *Pusa* is when a girl can't hold a boy's semen, it flows out of her. That is why some women cannot bear children.

(LESAANE, 28.12.1933): Semen changes into 'blood' when it gets into a girl's womb. If it does not mix properly with hers she won't get a child; she will excrete the semen, her womb cannot hold it.

(Mathee, 12.1.1934): *Pusa* means that when a man sleeps with his wife his semen flows out again after it has entered.

(Ntebeng, 13.1.1934): *Pusa* is a sickness inside a woman. They say this when a man meets a woman and leaves his blood in her, and she sends it back again; her womb stops the blood and throws it out.

*Pusa* was said to be due sometimes to anatomical abnormality, either innate (as suggested above) or produced by means of sorcery. The most usual explanation, however, was that it resulted from pre-marital promiscuity. Some people stated merely that if the girl had many lovers her womb became spoiled, because the different 'bloods' ejaculated into it 'disagreed' with one another. Others added that, in consequence, she was unable to retain the 'bloods' and kept on ex-pelling them.

Another alleged cause of barrenness was induced abortion. Most of the medicines used for this purpose (cf. Schapera 1940:223–4) did nothing more than 'spoil the woman's blood' for the time being, i.e. they did not prevent her from conceiving again. But some were said to cause permanent sterility: 'they polish (*-dila*) the womb, so that everything is smooth on top and the semen flows off' (Mmam-potele). The woman could also become and remain barren if she secretly buried the foetus in open ground:

(Mathee, 12.1.1934): There are many girls here who do not bear children after marriage. They are barren because when they were still young they led a loose life. Then they became preg-nant and, through fear of the consequences (wrath of their parents, expulsion from church membership, and mockery of other girls), they worked on their stomach for several days until the foetus (*madi*, blood) came out. The girl then wrapped up the 'blood' in an old underskirt, dug a hole, and buried it there, without telling her parents. This is called *goiphitlhela* (to hide oneself). After this she can no longer bear a child, no matter for with whom she sleeps. It is just like anthrax (*lebete*) in cattle: when a cow dies of anthrax, its spleen (*lebete*) is buried in a hole made in the ground, and then the disease will not attack the cattle again.

It should be added here that abortions, miscarriages and still-births all had to be buried in a particular way inside a hut, otherwise the mother 'will bear no more children'; they also had to be buried by women past the menopause, and not by one of child-bearing age, or 'she will stop having children' (Mathee, Mmasenwelo).

Kgatla believed also that a woman could be made barren by the actions of other people. This, informants said, usually took the form of sorcery (*boloi*). To achieve his aim the sorcerer (*moloi*) had to get hold of and 'doctor' something associated with the woman, such as her menstrual pads, the afterbirth of a child she had just borne, or the 'blood' that came from her if she miscarried. He could thus stop her from having any more children, or, if she was newly married, from having any at all. In an inheritance dispute heard in the chief's court in October 1935 (*Andrea Tlhowe* v. *Gaenaope*), a young widow asserted that she was barren because, soon after she was married, her father-in-law had stolen and doctored her husband's belt.

Sorcery sometimes caused the woman to menstruate excessively, 'so that her blood does not coalesce with the man's, but keeps on breaking up and coming out' (NATALE). It could also 'turn her womb upside down' (-*ribega tsala*), and so prevent the semen from getting in (SOFONIA, Manyama). Another possible effect was described as follows by Mmampotele (30.1.1934):

> When a girl menstruates one month but not the next, and then again, we call this *gokgora seome* (to eat a little food and satisfy one's appetite, but to become hungry again soon after-wards). Such a girl has been bewitched by means of the little animal *senanatswii* [a small variety of frog]. If she gets married, she will give birth to only one child, and then stop altogether. They will try to *remela* her [doctor her for barrenness], but she will not get healed.

As mentioned above, some forms of barrenness were considered incurable. This applied chiefly, but not only, to those caused by sorcery. Most other forms, it was said, could be cured. The treatment was known technically as -*remela* (from -*rema*, to cut or chop, e.g.

branches of a tree). The name, MAGANELO explained, 'does not mean that branches are cut for an enclosure in which husband and wife must live alone; it means that they must isolate themselves from bad ways and take care of each other, i.e. they must abstain from adultery until they bear a child.' The sexual taboo was confirmed by MAGOLENG, who said that if the husband violated it 'the wife's blood will break and she will be unable to conceive.' A child born as a result of the treatment was termed *ngwana wameremelo* (from *-remela*). 'People say it is more delicate than others' (MORUE).

Of six doctors questioned at various times (RAKGOMO, MAGOLENG, RAPEDI, SEPHARE, SEBAITSENG, and NATALE), only the first-named denied knowing how to deal with cases of barrenness. The others all said that their treatment consisted mainly in giving the woman medicines – 'to clean out her womb, which has been dirtied by a man with bad blood' (RAPEDI); 'to clean out her stomach' (SEPHARE); 'to dry her womb, so that the blood should not keep running out', i.e. to inhibit her menses (NATALE). Three (MAGOLENG, SEPHARE and NATALE) stated that the same medicines, or some of them, also had to be taken by the husband.

The medicines used invariably included portions, mostly roots, of one or more plants. Judging from the names given, some of which were esoteric, no two doctors relied on the same plants. SEBAITSENG, for instance, made his medicine from roots of *pelobotlhoko* (*Geigeria passerinoides*), whereas SEPHARE used roots of *mothata* (*Pappea capensis*) and *monokana* (*Heeria* sp) and leaves of *mosimama* (*Senecio laxiflorus*). Usually the medicine (sometimes whole, sometimes in powdered form) was either boiled or steeped in water. This the patient had to drink, once or twice daily, for periods ranging from 'three or four days' (MAGOLENG, NATALE) to 'a month' (SEPHARE) or 'until no longer needed' (RAPEDI). Some doctors (MAGOLENG, SEBAITSENG and NATALE) supplemented it with another medicine that was added to sorghum porridge, the staple food.

An additional ingredient of the medicines used by both SEBAITSENG and NATALE was the womb of a female goat that had borne one or more kids. It may be noted in this context that according to Chief ISANG (31.12.1933) some doctors also used a goat for diagnosing the cause of a woman's barrenness. They gave the goat medicines to drink, and made it lie next to her 'for half an hour or so'. Then they killed it, skinned it carefully, cut it open, and inspected the womb. From this they could tell what was wrong with the woman's womb, for instance if it was 'twisted' or had 'pimples or sores'. They knew accordingly what treatment to use. ISANG said he had seen this method successfully employed by a doctor named SEGAI.

The treatment sometimes included other features. Medicines were burned in a potsherd, next to which the woman had to sit, wrapped in blankets, 'so that she can -*aramela* (inhale) the smoke and have it round her body' (MAGOLENG, SEBAITSENG). Or the doctor might rub powdered medicine into small cuts he made 'on her belly, near the navel' (SEBAITSENG) or 'on the back, between the shoulder blades' (SEPHARE). NATALE used a homeopathic rite: he told the woman that after boiling the roots and removing them from the water she must bury the sodden mass in a hole dug in an antheap; then, while she continued drinking the water daily, 'the roots will start to swell, and so also will the womb.'

NATALE's treatment for *pusa* (see p. 174) seems worth recording more fully because of its ingenuity. Here is a paraphrase of his description (22.1.1934)

> He gave the woman a powder made from the roots of the bush *ntswelebogale*. She mixed some of it daily with a little porridge, which she and her husband had to eat early in the morning 'for about two weeks'. He also gave her a thick 'cork' (*sethiba*), whose main ingredient was 'the womb of a she-goat that has had kids once or twice'. Bits of the womb were roasted and powdered and, together with some *ntswelebogale* powder, were mixed with the goat's fat and moulded into shape. The woman had to insert this 'cork' into her vagina immediately after coition, as soon as her husband withdrew his penis. Its function was 'to prevent his blood from flowing out; the blood touches the cork, which makes it run back into her womb.' She kept it in position all night through, though if her husband wanted to 'use' her again that night she took it out immediately before coition and replaced it immediately afterwards. In the morning she took it out, wrapped it in a cloth, and 'hides it somewhere in the hut', ready to use again when needed. She continued using it like this 'until she knows that she is pregnant'.

It was less common, though by no means unknown, for a childless marriage to be attributed to a husband's impotence. The cause usually mentioned was the 'spoiling' of his blood through coition with a ritually-impure woman, especially a widow. He could then perhaps be cured by one of the treatments used in cases of infection by 'hot blood' (cf. Schapera 1940:194–6). An unfaithful husband could also be made impotent by the sorcery of his jealous wife. A third possible cause, mentioned only by LESAANE, was organic disease. He instanced a man named Bopapi, of Odi village, who suffered from *nkwana*, 'a sickness which ate out the innerparts of his nose, so that it became flat and he could not speak or breathe properly. This affected his main system: he would copulate, but he could not have an orgasm'.

Kgatla further believed that impotence is sometimes innate. It was then held to be incurable.

(Mathee, 12.1.1934): A man is sometimes born impotent (*moopa*). This can be noticed when he is still a small boy. Whenever he urinates his little penis does not rise (*ntsutswanyane yagagwe eseke etsoge*). So they say he has been fashioned like that by God, who did not give him strength (*obopilwe keModimo, mme osamha thata*), and when he sleeps with a woman he does not get an erection. When a man is like this, doctoring is of no use. He cannot be cured.

(LESAANE, 13.1.1934): When a boy is still young it is easily seen that he won't be able to beget children. By the law of nature his penis should be stiff when he urinates, and relax again afterwards. But if it dangles loosely when he urinates, then we know he won't be potent. Or if he does not get an erection when he sees girls, then we also know that he hasn't got any strength.

METHODS OF CONTRACEPTION

The interval between one birth and another was usually longer than is physically possible. An important reason was the rule that a woman should not become pregnant again before having weaned a sucking child. This she seldom did until it was able to walk steadily, at the age of about two or three years. Should she conceive sooner, it was said, the child at her breast would suffer.

Since at the time of my fieldwork few Kgatla yet reckoned their ages in terms of calendar years, I could not get much quantitative information about the spacing of births. The only fairly reliable data I have are for 26 families, each of three or more children whose dates of birth were recorded in the church baptism registers (1880–1935). According to this source, the intervals (in years) between successive births were numerically distributed as follows:

| Years | Births | Percentages |
|-------|--------|-------------|
| 1     | 5      | 4,3         |
| 2     | 50     | 43,5        |
| 3     | 38     | 33,0        |
| 4     | 15     | 13,0        |
| 5     | 6      | 5,2         |
| 6     | 1      | 0,9         |
|       | 115    | 99,9        |

The figures, because of their source, do not include records of mis-carriages and stillbirths. They are therefore not a complete guide to the spacing of pregnancies. Nevertheless it seems reasonable to con-clude from them that, in general, most children were born two or three years after their immediate predecessors.

A husband's often lengthy absence at work abroad must have helped to bring this about, assuming of course that his wife remained chaste while he was away. But a much more widespread, and older, cause was that the Kgatla knew and practised various methods of contraception.

The most common was coitus interruptus. This was variously termed *gontshetsa madi kwantle*, 'to take the "blood" outside'; *gotsholla mophateng*, 'to spill (the semen) on to the sleeping-mat'; or *gotsholla kwantle*, 'to spill (the semen) outside.' It was widely practised not only by married people, especially while the wife was suckling a child, but also by unmarried lovers. The necessary action had to be taken by the man; an unmarried girl, for instance, would sometimes yield to his advances only if he promised to do so.

(SOFONIA, 24.4.1931): When a boy wants to sleep with a girl she may at first refuse, saying, 'What will you do if I become pregnant?' He replies, 'Only fools make girls pregnant (*gok-gorisa dithomo*), I would not do so; I shall discharge outside you (*ketlantshetsa kwantle gagago*) the stuff that causes preg-nancy (*selo sesekgorisetsang*).' Then the girl agrees. The boy sleeps with her, and spills his semen outside (*otshollele moroto kwantle*). Then the girl thinks he is all right, he will never make her pregnant.

(Ntebeng, 13.1.1934): When a wife is still suckling a child her husband will try to ensure that he does not 'come' properly into her. Some men send their semen on to the ground; others put it in, but not properly, i.e. they withdraw the penis as they ejaculate. Or, if the woman herself does not want to become pregnant again, as soon as she feels that he is going to ejaculate she moves her hips slightly, so that his penis slips out of her vagina and the semen is spilled on to her loins. That is what I myself do.

(Tsholofelo, 25.1.1934): If a girl does not want to become pregnant when sleeping with a boy, she tells him not to stay on her too long, so that his *bonna* ('manhood', semen) should not come into her.

Ntebeng's statement about the woman herself taking evasive action was confirmed by other informants:

(LESAANE, 19.1.1934): Married women, when they want to avoid conception, feel from the stiffening of the man's body that he is about to ejaculate. Then they move their hips slightly, so as to throw out the penis and let the semen spill outside just at the mouth of the vagina.

(Manyama, 15.8.1934): When people have sexual intercourse it is the man who should stop himself from ejaculating into the vagina. But the woman can (also) stop it. When she feels him pushing more hurriedly, and so knows that he is about to ejaculate, she quickly turns on her side and pushes him off. But if you do this he usually quarrels with you and says, 'When I am enjoying myself you stop me by doing so.'

Should the man nevertheless ejaculate into her, the woman could try other expedients. According to male informants, 'immediately after copulation she goes outside and pisses to get rid of the semen' (SEIKANELO), or 'she turns on her belly after sleeping with the man, then his blood flows out and she cannot become pregnant' (NATALE). Female informants gave a little more detail:

(Ntebeng, 23.1.1934): If a girl does not want to conceive, she goes outside to urinate after the boy has slept with her, and so gets rid of his semen too. Or she lies on her belly, so that all the semen he has put into her must flow out.

(Marutshwi, 15.9.1934): As soon as the boy stops shaking on you [i.e. immediately after he ejaculates], you must not let him keep his penis inside. You quickly pull your thighs together and push him out; then you turn over quickly on to your belly, to let his 'blood' flow out. If you let him stop there it's your

own look-out (*kesagago*), you are going to get pregnant, because that thing of his [the penis] pushes the blood inside.

Another practice, described by two unmarried youths only, was
the use of medicines:

(SEGOGWANE, 5.2.1930): The woman eats the roots of the
*bogoma* shrub [*Setaria verticillata*], or she may grind the roots
of *phukutsa* [a purgative, unidentified] and put the powder
into water, which she drinks just after copulating.

(SOFONIA, 10.7.1930): *Magwane* (adolescent youths) sometimes give girls roots to chew, either before sleeping with them
or immediately afterwards, so that they won't conceive. Sometimes a boy takes the twigs of the *phukutsa* plant and boils
them in a pot. He then mixes the foam with hot water, which he
gives to the girl to drink straight after copulation. It prevents
her from having a baby.

The methods so far described were all traditional, and some were
said to be taught to children by their parents or other elderly relatives. In about 1930 youths who had either worked abroad or been to
school there also began to use condoms (which they called by
the English name 'French letters'). These they obtained in the towns,
or from local traders (one of whom first stocked them in 1932). They
regarded this method as more reliable than coitus interruptus, but
(as indicated below) girls apparently disliked it. I did not hear of its
being used by married people.

(MAGANELO, 21.8.1932): A few educated young men use
French letters when sleeping with girls. They say that some girls
like them, but that others object violently, through fear of one
breaking and bits coming into the womb.

(LESAANE, 18.1.1934): French letters are a recent innovation.
But girls regard them as very dangerous, having heard that
sometimes they get broken inside the girl and then she dies. If
you tell a girl that you are going to use one, she will utterly
refuse to let you sleep with her. That once happened to me. So
you never tell the girl, you just slip it on.

What some other people thought of condoms was shown in the
following incident, recorded by SOFONIA (12.9.1934). During a se-
duction case tried in Makgophana ward court, the girl alleged that
the youth, when asking her to sleep with him, produced *sengwe
sesetlhanyana*, 'something yellowish', which he said would prevent
her from conceiving. 'But I refused it, telling him I don't like it.'

Then one of the men in court asked that this particular bit of evidence should be ignored and not pursued further, 'because the chief would not like it, it had not been heard of in the village before'.

## REFERENCES

SCHAPERA, I. 1933 – Premarital pregnancy and native opinion: a note on social change. *Africa,* **6,** 59–89.
————1940 – *Married Life in an African Tribe.* London: Faber & Faber.

# TOWARDS AN APPRECIATION OF ZULU FOLKTALES AS LITERARY ART

*Trevor Cope*

The last chapter of Eileen Krige's careful and detailed description of Zulu traditional life, *The Social System of the Zulus*, concerns Zulu folklore. In it she mentions some of the characters (humans, animals, monsters) and episodes (miraculous births, trickeries, pursuits and escapes) of Zulu folktales, and paraphrases some of the stories. She shows how these stories relate to the context of social life, and gives an impression of the style of their narration. Nevertheless, the verdict of the average reader on these stories could well be 'little art and less literature'. In this tribute to my past teacher and present friend, I wish to expand on this chapter of her work, and show that Zulu folktales involve great art and deserve the name of literature.

My contribution is based on the study of texts only, and I have concentrated therefore on the structural aspect of the folktales rather than on their narration in performance or their relation to context. My object is to illuminate the nature of the art and to give grounds for the critical appreciation of its products, from this structural point of view. I readily admit the tentative nature of this essay: I hope it stimulates others to investigate further along these lines.

## ZULU FOLKTALES AS PERFORMANCES IN CONTEXT

African folktales suffer a great reduction when they are reduced to texts. Not only are the non-verbal aspects unrepresented – mime and movement, gestures and expressions, for all means of human communication contribute to this solo dramatic act – but also the verbal aspects of vocal imitations, inflections and intonations. A further factor, not so often appreciated (but see Dundes (1969) where he says that context should be recorded as well as text), is the effect of the context on an art where the performer is so intimately in tune with the audience.

Lately, however, there have appeared two books which present the texts of Xhosa folktales in ways designed to lessen these limitations. The Xhosa writer, Jordan (1973), adapts the texts to the needs of the reader by attempting to write into them something of the subtlety of unwritten communication. He describes appearances and mannerisms, the responses to suggestions and the reactions to situations, which are not normally verbalized. The book is introduced by Scheub, who helps the reader to appreciate the art of folktale narration. Scheub subsequently brought out his own publication (1975), in which the texts are transcribed as faithfully as possible from performances recorded in the field, with indications of pauses and exclamations, and descriptions of situation and audience. They do not read as well as Jordan's tales, but they reflect something of the reality of narrative events.

Zulu is not as fortunate as Xhosa in the reflection in written literature of its oral prose stories. The productions of Ntuli (*Izinganekwane*, 1939) and Mbatha & Mdladla (*UChakijana*, 1936), contain rather brief and simple versions written in contexts devoid of audience by men (instead of spoken by women) for children (instead of children together with adults), and the transcriptions of Callaway (1868) and James Stuart (1919) are perhaps rather too long (no audience to control the performance?) and contain virtually no animal stories (not suitable for the white man?). In these ways text reflects context. Scheub's collection contains no animal stories either, perhaps for the same reason, but it does seem that they have fallen out of favour in recent times. Marivate (1973) in his study of Tsonga tales actually says so.

'ANIMAL' STORIES AND 'HUMAN' STORIES

There are two words for Zulu folktales, *izinganekwane*, which suggests simplicity and suitability for children (*izingane*), and *izinsumansumane*, which refers to strange fantastic stories. The former could describe 'animal' stories, and the latter 'human' stories, but in fact *izinganekwane* is nowadays the normal word for folktales of both types, and *izinsumansumane* refers to strange, incredible or ridiculous stories in general. The two types of tale are nevertheless distinct.

'Animal' stories (which comprise one-third of *UChakijana* and two-thirds of Ntuli's book) are distinct from 'human' stories in that although the animals behave in every way like humans in the real world, they represent not individual people but human character types (the sly jackal, the greedy hyena, the ponderous, dull and dutiful elephant); whereas in 'human' stories the humans are real people (not representations of character types) in a world partly real and partly fantastic, who are required to interact with strange creatures and monsters as well as with one another. There are humans (but not monsters) in the animal stories, where they represent the most negative type of character; and there are animals (as animals, not as representations of humans) in the human stories, small animals like birds, who, together with young girls and old women, play the part of the mediator or agent towards resolution. The animal stories may be described as comic satires: they give a critical yet tolerant and humorous assessment of human nature. The human stories, on the other hand, seem to express the concern of man's sense of insecurity, his anxieties, fears and doubts. They are serious and complex, employ symbolism and present polarities, and could be regarded as philosophical statements.

The trickster is the main actor in the animal stories. This irreverent and irrepressible character stands half inside and half outside society and from this position clearly and cruelly exposes the weaknesses of human nature as represented by the animals. At the same time, he provides a vicarious escape, self-indulgent and full-blooded, from the restraints of society. The trickster never occurs in a human story. When the authors of *UChakijana* (the name of the trickster, indicating a type of stoat or weasel) want to turn from animal stories to human stories, they deliberately arrange for Chakijana to go away 'up country'. At the end of the book when they want to bring him back, presumably for the sake of the title of the book, they introduce him into a human story as the agent for returning a woman from a strange, distant and dangerous situation to the security of her home, a role which the trickster can never play. Similarly in the first string of stories in Callaway's *Izinganekwane*, the trickster (Hlakanyana here, a half-human rather than an entirely animal trickster) plays his tricks not on a variety of animals in accordance with their characteristics of pride or greed or gullibility, but on half-human ogres. These creatures (*amazimu*) are the terrifying representations of evil in the human stories, but here they are simply the props for the episodes. In themselves they are completely negative, and the episodes consequently lack colour and contrast. This cycle of stories, summarized by both Eileen Krige (1936) and Alice Werner (1933), is not only lengthy, but somewhat monotonous, a reflection, I suggest, of the circumstances of its performance.

## A ZULU FOLKTALE TEXT

As an example for preliminary analysis, I have translated Sections 15 and 16 from *UChakijana* (Mbatha & Mdladla 1936):

(1) Once upon a time a woman went to cultivate the land. She hoed and hoed, and there came a bird which said, 'Tshwiyo! Tshwiyo! This is the earth of my sister, which is cultivated by lazy people and not by diligent people!' The little clods went *mbe mbe* (tight, tight), the little hoe-handle went *phoqo phoqo* (snap, snap). The clods returned to their places, and the hoe-handle broke. [The bird's song in Callaway's version goes: 'Tshiyo, tshiyo, tshiyo! This is the earth of my father, which I always refuse (to allow to be cultivated). You have acted in opposition to me. Little clods, go tight. Little seeds, scatter. Little hoe-handle, snap. Little hoe, fly off'.]

The woman returned home and reported to her husband the strange events which had happened to her. Her husband scolded her and said, 'You are lying, it is because of laziness'. The next day the woman returned to the field, and the same events took place. The bird came and said, 'Tshwiyo! Tshwiyo! This is the earth of my sister, which is cultivated by lazy people and not by diligent people!' The clods returned to their places, and the hoe-handle broke.

She returned and reported to her husband, and he replied that he would go and see for himself this strange event. The woman returned to the field on the third day, accompanied by her husband. The bird came out and said, 'Tshwiyo! Tshwiyo! This is the earth of my sister, which is cultivated by lazy people and not by diligent people!' The little clods went tight, the little hoe-handle went snap.

(2) The man set off with speed to chase the bird. The bird fled, and finally arrived at the home of all the birds in the reed-bed. When the man arrived he was no longer able to see the one he was chasing.

(3) And so he was continually catching and releasing again. As soon as he caught a bird, it said, 'Why do you catch me and leave him?' As fast as he caught them, they answered with this question, until he finally caught the one. This one was simply silent.

The man said, 'Maas bird, maas bird, make maas for me to see'.
The maas bird went squirt, and the man held out his hands and ate.
He returned home with this bird.

(4) When the man arrived home, he told his wife to wash a big pot
and put it at the back of the house. The pot was nicely prepared and
placed there, the bird was put inside, and the pot was covered; and
then the children were told not to dare to uncover the pot. There were
two children, a boy, Demane, and a girl, Demazana.

Every morning and afternoon the mother would open the pot and
find it full of maas. She would stir it up, and she and her husband
would eat, the children not getting even a smell of maas.

One day when the man and the wife had gone out to cultivate,
Demazana said, 'Let us see what is in this pot which we were told not
to uncover'. And indeed Demazana uncovered it and found it absolutely full of maas. She said, 'Gosh! It is full of creamy maas!'
She took the bird out and put it down, and joyfully devoured the
maas of her parents.

(5) The bird went and sat on the hearth. Demane said, 'Demazana,
Demazana, here is father's bird going away'. 'Wait brother, I am
still swallowing a mouthful', said Demazana.

The bird went and sat in the doorway. Demane again said, 'Demazana, Demazana, here is father's bird going away'. Demazana
answered with that same expression, and said, 'Wait brother, I am
still swallowing a mouthful'.

The bird went and sat on the screen (outside the doorway). Demane
again said, 'Demazana, Demazana, here is father's bird going away'.
'Wait brother, I am still swallowing a mouthful', said Demazana.
And so the bird simply flew away.

Section 17 continues as follows:
(6) The children substitute a wagtail for the maas bird in the pot, and
the parents subsequently find the pot full of black defecation instead
of maas.

(7) The parents lull the children to sleep and then drive sharpened
fire-heated stakes through their heads from ear to ear. The children
wake up and rush off and plunge into a pool – 'the stakes cooled
down and they pulled them out and threw them away and set out.

They travelled and travelled and travelled, until . . .', and so on to an encounter with an ogre (Section 18). [Note that the parents' action is how witches are supposed to convert resurrected bodies into mindless familiars (Krige 1936:326; Berglund 1976:279), and the children's entry into the pool is how divination initiates are supposed to contact their tutelary spirits (Berglund 1976:140–50)].

A PRELIMINARY ANALYSIS

There are clearly two dimensions to this 'human' story, the horizontal dimension of the *sequence* of events where we could investigate the syntagmatic structure of the narrative in terms of the relationship between the episodes, and the vertical dimension of the *pattern* of events where we could investigate the paradigmatic structure of the narrative in terms of the opposition of forces and the balance between them.

On the vertical dimension, the forces of man and nature, or of cultural control and natural profusion, appear to be ranged in opposition. The woman cultivates and nature negates her efforts through the medium of the bird, who accuses her of being too diligent. Her husband accuses her of being too lazy, and she returns to the field to try again, with the same negative result. The pattern is repeated three times. On the third day the man takes over, but his efforts at control are similarly thwarted by the profusion of nature at the reed-bed, the source of life in Zulu mythology. He is overcome by the profusion of birds as his wife was overcome by the profusion of weeds. [Weeds are not mentioned in this version, but they appear significantly in other versions, where the bird is known as *inyoni yokhula* 'weed bird'.] The pattern is repeated for the fifth time when the man finally gains control of the bird and seeks to exploit it, for the bird is the source of maas in profusion. Nature reasserts itself when the bird flies away through the medium of the children. The maas bird (*inyoni yamasi*) is different from the weed bird (*inyoni yokhula*): it represents nature, whereas the weed bird is the mediator, the bringer of balance.

| MAN | in opposition to | NATURE | – | MEDIATOR |
|---|---|---|---|---|
| woman | | earth | | bird |
| man | | reed-bed | | bird |
| parents | | maas-bird | | children |

Thereafter the children try to save themselves in a futile way which the parents directly discover. The parents then impose upon the children a hideous unnatural control from which they are released by the natural means of water. It is likely that other polarities are represented in this last section:

> parents conceal white maas from children
> children reveal black defecation to parents,
>
> parents reduce/destroy children with hot stakes
> pool releases/restores children with cool water,
>
> parents act like witches imposing power over victims
> children act like initiates drawn to power by spirits,

but the expression of the nature – culture polarity is perhaps still to be seen:

> cultural control of nature, mediated by agent
> children impose upon wagtail, released by parents
> parents impose upon children, released by water.

On the horizontal dimension, there are seven episodes linked together to form the narrative. The first episode has as its core the song of the bird expressing an interdiction which the woman violates, and which brings about the consequence. This sequence is repeated three times, in typical folktale fashion, progressively involving the woman's husband. He initiates the very brief chase sequence: the flight and the pursuit and the escape of the bird by entering into the family of its fellows. The third episode in which the man catches the bird is also very brief and undeveloped, and leads unexpectedly and unconvincingly to the revelation of the bird as the maas bird. This episode provides the link between the bird of the field and the reed-bed, and the bird which produces maas, but it is a clumsy link – the ideal is surely a smooth transition. The maas bird episode (4) follows the formula of the first episode: interdiction – violation – consequence, but there is a subordinate motif of deception embedded in it, which functions as an internal link with the sixth episode in which the children attempt a counter-deception on the parents by substituting a wagtail for the maas bird. The fifth episode has as its core the dialogue between brother and sister, repeated three times with increase in tension as the bird moves closer to flight.

The sixth and seventh episodes both follow a formula of deception, but the children's pathetic attempt at deception – a reflection in every way of the parents' deception over the maas bird – contrasts strongly with the parents' calculated deception and terrible treatment of their children. 'They travelled and travelled and travelled' is clearly an external link between two completely separate parts of the story.

Of the seven episodes, the first and fourth with their images of the bird of the field and the bird which produces maas, are the principal episodes, on which the second and the fifth follow in consequence and to which the third acts as a transitional link. The sixth and seventh episodes go together, picking up the internal link of deception in the principal episode of the maas bird. Thus: $(1 + 2) + 3 + [(4 + 5) + (6 + 7)]$.

There are suggestions in this preliminary analysis of the horizontal dimension, relating to 'episodes' and 'sequences', 'cores' and 'images', 'formulas' and the linking of episodes into a unitary narrative. The study of this aspect of structure is designated 'morphological analysis' to distinguish it from the type of 'structural analysis' practised by Levi-Strauss, but it is no less structural. Although the study of the paradigmatic dimension contributes to literary appreciation, it is primarily a philosophical approach. Whatever the anthropological, psychological or philosophical significance of folktales, they are essentially literature, and the storyteller is essentially a literary artist. Morphological analysis gives the greatest insight into folktales as oral literature composed in performance, and it is this approach I propose to follow and develop.

THE MORPHOLOGICAL STRUCTURAL MODEL

Propp and Dundes are the names most closely associated with the analysis of the morphological structure of folktales. Propp's study of Russian fairy tales (1958) shows that the structural elements or 'functions' of a specific type of folktale are constant, however great the variety of the representations or 'terms' of these functions, and that the functions are limited in number and ordered in sequence. Thus, from the great variety of villains in Russian fairy tales, he abstracts the significant narrative unit or 'function' of villainy, which

takes its place in a sequence of functions such as interdiction, violation, pursuit, escape, rescue, recognition, punishment, etc. Not all
functions occur in all tales, but the functions necessarily follow one
another in set sequence. Dundes applies this thesis to North American folktales (1964), and sets up the functions relevant to these tales
and the sequence in which they occur. He points out that the functions are the emic units in folktale morphology, and the terms of the
functions the etic units. According to Dundes (1963), the functions
of North American folktales are far less in number than in the Russian fairy tales: he suggests about eight, whereas Propp establishes
thirty-two (counting his controversial 'lack' function as a function in
its own right). The Zulu folktales also seem to show fewer functions,
but they exhibit complexity at higher levels.

Dundes (1962) adopts the model of structural linguistics established by Pike (1954) in which he suggests its applicability to other
areas of human behaviour – the model itself is most clearly set out in
Cook (1964) – and indeed the three modes of feature, manifestation
and distribution are as relevant to the morphology of folktales as to
the morphology of languages: the feature mode determines the emic
units, the manifestation mode describes their etic representations,
and the distribution mode their contextual occurrence. So in gram-
matical morphology, morphemes are manifested by variants and
distributed according to rules of order, e.g. the English plural mor-
pheme is a suffix by distribution, which occurs as either *s* (cats) or
*z* (dogs) or *iz* (horses) in manifestation.

Although Dundes applies the 'mode' axis of Pike's tagmemic
model to folktale structure, he does not apply the 'level' axis. He
shows that there are significant sequences of functions such as interdiction – violation – consequence, but does not establish these sequences as higher level narrative units. Propp also perceives that
some functions are more closely related to one another than to others,
and that the folktale proceeds by means of these groups of functions
which he terms 'moves'. He also mentions 'sections' of the folktale, and yet he fails to recognize the overall hierarchical structure
of the folktale. Marivate (1973) comes closest to the recognition of
hierarchical structure with his 'patterns of motifemes' and 'combinations of motifeme patterns' ['motifeme' is Dundes's term for
'function']. The linguistic analogy is obvious: just as morphemes
combine in rigid order to form words, so functions combine in
function sequences; and just as words combine to form sentences,

so sequences combine in sequence combinations. As in Pike's tagmemic model, emic units (e.g. words, or folktale sequences) are
analyzed in terms of the distribution of their constituents at the next
lowest level (morphemes, or folktale functions), and distribution
combinations (e.g. of morphemes, or of folktale functions) constitute
emic units (words, or folktale sequences) at the next highest level.
Thus the order of functions constitutes the emic unit of the *sequence*,
and the order of sequences constitutes the emic unit of the *combination*.
I propose to use the terms function, sequence and combination for
the narrative units at the three levels of the hierarchy. [It is convenient but arbitrary to limit the hierarchy to three levels. In fact, just
as some functions are more closely related to one another than to
others, so some sequences are more closely related to one another
than to others, and there are sub-combinations within the combination analogous to phrases within the sentence. These units could be
called 'stages', for they are the stages by which the narrative proceeds. However, limitation is necessary, and I do not discuss stages
here]. A 'term' is the manifestation of a 'function': it is the word
used by Maranda in two publications (1971a, 1971b), although I
cannot trace it in Propp himself. Thus the *function* of villainy is ful-
filled or represented or manifested by the *terms* of dragon, monster,
wolf, witch, sorcerer, etc., in Russian fairy tales. For the levels of
narrative structure I suggest the terms motif, episode and narrative.

## MODES

|   |   | *Feature* | *Manifestation* | *Distribution* |
|---|---|---|---|---|
| L | *Motif* | (emic unit) function (cf. morpheme) | (etic unit) term | order of functions = *sequence* (see feature at next level) |
| E V E L S | *Episode* | sequence (cf. word) | realization in terms of func-tions | order of sequences = *combination* (see feature at next level) |
|   | *Narrative* | combination (cf. sentence) | realization in terms of sequences | contextual situation? |

THE INDIVIDUAL CONTRIBUTION

Whereas Russian fairytales are apparently rigidly ordered through-out, Zulu folktales are not. The tradition orders the sequence of functions at the episode level, but it is the storyteller who determines the combination of sequences at the narrative level, and this is where the art of composition mainly lies. An episode or function sequence could constitute a tale in itself, e.g. interdiction + violation + con-sequence, but Zulu tales are never so simple in structure. The epi-sodes combine to form such complex structures as [(int + viol + cons) + (flight + escape)] + (seek and find) + { [(int + viol + cons) + (flight + escape)] + [(deception sequence) + (deception se-quence)] }, which is the structure of the folktale already discussed. The syntax of the Zulu folktale is the test of the creative imagination of the storyteller. The Russian fairytale is a sequence of functions of which the teller has a total of thirty-two from which to choose, whereas the art of the Zulu storyteller lies not in the choice of functions to combine into sequences (for both functions and sequences are determined by tradition), but in the choice of sequences to com-bine into a coherent and integrated narrative. The tale is a combina-tion of sequences of which there may be about eight, comprising perhaps up to twenty functions. There is no limit to the variety of combinations, which is the sphere of individual creativity.

Oral literature is different from written literature in that it is com-posed as it is performed, according to a tradition which is fairly rigidly laid down. Furthermore it is performed and appreciated by the community, unlike written literature which is restricted as to writers and even as to readers. We in the Western world have largely lost the appreciation of language in daily life, especially its creative aspect (Doke (1948) describes so well the role of language in Bantu socie-ties), because of our loss of a universal oral literature. Ruth Finnegan (1970) plays down the role of tradition and the significance of com-munal literary activity, in reaction to scholars such as Lestrade (1937) who emphasized these aspects at the expense of the individual contribution, but in fact oral literature is a blend of tradition and creativity, memorization and improvization, the communal and the individual. Whiteley (1964) debates the nature of the individual con-tribution, but he comes to no clear conclusion because of 'lack of information', a lack which scholars such as Mbiti (1966), Finnegan (1967) and Evans-Pritchard (1967), later contributed to fill. The appreciation of Zulu folktales requires an understanding of the nature and proportion of the balance between these elements. No literary criticism is possible otherwise.

## THE BALANCE BETWEEN TRADITION AND CREATIVITY

Tradition determines functions and sequences, but the individual determines the terms of the functions and the realization of the sequences: the manifestation mode is always the sphere of the performer. Tradition determines the function of villainy, but who fulfils it is left to the storyteller. There are traditional villains, but the choice is so wide (the Russian tradition provides nineteen varieties of villainy!) as to be virtually unlimited. The Zulu trickster offers his services as nursemaid to a woman, a lion, a leopard, a duiker, a jackal, to anyone, in fulfilment of the function of 'trickster contract'. Tradition determines that the contract is followed by a fraudulent trick from which the victim suffers and the trickster triumphs, but the realization of the sequence is left to the storyteller.

Tradition does not determine the distribution of sequences in the combination which constitutes the total narrative: individual creativity has full play in the determination of the syntax of the folktale. Here it is not only the manifestation that is left to the storyteller, but the determination of the feature itself, the combination, by arrangement and distribution of sequences. Intelligence, imagination, and great literary skill are required in the choice and fusion of sequences into a unitary narrative during the course of the performance.

The distribution mode at this final level of the total narrative or complete performance is where text interacts with context: the situation which gives rise to the performance and to which it is a response. Just as linguistics recognizes in discourse analysis a level higher than the sentence, so in the literary analysis of folktales there is an area beyond the present reach of the subject, where literature and anthropology could jointly contribute.

# THE CONSTITUENT STRUCTURE OF THE FOLKTALE

|   | Communal traditional constituents | Individual creative constituents |
|---|---|---|
| L *Motif* | function (feature) | term (manifestation) |
| E | order of functions (distribution) | – |
| V *Episode* | sequence (feature) | realization of sequence (manifestation) |
| E | – | order of sequences (distribution) |
| L *Narrative* | – | combination (feature) |
|   | – | realization of combination (manifestation) |
| S | contextual situation? (distribution) | contextual situation? (distribution) |

## STYLE AND THEME

No literary treatment of Zulu folktales would be complete without some mention of style and theme. Here again there is a balance between what is traditional and what is individual.

The traditional style is strictly narrative, with dramatic interludes by means of direct speech, dialogue and song, and the impression of direct action through the use of ideophones. There is no comment, no reflection, no description. Although there is room for variety within this tradition, the *individual* style is mainly a matter of mime and movement, vocal inflection and mimicry. Alice Werner (1933:106) writes that 'the brief statement leaves to the imagination the clamour, the turmoil, the frantic struggles' – to the imagination of the audience as well as the storyteller, who expresses herself in many unwritten ways when she describes the actors and the actions. (The storyteller is usually a woman).

The traditional theme of the human stories is the threat to security, the presence of evil in the world, and the desire for harmonious relations within society and between man and nature. The nature – culture polarity is expressed in the human stories, but not in the animal stories. The representation of humans by animals may seem to be the expression of this theme, but the animal stories deal only with human nature, and they are far less complex in structure. The *individual* theme may be the greed of a father, the fear of a mother, the terror of children captured by cannibals. Thus does the storyteller set an individual stamp, in both style and theme, on the traditional material.

ZULU FUNCTIONS AND SEQUENCES

The functions relevant to Zulu folktales have yet to be determined. Marivate (1973) applies Dundes's few functions to Tsonga folktales, but it is possible that these functions are not suitable for Zulu folktales, especially the complex human stories. They are certainly not sufficient, and the number of functions relevant to Zulu folktales is likely to be closer to eighteen than eight. The Herskovitses in their study of Dahomean Narrative (1958) use the title of False Friendship to classify and describe a number of morality tales, hunter stories and trickster stories, and Dundes (1971) notes that it is a common theme throughout Africa. Folktales reflect cultural concerns. Beidelman (1961, 1963) has shown how Kaguru tales reflect the concern of the conflicts of matrilineal relations, and in False Friendship we see the reflection of the concern of the obligations of friendship. In North America, friendship provides no frame for folktales. There we find the violation of a supernatural sanction instead of the violation of a personal relationship. In Zulu folktales, the false friendship between the hyena and the jackal is different from the false friendship between the trickster and his victims. The hyena and the jackal make a contract to hunt together, and although they constantly violate it and deceive one another, they constantly renew it in the hope of future benefit. The one is not necessarily on the spot at the time of the deception, and the other is always aware that he has been deceived. On the other hand, the trickster contract is always slanted at the outset, for the trickster's intention is clear, and the victim is completely innocent. The violation is a cruel fraud and the deception a heartless gloat. The trickster is always on the spot to enjoy the situation, and the victim is not necessarily aware of the trickster's crime. Either we would have to recognize 'contract' and 'trickster contract' as different functions in different sequences, 'false friendship' and 'trickster false friendship', or treat the trickster function and sequence as etic manifestations of the basic emic units, conditioned by the presence of the trickster.

Here is an extract from Callaways's version of *asiphekane* 'let us cook one another': The woman takes Hlakanyana out of the pot when he asks to be taken out, and gets into it herself. When she begs to be taken out, saying, 'I am burnt to death', he says: 'No, indeed, you are not yet burnt to death. If you were burnt to death, you could not say that you were burnt to death. I understand for I am a man, and if a person says he is burning to death, he is not yet burnt, and if he is burnt to death, he does not say he is burning, he is burnt to death, and that is the end.' She then says she is being cooked, and he says: 'No, you are not yet cooked. There you are saying that you are being cooked, but I know that . . .', and so on, until the woman dies. Does she realize that Hlakanyana is deliberately boiling her to death? And so he triumphs, for the woman had been told to watch over him for her son, his captor, to eat later. This extract represents the 'gloat' function of the 'trickster false friendship' sequence.

## SOME SUGGESTIONS FOR ZULU FUNCTIONS AND SEQUENCES

*Sequences*                          *Functions*

obedience:          command + obedience + consequence
violation:          interdiction + violation + consequence
chase:              flight + pursuit + ploy + escape
contrary result:    boast + challenge + deception + defeat
                    (e.g. how the tortoise won the race)
false friendship:   contract + violation + deception + consequence
                    (e.g. why the hyrax has no tail)
trickster false
  friendship:       trickster contract + fraud + gloat + triumph

### ORAL FORMULAS

These function sequences are structural formulas for the composition in performance of Zulu folktales. The role of formulas has been

widely recognized in oral poetry, following the research of Parry and
Lord in Europe (1960), but apparently not in oral prose. There are
also formulas for the manifestation of functions. Although the storyteller is free to fulfil the functions as she pleases, the tradition provides
a stock of actors and actions from which she may choose. As Eileen
Krige observes (1936:355), whenever a delay is needed, the villain is
sent to fetch water from the river with a leaky calabash; and there are
'common means of escape', which I would regard as formulas to
fulfil the function between 'pursuit' and 'escape': ploys such as
climbing trees, crossing rivers, lighting fires, always in unusual ways.

Zulu praise poetry also has two such types of formula. First there
are structural formulas (emic features), e.g. noun-verb initial link
parallelism (Cope 1968:43), as in these praises spontaneously composed in honour of Eileen Krige:

> The ferreter out of information at our place at Thusini*
> Who ferreted out the information relating to fertility**

> [* The brass ball or golden globe at the top of the dome
>    of Howard College, hence the university campus in Durban]
> [**See Krige 1967 to 1970]

And then there are phrase formulas (etic manifestations), e.g. 'the
ford with slippery stones where people slipped as they tried to cross'
(diplomatic shrewdness), 'the pile of rocks which sheltered elephants
in bad weather' (powerful protection), 'the stick which struck water
and mud appeared' (forcefulness), which are available wherever
appropriate, as with the stock actors and actions of Zulu folktales.

Ruth Finnegan (1970: Chapter 13), in a chapter which is a mile-
stone in the appreciation of oral prose narratives, stresses the importance of the individual creative artist in the spontaneous composition of oral literature, but, although she mentions 'stock characters' (345 and 355) and even 'the combination of motifs and episodes' (387), she does not state specifically how 'spontaneous
composition' operates. Propp has 'thirty-two functions all carefully
packed with its name labelled clearly on each', but, like the baker
when he sets off to hunt the snark, Finnegan leaves them behind
on the beach, or rather in a footnote, as 'too formalistic' (353).
Scheub (1970, 1975) makes no reference to morphological analysis
at all. He offers 'the technique of the expansible image' (see below),

but he again does not state specifically how it operates. The role of oral formulas is of paramount importance in the composition and performance of Zulu *izibongo* and *izinganekwane*, and we should direct our judgement in the literary criticism of oral literature to the effectiveness with which they are used.

## FOLKTALE IMAGES

Scheub (1970, 1975) has contributed greatly to the appreciation of the folktale tradition. He stresses throughout (as does Finnegan) that the folktale is a performance, and that the text is only the bare bones of it. The performance, of course, is as different from the text as the performance of a symphony is different from its score, but musicologists can nevertheless appreciate the structure and musical value of a symphony by studying its score, as we can partly appreciate a folktale by studying its text. Scheub contributes to our understanding of the balance between memorization and improvization, between what is inherited and what is created, with his concept of the 'expansible image'. He shows that at the heart of a folktale episode is a core song, proverb or expression, which, with its associated details of actors and actions, forms a core image which is expanded during performance by the exercise of the imagination, into a work of literary art. His concern at this level of the episode is the semantic input rather than the frame (structural formula) the input is put into, although there are certainly structural implications in his 'expansible image', just as there are semantic implications in Propp's functions.

This concept of the expansible image is easily illustrated by two Zulu proverbs, *sobamba elentulo* 'we will stick to (the word of) the lizard', which is the core of a story relating to the origin of death (therefore technically a myth – Callaway does not include it in his *Nursery Tales* but in his *Religious System*), and *sobohla Manyosi* 'it (the stomach) will subside, Manyosi', which is the core of a legend relating to a man who lived at the time of Shaka. The core *sobamba elentulo* calls to mind the story of the lizard and the chameleon sent by Nkulunkulu with their different messages relating to life and death. The lizard darts quickly, the chameleon treads slowly and diverts its attention constantly to red berries. The lizard arrives first with its message of death, the chameleon arrives too late with its message of life: 'We have already received the message of the lizard, and we must stick to it'. If the interest were only in the 'paradigmatic aspect' of the story, with its polarities of lizard and chameleon, life and death, lightness and darkness, and the role of the red berries, it would not matter how the tale was told, but from the literary point of view, the way in which the teller expands the core image is of prime importance.

Similarly the core *sobohla Manyosi* provides the core image of Manyosi and his enormous stomach, and his ability to consume a goat at a sitting, washed down by beer in great quantity. The delight of this story is the 'contrary conclusion' that Manyosi's stomach did not subside, and he pointedly named his son 'Sobohla'. [I have discussed elsewhere (Cope 1968:54–7) the Zulu inclination to the 'contrary conclusion': the Zulu sense of humour makes much of it.] There are also the images encapsulated by the core expressions *uBheje useNgome* 'Bheje is in the Ngome forest' and *uBhongoza uholela oPhathe* 'Bhongoza leads into an ambush at the Phathe gorge', which bring to mind the events which gave rise to these expressions. These images are expanded in narration, but these stories are not folktales: they have neither the style nor the theme, they use no oral formulas, and they do not reflect the composite structure of folktales. However effective the core may be as a summary to be expanded in performance, it is not sufficient in itself to account for a folktale. The tradition accounts not only for the core and the core image (the semantic component), but also for the formula of expansion (the structural component). Improvization creates the tale from these traditional elements stored in the memory.

The proverb *imbila yaswela umsila ngokulayezela* 'the hyrax lost its tail by sending messages for it', is the core of a folktale which deals with the distribution of tails. It is expanded according to the formula (function sequence) of False Friendship. The hyrax being too lazy to go for himself, makes a *contract* with a jackal or a monkey (or other actor) to go and get his tail for him. The animal gets the tail: the *violation* is that he eats it or attaches it to his own tail (or other action), and the *deception* is that he tells the hyrax that he was unable to get it and that the hyrax has to go himself after all. The tails are now finished, and the *consequence* is that the hyrax has no tail. There is much scope here for the imaginative treatment of conversations and situations, which a text can only partially represent.

Repetition plays an important part in oral literature, and Scheub regards it as the main means of expansion of the core image. I have shown that it is rather the structural formula that is the means of expansion. Repetition is as much a stylistic effect as a structural technique. The 'trickster nursemaid' image is expanded by means of the 'trickster false friendship' formula: the trickster offers his services as nursemaid (*contract*), and then kills and eats the children (*fraud*), and reserves some of the meat for the mother to eat and then taunts her with what she has done (*gloat*), and then runs away singing his praises (*triumph*). This sequence is usually followed by a 'chase' sequence, the final function of which is 'escape'. The 'trickster nursemaid' episode may be related about a leopard with two children (Callaway), a duiker with three children (Ntuli), a woman with ten children (Mbatha & Mdladla). In the last case there is no repetition at all. In the second case (Ntuli) there is a threefold repetition, word for word except for effective slight variation: the first account introduces, the second establishes, and the third both concentrates the tension and leads to the climax which necessarily follows, for there are only three children. In the first case (Callaway), there is also no repetition. There are two children, but twofold repetition is most effective when there is a contrast between the two actors: the one is clever and the other is stupid, or the one is generous and the other is selfish, and the two accounts are identical except that all the responses are different, and the final result is naturally quite different. In Zulu folktales, repetition is used probably less often in the realization of the core image.


## LINKING

Scheub's 'core' relates to the narrative unit of the function at the level of the motif (usually to the final function of 'consequence' or 'escape' or 'triumph'), and his 'core image' relates to the narrative unit of the sequence at the level of the episode. (See the table on page 192 above.) His greatest contribution, however, to the appreciation of the literary art of the storyteller, is his exposition of how she operates at the narrative level in the choice and integration of episodes: how she constructs the narrative unit of the combination. The feature of the episode comprises the mainly structural component of the sequence and the mainly semantic component of the image, both of which are determined by tradition: but whereas tradition determines images and sequences, it is the performer who determines the combination in both its semantic and structural aspects. In the process of performance the storyteller links the episodes together both internally and externally. External links bring about transitions between episodes, usually by the hero travelling from place to place, so that a physical movement marks a transition. Internal links are references to past and future episodes (the story-teller scans the repertoire for future images in the process of performance, as Scheub says). The episodes are fairly loosely linked together, both internally and externally – Mofokeng (1951) comments on this looseness of structure.

To the literary criticism of Zulu folktales we may now add the consideration of linking: how effectively are the sequences internally and externally linked to form a narrative combination? The external link usually involves the hero, but it may bring about a change of hero, as when Chakijana goes away 'up country' (*uChakijana*, No. 9) and the authors turn from him to his human sister Hliziyonkulu, who then sets off on her marriage journey. Her father warns her not to step on an ant-heap (*interdiction*), but she does (*violation*), and there appears an *imbulu* who demands her clothes and forces her to become its servant (*consequence*). They travel on, which serves as the link to the 'false bride' image and sequence, with its reversal of roles, miraculous revelations, and restitution through the agency of a young girl; or in Callaway's version, an old woman with no legs. The agent is always weak and insignificant, 'a protest of weakness against strength' suggests Junod (1927:224), but superficial insignificance is the nature of mediation in the Levi-Straussian sense.

The external link need not involve a movement from place to place. In Callaway's Hlakanyana cycle, when the trickster has cooked the old woman, the link is achieved when he dons her clothes and impersonates her to her son (*trickster contract*), and persuades him to eat the meat (*fraud*), and allays his suspicions as he recognizes arms and legs (*gloat*), and triumphs over the man who had intended to eat him (*triumph*: 'and so you eat your mother', the core of the image, which is as memorable as the core of the previous image, 'let us cook one another', as these expressions relate only to folktales!). A 'chase' sequence follows: 'flight' and 'pursuit', the 'ploy' (the man throws him across the river) and the 'escape' (*wangiweza phela* 'and so you saved me indeed'). And the trickster goes on his way (external link). Although Callaway's Hlakanyana cycle is unsatisfactory in some ways, mainly in that the dupes are all ogres instead of a variety of animals, it is clearly an orally composed performance and as such illustrates the nature of Zulu folktales better than the written accounts of the Zulu authors. Therefore we will continue with the tricks of Hlakanyana, to illustrate further the operation of linking.

Some episodes later he meets an ogre, whom he greets as his *malume* (maternal uncle) and gains the response 'child of my sister', and so the contract is made. He offers the ogre some meat from the leg of the leopard he had killed in the previous episode (internal link), which confirms the contract. They build a house together, and Hlakanyana knots the ogre's hair into the thatch so that he is trapped on the roof (*fraud*). He feasts on the ogre's food while the ogre implores his help (*gloat*), and when he is dead Hlakanyana says, 'Uncle, why are you so silent?' (*triumph*). And he goes on his way (external link). He meets another ogre carrying a musical calabash, who refuses to respond to him. 'How am I your uncle?' he asks. Hlakanyana tries to bluff him, but he insists that 'I can never agree that you are my sister's child'. So there is no contract, but a link has been laid down. He then meets another ogre who accepts him as his nephew (*contract*). The ogre with the musical calabash reappears (internal link), and Hlakanyana uses him as a means of outwitting the other ogre (*triumph*). We now await with anticipation the episode of the ogre with the musical calabash. It comes – and it ends: 'Speak, my uncle, why are you so silent? Please play your calabash for me?' (*triumph*).

The episode ends, but the narrative does not end: it goes on as long as the bond between the storyteller and the audience is strong. Zulu folktales, like Zulu songs, do not demand attention for a prescribed duration. The audience determines the duration of the performance, and the storyteller concludes when the audience begins no longer to participate or respond or agree (*vuma*); just as the solo singer concludes when the chorus ceases to join in (*vuma*), as one by one they wander away to attend to other matters.

## REFERENCES

(O.L.A.L. = Oxford Library of African Literature, Oxford: Clarendon Press)

BEIDELMAN, T. O. 1961 – Hyena and rabbit: a Kaguru representation of matrilineal relations. *Africa* **31**, 61–74.
————1963 – Further adventures of hyena and rabbit. *Africa* **33**, 54–69.
BERGLUND, A. I. 1976 – *Zulu Thought-Patterns and Symbolism*. London: Hurst.

CALLAWAY, H. 1868 – *Nursery Tales, Traditions and Histories of the Zulus, vol. 1: Izinganekwane*. London: Trübner.

COOK, W. A. 1964 – *On Tagmemes and Transforms*. Washington: Univ. of Georgetown Press.

COPE, A. T. 1968 – *Izibongo: Zulu Praise Poems*. O.L.A.L.

DOKE, C. M. 1948 – The basis of Bantu literature. *Africa* **18**, 284–301.

DUNDES, A. 1962 – From etic to emic units in the structural study of folktales. *J.Am. Folklore* **75**, 95–105.

————1963 – Structural typology of North American folktales. *SWest. J. Anthrop.* **19**, 121–30.

————1964 – *The Morphology of North American Folktales*. Helsinki: Suomalainen Tiedeakatemia.

————1969 – Texture, text and context. *Sth. Folklore Q.* **28**, 251–65.

————1971 – Friendship as a structural frame in African folktales. In *Structural Analysis of Oral Tradition* (eds.) Maranda, P. & Maranda, E. K.

EVANS-PRITCHARD, E. E. 1967 – *The Zande Trickster*. O.L.A.L.

FINNEGAN, R. 1967 – *Limba Stories and Storytelling*. O.L.A.L.

————1970 – *Oral Literature in Africa*. O.L.A.L.

HERSKOVITS, M. J. & HERSKOVITS, F. S. 1958 – *Dahomean Narrative*. Evanston, Illinois: Northwestern Univ. Press.

JUNOD, H. A. 1927 – *The Life of a South African Tribe*. London: MacMillan.

JORDAN, A. C. 1973 – *Tales from Southern Africa*. Los Angeles: Univ. of California Press.

KRIGE, E. J. 1936 – *The Social System of the Zulus*. London: Longmans.

————1967 to 1970 – Papers and Seminars on Zulu songs, rituals, beliefs and concepts relating to fertility, health, morality and religion.

LESTRADE, G. P. 1937 – Traditional literature. In *The Bantu-Speaking Tribes of South Africa* (ed.) I. Schapera. London: Routledge.

LORD, A. B. 1960 – *The Singer of Tales*. Cambridge, Mass: Harvard Univ. Press.

MARANDA, P. & MARANDA, E. K. 1971a – *Structural Models in Folklore*. The Hague: Mouton.

————1971b – *Structural Analysis of Oral Tradition*. Philadelphia: Univ. of Pennsylvania Press.

MARIVATE, C. T. D. 1973 – Tsonga Folktales. Univ. of South Africa, Pretoria: unpublished M.A. thesis.

MBATHA, A. H. S. & MDLADLA, G. C. S. 1936 – *UChakijana Bogcololo*. Durban: Griggs.

MBITI, J. S. 1966 – *Akamba Stories*. O.L.A.L.

MOFOKENG, S. M. 1951 – Sotho Folktales. Univ. of Witwatersrand, Johannesburg: unpublished M.A. thesis.

NTULI, F. L. 1939 – *Izinganekwane nezindaba ezindala*. London: Longmans.

PIKE, K. L. 1954 – *Language in Relation to a Unified Theory of the Structure of Human Behaviour*. Glendale, California: Summer Inst. of Linguistics.

PROPP, V. 1958 – *The Morphology of the Folktale*. Bloomington: Univ. of Indiana Press.

SCHEUB, H. 1970 – The technique of the expansible image. *Res. Afr. Lit.* **1**, 119–46.

————1975 – *The Xhosa Ntsomi*. O.L.A.L.

STUART, J. 1919 – Izinganekwane. (Unpublished typescript.) Durban: Killie Campbell Library of Africana.
WERNER, A. 1933 – *Myths and Legends of the Bantu*. London: Harrap.
WHITELEY, W. 1964 – *African Oral Prose*. O.L.A.L.

# ZULU CLAN PRAISES*

*Douglas Mzolo*

INTRODUCTION

Clan praises constitute a type of praise-poetry common amongst
South African Bantu-speaking societies, but they have largely escaped
the attention of scholars of traditional oral literature. Only one
collection of such praises is available, from the (Cape) Hlubi, and
that in a purely vernacular text (Ndawo 1939) which is not very easy
to find. Consequently clan praises scarcely figure in such intensive
studies of praise-poetry as may be found in the unpublished theses of
B. W. Vilakazi (1946) and Raymond Kunene (1962), or in published
works on the Tswana (Schapera 1965), the Southern Sotho (Kunene
1971) and the Zulu (Cope 1968) or in more general studies of African
oral literature, such as Finnegan's (1970). One merely finds statements like Jordan's (1957:102) that 'every clan amongst the Hlubi
has its own praises' or Finnegan's (1970:122): 'although normally
addressed to distinguished human beings, praise-poems can be concerned with almost anything – animals, divining-bones, beer, birds,
clans'. Hence, as David Rycroft (1974) has remarked, generaliza-
tions and conclusions are made on the basis of the type of poetry
that has been widely collected and documented to the neglect of the
lesser known material. He further remarks that clan praises differ
both in function and style from individual praise-poetry and instances Shona clan praises as the most important form of oral poetry
among the Shona. He concludes by saying that 'it will not be possible
to gain a clear picture of the relative importance of clan praises
until a great deal more research has been carried out'. The present
study of Zulu clan praises is therefore directed towards an investigation of this genre of praise-poetry, in order to begin filling this
gap in our knowledge of Zulu and, more widely, of African oral
literature.

*This article which I am glad to include in a collection for Professor Eileen
Krige, summarizes some of the material in my unpublished M.A. thesis, *A
study of Nguni Clan Praises in Natal and Zululand*, Univ. of Natal, Durban,
1977.

## THE CLAN

One view of the Zulu clan is that it 'was but a magnified family, consisting of offspring of a single forefather, the clan's founder' (Bryant 1949:421–2). This view implies a continuous process of expansion by which a traditional, patrilocal, polygynous, extended family has given rise over the generations to a whole series of such families linked by the patrilineal ties between their male heads. However, it is not now the case that all the numerous members of one clan can trace their connections to each other by patrilineal descent from a common ancestor. Nor is the clan as a whole a localized group; its members can be found widely scattered throughout the province of Natal and elsewhere in South Africa.

In such circumstances, how is the clan identity preserved? Sometimes clues to the identity are provided by such practises as piercing and extending the ear-lobes (*ukuklakla*) or making incisions on the face (*ukuklakla ebusweni* or *ukugcaba*), because members of certain clans are nowadays more likely than others to retain these practices. For example, members of certain clans still tend to have their earlobes pierced, whereas other clans do not have this practice. But a much more certain means of identification is always the patrilineally inherited clan name, as well as the address-names and praises associated with it.

The clan name itself (*isibongo*) is usually taken to be the name of the clan's founder or perhaps of some particularly famous former member of it. It is noticeable, though, that the supposed founders' names are quite often also those of natural phenomena, as, for example, *uZulu* ('sky'), *uMkhize* ('drizzle'), *uLuthuli* ('dust'), *uNdlovu* ('elephant'). There are several ways in which a person may use the clan name to reveal his clan membership. Sometimes he may say, *NgingowakwaMkhize*, meaning 'I belong to the Mkhize clan', but using the locative form *kwaMkhize*, implying 'the place of Mkhize'. Indeed, this 'place' associated with the clan may be specified by another name, different from that of the clan founder. Thus the members of the Mkhize clan are also known as *abaseMbo*, 'they of the place called eMbo', while members of the Ngcobo clan may be either *abasemaQadini* or *abakwaNyuswa*, meaning 'they of the amaQadi or Nyuswa place'. It is therefore possible to ask for a stranger's clan by saying, *Ungowaphi?*, meaning literally, 'Of what place are you?' The answer might be *NgingowaseMbo*, 'I am of the place called eMbo', i.e. of the Mkhize clan, or *NgingowasemaZizini*, 'I am of the place called emaZizini', i.e. of the Miya clan. These usages imply that there is an association between clans and particular places, but the association is now the concentration of clan segments in certain areas rather than the exclusive occupation of them by whole clans.

In addition to the clan name (*isibongo*), there is the *isithakazelo*, i.e. address name. Every clan name has its *isithakazelo*. The address name is held in high esteem, to the extent that a person is respectfully addressed not by his clan name, *isibongo*, but by the address name, *isithakazelo*, e.g.:

| | | |
|---|---|---|
| *Zulu* | = | *Mageba!* or *Ndabezitha!* |
| *Ngema* | = | *Madlokovu!* |
| *Mchunu* | = | *Macingwana!* |
| *Mzolo* | = | *Dlangamandla!* |
| *Ndlovu* | = | *Gatsheni!* |

These address names might have been the proper names of the clan founder or simply the names of well-remembered and admired ancestors of the clan. It is also worth noting that some people adopt these address names as surnames, e.g. *Qwabe* is the parent clan-name: *Gumede* is the *isithakazelo* which is now adopted by some Qwabe as their surname. Then there is *Khuzwayo* which, though not *isithakazelo*, is the surname related to Qwabe as reflected in the clan praises of Qwabe. In some of these cases it is possible that some early, prominent clan member, other than the clan founder, attracted a large personal following to himself and that his name came to be adopted as the surname by that section of the clan, although it still retained ties with the parent clan. So, for example, Makhathini may have been an eminent member of the Zulu clan whose name is now used by some members of that clan. On the other hand, the adoption of the *isithakazelo* as the surname may be very much a matter of individual choice, so that for example many persons whose *isibongo* is *Hadebe* now prefer to call themselves by the *isithakazelo*, *Mthimkulu*. Indeed the use of the address name is so widespread that a clan name is seldom used when addressing a person. Everybody is familiar with the *isithakazelo* of the clans in the neighbourhood. If a person meets another familiar person, greeting will be formal and they will simply use the *isithakazelo*, viz., *Gatsheni!* for *Ndlovu* or *Mageba!* for *Zulu*.

Similarly when a stranger calls at someone's kraal, he will always shout out at the top of his voice and utter *isithakazelo* of that kraal, saying, for example, *Eh! Gatsheni!* referring to *Ndlovu* clan, or

*Macingwana!* for *Mchunu* clan. This was in fact a method of making the members of the other family aware that there was some stranger expecting attention. It did not matter whether the people in that family were indoors or outdoors, the stranger was expected to make the salute. This is the same thing in our contemporary society as knocking at the door before entering. The use of address names is a polite expression which also demonstrates respect for that particular member of a clan. Married women never address their husbands by name or clan name, *isibongo*, but instead the address name, *isithakazelo*, or the regimental name is used.

The present clan system, including the clan names, the address names and the praises, is thus the product of a long and complex history, during which clans have produced sub-clans or have even been completely divided. Moreover, clans have become dispersed and, in the contemporary, cosmopolitan society undergoing rapid urbanization and industrialization, often have little meaning for many Zulus. However, much of the system does still survive, especially in the rural areas, where local concentrations of clansmen may be found and it is amongst them that clan praises are still to be heard and collected, as the following samples will show.

THE CLAN PRAISES

Clan praises are the attribute of a collection of individuals, whereas other types of praises are individualistic in nature and belong to a particular person. Praises of the clan are shared by every member of the clan. Where the clan system still persists, all the members of the clan know their praises or are expected to know as much of them as possible, whereas with the individual praises nobody is under the obligation of knowing them except the individual concerned or the reciter. Some clansmen, in addition to mastering their praises, even go to the extent of knowing the praises of the other clans in the neighbourhood.

Clan praises are normally preceded by address names, *izithakazelo*. Before reciting the praises *izithakazelo* are uttered first, as for example:

| | | |
|---|---|---|
| XULU! | = | The clan name |
| Donda! | | |
| Gxabhashe! | = | The *izithakazelo* |
| Makhathini! | | |

followed by the clan praise:

| | |
|---|---|
| Phuhla phansi njengekhowen-dlovu. | Break through the soil like the largest mushroom. |
| Wena owashaya udaka. | You who splashed mud. |
| Waveza abantu nezinkomo. | You produced cattle and people. |
| Wena waseNkweleni. | You of Nkweleni. |
| Wena owehla phansi ngesilulu, | You who came from below by means of a large grain basket, |
| Ngoba bonke abantu bavela ngawe. | Because all people came because of you. |
| Wena Donda! | You, Donda! |
| Madango! | Madango! |

THE PRAISER

Praises of chiefs are recited by professional bards, *imbongi*, who are specialists. Other individual praises can be recited by anybody or by the individual concerned. These do not need a specialist; the same applies to the clan praises. These do not require the services of a specialist because every member of the clan is expected to know them well, or at least to have some knowledge about them. On important occasions, however, some sort of specialist may be called upon to deliver the praises of the clan simply because of his proficiency. He may therefore not necessarily be a member of the same clan. For more serious occasions like rituals, it is the prerogative of the kraal-head to deliver the praises of the clan.

Praises of chiefs, or other individuals, are memorized, and there-fore the essential qualification of the praiser is the ability to memorize. He memorizes the genealogies of ancestors, events, history, qualities of the person praised, his achievements or his failures and weaknesses expressed in a subtle manner. There may, to a limited extent, be im-provisation or original composition which the professional praiser may add and which are therefore not repeated from memory. His creativity as a specialist emerges. As a rule clan praises are rather short, so that memorizing them is not a problem. There is no com-position here; it is purely a matter of memory.

'Persons of but modest rank in Bantu society usually compose their own praise-poem, and the praise-poems of their cattle, while those of higher status have theirs composed by professional bards' (Schapera 1965:12). It is not clear who composes clan praises. They are merely transmitted orally from generation to generation. Occasionally there are indications that some phrases or little bits are added to the existing clan praises, but it is not clear who composes these little bits, whereas with personal praises new ones are added all the time by one's associates and by oneself. In this manner they accumulate and become longer and longer, whereas praises of clans are as a rule short and remain so.

### THE ACT OF PRAISING

Before the professional bard commences his performance he does not directly embark upon his main task. He prepares his audience first in order to get people in the right mood. The audience must be orientated to this event. He makes some introductory remarks. Similarly before concluding he makes a suggestion of some kind for the audience to realize that he has come to the end of his performance. The same thing applies to the clan praises. The officiator will always commence by saying a few words relating to the occasion and then recite the clan praises. He also concludes by adding his own words. In essence, praises, whether individual or clan, must be recited in relation to some context, and not in isolation.

As to the actual delivery of chiefly or other individual praises, the performer does not use his vocal pitch as in normal speech. He recites at the top of his voice and at great speed. The raising of the voice is necessary in order to be audible, because the performance normally takes place in the open before a large audience, although this depends upon the occasion. Clan praises are normally recited to a small audience and the raising of the voice is unnecessary. The performer uses normal speech. The voice may be raised slightly on big ceremonial occasions when a number of people are present, especially during weddings.

When the professional bard performs, he is dressed in special attire. He does not stand still, but moves up and down and makes dramatic movements. The clan praiser stands still and makes no dramatic actions and wears no special attire for the occasion. He talks with dignity and with respect especially when propitiating the ancestors.

The reaction of the audience is worth noting. In the case of individual praises the audience may be filled with emotion and now and then people utter shouts of approval and encouragement, such as to say *musho* i.e. 'praise him the more'. In the delivery of clan praises, the audience generally listens in complete silence until the officiator finishes. Sometimes, on special occasions, such as weddings where there is rejoicing and excitement, women fail to contain themselves and may burst out with shrill cries of ululation.

## SOCIAL FUNCTIONS OF CLAN PRAISES

*As a cohesive force of the clansmen.* Clan praises pervade the social life of the Zulu people. They are a cohesive force which binds the members of the clan together into a social unit and gives it solidarity. This is also evident in the classificatory kinship system of the Zulus. Members of a particular clan regard one another as father, brother, son, etc. They feel more sympathetic towards one another than towards members of another clan, less sympathetic to a member of another group, viz., Sotho, and even less to a foreigner. If an invitation is extended to guests for any occasion, the clansmen are considered first, then other relatives and friends come next. The clansmen, by virtue of belonging to a clan, gain the freedom of activity in the kraal of another clansman. They observe no food taboos there; therefore they feel at home. In the contemporary urban setting, some clans even go to the extent of organizing themselves and come together periodically to discuss matters of common interest.

*To express appreciation.* If a member of the clan performed or rendered a service which merits appreciation, it is not enough simply to say *Ngiyabonga*, 'I thank you'. The one who expresses thanks goes further and recites some, if not all, the clan praises. For some achievement, such as when a mother gives birth to a first born son or even just an ordinary baby, some words of appreciation are expressed and in addition clan praises are recited; saying, 'you have done well you of so-and-so', etc. In other words, the praises in this context are an expression of congratulation. A person who is praised in this manner feels highly honoured and this serves as an incentive to him to strive to do better in future or to maintain a high standard of performance.

*On ceremonial occasions.* One of the most important ceremonial occasions in Zulu society is the wedding. On such an occasion the father or the guardian of the bride, in presenting the daughter, will always say a few words about their daughter concerning her up-bringing, the family from which she comes, etc. and then end up with reciting clan praises. Similarly, the father of the bridegroom, in reply, will say a few words of welcome into the family and then proceed to recite the praises of his clan.

*For ritual purposes: Ukubuyisa ritual.* After the death of a clansman, especially if he was the kraalhead, a ritual ceremony known as *ukubuyisa*, the bringing home of the spirit of the deceased, is observed. This ceremony takes place after a few years. It is a ceremony whereby the bridge between all the ancestors and the living is created. Professor Krige mentions that, 'on this occasion the name of the deceased is included in the praises of the ancestors for the first time after his death, and he is specially asked . . . to come back and look after his people' (Krige 1957:169). The person who officiates on this occasion is the nearest of kin. In the words he has to say, he will remark, 'we are bringing you back so-and-so'; thereafter he will start reciting the dead man's personal praises and end up with the praises of the clan. As this is a religious occasion, solemnity, dignity and respect are essential. Recitation of either clan praises or personal praises on this occasion is done steadily and respectfully in natural speech and speed. The audience on such an occasion stays silent until the officiator comes to an end. After this ceremony, the deceased person for whom the ritual was performed is included in the list of the ancestral spirits of the family. In other words, the recitation of the clan praises for ritual purposes is a sort of prayer and intercession directed to the ancestors.

## LINGUISTIC FEATURES

*Pronouns.* Those used in the personal praises refer to the third person, viz., *u-* or *yena* for 'he/she' and *ba-* or *bona* for 'they'. As clan praises are usually an address to the second person, here you find pronouns of the second person, viz. *wena* > 'you', *nina* > 'you'. In a different context first person pronouns may be employed in the clan praises in the plural form, which suggests belonging to a clan, viz. *singabakwa* . . . 'we are of so-and-so'.

*Possessives.* As there is no sense, with the personal praises, of belonging to some collectivity, the use of possessive pronouns is rare.

With clan praises the feeling of belonging to someone is vital. Clan praises have constant references to 'we of so-and-so' or 'you of so-and-so', e.g. the Mchunu clan: *nina bakwaMacingwana kaPhakade akagugi* – 'you people of Macingwana, the son of Phakade who never grows old' . . . or *Singabakwa* . . . – 'we are of so-and-so'.

*Vocatives.* As the clan praises are addressed to second persons, nouns take the form of the vocative in which the noun occurs without an initial vowel (sometimes there is a tonal difference). In most cases clan praises commence with address names, and even in the recitation itself some names of ancestors occur and all these are in the vocative, e.g. *uZulu* = Zulu! *uMageba* = Mageba! *uNdabezitha* = Ndabezitha!

*Vowel elision.* As the individual praise-poems are recited at a very fast speed, final elision (which is normally optional, depending upon the speed of speech) becomes compulsory, e.g. *ilemb' eleq' amany' amalembe* in Shaka's praises meaning 'The axe that surpasses all others'. Such a feature is vital in the interest of metrical rhythm in the recitation. In normal or slow speech it is *ilembe eleqa amanye amalembe* which destroys the metrical rhythm. In reciting clan praises, final vowels are not usually discarded, because the recitation is as effective in normal speech as in quick speech; it is not a context of high emotional excitement, but is quiet and serious. On joyful occasions, however, where there is excitement and high emotion, final vowel elision may be practised.

## LITERARY OR POETIC QUALITIES

*Personification.* In many instances one comes across impersonal nouns personified. This is achieved by simply discarding the initial vowel of the noun in the prefix and replacing it with the vowel *u-*, the singular form of the personal class of nouns in Zulu. Such nouns are now transferred to the personal noun class 1a:

    e.g.   *isiduli* (ant-heap) *uSiduli*
           *ivila* (sluggard) *uVila*

These nouns still retain their concordial agreements as if they were still in their original class of nouns:

    e.g.   *uSiduli si-* and not *u-*
           *uVila li-* and not *u-*

The same principle is applicable to the clan praises as well:

e.g.   *isigoloza* (the one who stares) – *uSigoloza* for Hadebe
      praises

     *inyanda* (bundle of something) – *uNyanda* for Mchunu
      praises

     *ichibi* (lake) – *uChibi* for Mkhwanazi praises

Here again the noun often occurs without its initial vowel in clan
praises, because the vocative is used, as in direct address.

*Imagery.* As imagery constitutes the major ingredient of poetry,
praise-poems and clan praises are rich in this respect. Dingane is referred to as the deep quiet pool, which seems calm, but drowns a
person as he bathes in it:

> *isiziba esinzonzo sizonzobele*
> *siminzisa umuntu ethi uyabhukuda*

Shaka is described as 'the axe which surpasses all the other axes in
sharpness':

> *ilemb' eleq' amany amalembe ngokukhalipha*

or Shaka is referred to as 'the joke of the women of Nomgabhi':

> *uteku lwabafazi bakwaNomgabhi*

Corresponding imagery occurs in the clan praises. For example, the
Chiya clan:

> *Abakwahlamba ngentusi*
> *Abanye behlamba ngamanzi*

(The people who use milk to wash themselves while other people
wash themselves with ordinary water). This phrase implies that they
had numerous cattle from which they obtained plenty of milk.

Or Chiya again:

> *Abakwasihlahla esabanda amagwala*

(The tree behind which the coward took refuge), suggesting that during the military times of Shaka, for example, Chiya people protected those who were fleeing from the wrath and destruction of Shaka.

The Xolo clan:
they refer to themselves as 'the heavy brass-button armlet which
is on the upper arm, which men fail to loosen':

> *Abakwasinda elimqosho*
> *Lisenhla nengalo*
> *Lehlula amadoda ukulikhwishilila*

Or they say, 'We are the mist that rises so very high as to touch the
sky':

*Singabakwankungu ende*
*Ebambelele ezulwini*

*Alliteration.* The Zulu language, by virtue of its alliterative gram-
matical concords, achieves alliteration naturally, e.g. in Dingane's
praises:

*isiziba esinzonzo sizonzobele*

(The deep silent pool of water, it looks calm), where the natural
alliteration of *s* in the prefixes is reinforced by the alliteration of
*z* in the stems. There may also be a deliberate introduction of alliteration in reinforcing imagery, e.g. as in Shaka's praises:

*Sidlukula – dlwedlwe*

*siyadla sindlondlobele*

(Snatcher of the staff; he attacks, he is ready to attack).

The same situation in clan praises occurs where alliterative gram-
matical concords are unavoidable. Deliberate alliteration here too is
common, but not as widespread as in the praise-poems. Natural
alliteration, e.g. Mkhize's clan praises:

*Kwasibi-side simaphandla*

*Siphadle abaNguni bavungama*

(The people of the long straw which dazzles; it dazzled the Nguni
people until they grumbled).
Deliberate alliteration, e.g. Ngema's clan praises:

*UMadlokovu.*

*Owadlokovula imifula*

(Madlokovu: who ran wildly like the rivers).

PARALLELISM AND TECHNIQUES OF LINKING

About Zulu traditional poetry Professor Cope (1968:39) states,
that 'the effectiveness of imagery is greatly increased by the judicious
use of repetition' of various kinds. He has analysed in detail the repetition techniques known as parallelism. It is an effective technique
whereby one verse is automatically linked to the next one. The following examples out of the praise-poems illustrate parallelism.

Shaka's praises:   *Uteku lwabafazi bakwaNomgabhi*

*Betekula behlezi emlovini,*

which illustrates noun-verb initial linking: *uteku* = joke, *betekula* = they were joking.

(The joke of the women of Nomgathi; joking as they sit in the sheltered place.)

> *UMahlom' ehlathini onjengohlanya*
> *Uhlanya olusemehlweni amadoda,*

which illustrates cross – linking with *uhlanya*, and also, incidentally, a wonderful *hl* alliteration

(He who armed in the forest, who is like a madman; the madman who is in full view of the men).

Clan praises also share this technique of parallelism with the praise-poems, e.g.

MKHIZE:       *Kwasibi-side simaphandla*
                       *Siphandle abaNguni bavungama*

(of the long straw which dazzles; it dazzled the Nguni people until they grumbled),

illustrating cross-linking, which also occurs in personal praises and is a very common type of parallelism in clan praises, but is still not as common as negative-positive initial parallelism. Examples of this initial parallelism are:

MAZIBUKO:       *Abangaweli ngazibuko*
                           *Abawela ngezimpambosi zemifula*

(They do not cross at the drift; they cross at the deviations of the river).

MADONDO:       *Abangawudli umbilini*
                           *Udliwa abalandakazi*

(They who don't eat the entrails of a slaughtered beast; they are only eaten by in-laws on the wife's side).

CHIYA:       *Abakwahlamba ngentusi*
                   *Abanye behlamba ngamanzi*

(They who wash with milk while others wash with water), which is an illustration of parallelism in content rather than in form.


ORAL FORMULAS

It was Lord who recognized that the composition and performance of an oral piece of literature evolve around formulas. He defines a formula as 'a group of words which is regularly employed under the same metrical conditions to express a given essential idea' (Lord 1960:4), while Charles Bird defines a formula as 'a kind of abstract pattern sentence into which the singer can substitute a greater number of words, creating a line that will meet the metrical requirements of the poem' (Bird 1972:283).

Praise-poems as well as clan praises adhere to this pattern. These formulas can be classified into two types, viz. parallelism and techniques of linking representing one type and fixed phrases in common usage representing another. Parallelism and techniques of linking have been dealt with above. In the clan praises fixed phrases occur which are shared by a number of related or unrelated clans; this feature is widespread and is an accepted cultural phenomenon; for example the unrelated clans Sibiya, Ngcobo, Ngema, together with the related clans Biyela and Ntshangase, all share this phrase

> *Sibiya ngankomo*
> *Abanye bebiya ngamahlahla*

(Builders of fences by means of cattle; while others make fences by using tree branches).

The phrase suggests possession of many herds of cattle as a status symbol, and wealth in terms of cattle.

Similarly, the clans Ngocobo, Mkhize, Myeza, Shelembe, all share the phrase:

> *AmaLala,*
> *Alala nomunwe engquza*

(The Lala people who sleep at night with the finger stuck in the anus).

This was an alleged former custom of these people. The unrelated clans Khumalo, Mabaso, Hlongwane together with the related clans Qwabe, Gumede, Khuzwayo share the phrase:

> *Abadla umuntu bemyenga ngendaba*

(People who cheat a person by enticing him into a story).

This suggests people who have skill or diplomacy in getting the better of another person.


DEVELOPMENT INTO STANZAS

Jordan Ngubane (1951:4) recognized a development within 'loose' stanzas in praise-poems. He notes that with the early bards the stanzas were short and could be analysed into two parts: the introduction where the bard stated his theme and the dissertation where he developed his argument. He describes this type of stanza as incomplete. He states, however, that during the period immediately preceding Shaka, a third part of the stanza, the conclusion, was introduced,

but this was very rare. It was only during and after the reign of Shaka
that the conclusion became the rule. He cites a typical example by one
of the bards, Mshongweni, in the praise-poem of Shaka as follows:

INTRODUCTION:     *Uteku lwabafazi bakwaNomgabhi,*
                      (The joke of the women of Nomgabhi)

DISSERTATION:     *Betekula behlezi emlovini,*
                      *Beth' uShaka kakubusa, kawubaNkosi*
                      (Joking as they sat in a sheltered spot saying
                      that Shaka would not rule, he would not
                      become king)

CONCLUSION:     *Kanti ilapho ezawunethezeka*
                      (Whereas he was then about to prosper)

Professor Cope (1968:54), using the same illustration, analyses it as
follows:

STATEMENT:     The joke of the women of Nomgabhi
EXTENSION:     Joking as they sat in a sheltered spot
DEVELOPMENT:     Saying that Shaka would not rule, he would
                      not become chief
CONCLUSION:     Whereas it was the year in which he was
                      about to prosper.

In clan praises, stanzas are not as highly developed as in praise-
poems. There are loose stanzas here and there which can be regarded
as incomplete, viz.:

MADONDO

STATEMENT:     *Abangawudli umbilini*
                      (Those who do not eat the entrails of a
                      slaughtered beast)
EXTENSION:     *Udliwa abalandakazi*
                      (They are eaten by in-laws on the wife's
                      side)
CONCLUSION:     *Besaba izisu ukudumba*
                      (Because of fear that their stomachs will
                      swell)

Here the extension has been achieved by initial linking of negative
and positive forms of the verb.

MNGUNI

STATEMENT:     *Wena wakalulwandle aluwelwa*
                      (You of the uncrossable sea)

EXTENSION:               *Luwelwa zinkonjane*
                         *Ezindiza phezulu*
                         *Abantu abaluweli*
                         (It is crossed by swallows, which fly above,
                         people never cross it)

This stanza has no conclusion. The extension part is long and achieved by cross-linking of negative and positive forms of the verb.

In this collection of clan praises, there is one typical example of a highly developed complete stanza:

MIYA

STATEMENT:               *SingabakwaSidinane*
                         (We are the people of Sidinane)

EXTENSION:               *Ngokudina abalandakazi*
                         (Through annoying the in-laws on the wife's
                         side)

DEVELOPMENT:             *Ngoba uSidinane wayehlaba inkomo yemithi*
                         *Ethi inkomo kayimithi*
                         *Umuntu kuphela omithayo*
                         (Because Sidinane used to slaughter a cow in
                         calf
                         Saying a cow does not become pregnant
                         It is only a human being who becomes preg-
                         nant)

CONCLUSION:              *Inkonyane iyocobela ubendi*
                         (The calf will be cut up into small pieces for
                         cooking brawn)

In this illustration, the development is long and achieved by final linking with the repetition of the word *mithi*.


CONCLUSION

Even from this summary account, it can be seen that clan praises are a genre which shares some, but not all, characteristics with individual praise-poems, and which serves functions in Zulu society that differ considerably from those of other kinds of praises.

# REFERENCES

BIRD, C. 1972 – Heroic songs of the Mande hunters. In R. M. Dorson (ed.) *African Folklore*. Bloomington: Indiana Univ. Press.

BRYANT, A. T. 1949 – *The Zulu People*. Pietermaritzburg: Shuter and Shooter.

COPE, A. T. 1968 – *Izibongo: Zulu Praise Poems*. Oxford: Clarendon Press.

FINNEGAN, R. 1970 – *Oral Literature in Africa*. Oxford: Clarendon Press.

JORDAN, A. C. 1957 – Towards an African literature: II. Traditional poetry. *Africa South* 2, 1, 97–105.

KRIGE, E. J. 1957 – *The Social System of the Zulus*. Pietermaritzburg: Shuter and Shooter.

KUNENE, D. P. 1971 – *Heroic Poetry of the BaSotho*. Oxford: Clarendon Press.

KUNENE, R. M. 1962 – An analytical survey of Zulu poetry. Durban: unpublished M.A. thesis, Univ. of Natal.

LORD, A. B. 1960 – *The Singer of Tales*. Cambridge, Mass.: Harvard Univ. Press.

NDAWO, H. M. 1939 – *Iziduko Zama-Hlubi*. Lovedale: Lovedale Press.

NGUBANE, J. 1951 – An examination of Zulu tribal poetry. *Native Teachers' Journal* 31, Oct., 3–6.

RYCROFT, D. 1974 – African praise poetry. London: unpublished.

SCHAPERA, I. 1965 – *Praise-Poems of Tswana Chiefs*. Oxford: Clarendon Press.

VILAKAZI, B. W. 1946 – Oral and written literature in Nguni. Johannesburg: unpublished D.Litt. thesis, Univ. of Witwatersrand.

# THE MONARCHY AND THE MILITARY IN SWAZILAND*

## Hilda Kuper

In September 1968 Swaziland received international recognition as an independent kingdom under Sobhuza II. It was largely through his leadership that there was a peaceful transition from rule through a minority of White officials implementing British policy, to rule by a Black majority guided by its own national and cultural ideals. The population, though predominantly Swazi-speaking and Swaziland born, includes Whites, Eur-Africans (Coloureds) and non-Swazi Africans under the authority of Sobhuza as head of state and as Ngwenyama (Lion), King of the Swazi. The tiny kingdom, land-locked between South Africa and Mozambique, became the 28th member of the British Commonwealth, the 40th member of the Organization of African Unity and the 120th member of the United Nations. Since then, Sobhuza, with the backing of his people, has re-pealed the Independence Constitution drafted by the British and has extended traditional structures of control.

Swaziland is one of the few post-colonial African countries which has experienced neither violence nor despotism. I interpret violence as non-legitimated coercion, despotism as the exercise of arbitrary control wielded by an individual with access to physical force, and authority as a form of control based on consent and legitimated force. To quote from MacIver (1947: 16): 'Without authority force is destructive violence, spasmodic, undirected, futile. Authority is responsive to the underlying social structure. The force of government is but an instrument of authority, vindicating the demands of an order that force alone never creates.'

In this article, I describe the relationship between the authority of a monarchy and the organization of force at different stages in the reign of Sobhuza II. In such a study the historical perspective is essential. Swazi culture is not only deeply rooted in a well-remem-

*I wish to acknowledge the support I received from the Centre for Advanced Study in the Behavioural Sciences and from the National Endowment of the Humanities as a Fellow of the Centre 1976–77, on leave from the University of California, Los Angeles.

bered and also idealized past, but Sobhuza himself deliberately refers to traditions and customs in planning for the future. An institution to which he has devoted particular attention is the *libutfo* (age-class system). In a previous publication (Beemer 1940), I discussed the traditional organization and its transformations through internal and external influences before World War II; since then, the process has been continued, but a brief summary of the earlier periods is essential.

During the eighteenth and nineteenth centuries the Swazi nation developed a particular way of life within a broad framework of contact between Nguni – and Sotho – speaking peoples who had migrated into Southern Africa. By the use of diplomacy as well as military strategy, hereditary leaders of the present royal clan, the Dlamini, absorbed peoples of numerous other clans into a single political system. A complex centralized government was developed under a dual monarchy with the Ngwenyama, always of Dlamini descent, sharing power with the Ndlovukazi, his mother, real or surrogate. Local clans which submitted without resistance were allowed to retain a strong measure of independence. Those that were defeated were not exterminated. The Dlamini attached a sanctity to hereditary chieftainship and if an heir survived, acknowledged him as a foundation on which the conquered could rebuild their identity under Dlamini sovereignty (Kuper 1947: 14–18). In this way allies were made of once powerful enemies, and victories were propaganda for Dlamini royalty.

Though the Swazi are related to the Zulu, whose military system has been so well described by Eileen Krige (Krige 1950), the political system developed under the leadership of Sobhuza I contrasts strongly with that of Shaka, who was his contemporary. Sobhuza entered into alliances; Shaka wanted no allies. Sobhuza believed in the power of persuasion; Shaka ruled by terror (Walter 1969). When the Swazi nation was at the height of its power, there were structural restraints on monarchical despotism through an elaborate system of councils and a network of cross-cutting ties between the King, his mother, the chiefs, the princes, governors and the ordinary people (Kuper 1947). Even in the reign of Sobhuza's son, Mswati, the greatest of the Swazi fighting kings, there was less destruction by violence, and more peaceful incorporation.

Following the Zulu model, Mswati reorganized the regiments on the basis of age, which was more inclusive and effective than locality or kinship alone in unifying different components of the hetero-geneous nation. Local age contingents (*emabutfo*) mobilized at royal villages strategically placed throughout the country. At least two royal villages were established in each reign; the first being the *umpakatsi*, the ritual capital and residence of the Ndlovukazi; the second, *lilawu*, the administrative headquarters established for the King on maturity. These villages, the largest in the land, were inhabited by families, as well as warriors, again unlike Zulu rulers whose capitals were predominantly great military camps (Gluckman 1960).

Swazi who chose to live in barracks at royal villages had special duties and were entitled to special recognition. Warfare itself was intermittent and the entire army was never in action at the same time. The *emabutfo* were essentially multifunctional associations. The members served as state police (maintaining order and enforcing the King's decisions), court messengers, labourers, builders, maintenance men, cultivators of royal fields and herdsmen of royal cattle; they included experts in technical skill and specialists in ritual. In this pre-capitalist economy workers received no fixed rate of pay, but expected to be 'rewarded' with beer and meat and, occasionally, more substantial gifts.

Since every male was automatically enrolled into the age-class system, there was no sharp division between the soldier and the citizen and the staff of the army was not sharply distinguished from other officials dealing with daily affairs. It was assumed that men who showed leadership in battle would show strength and responsibility in the routine of government. The age-class system encouraged communal responsibility more than individual initiative, and though heroes in battle were honoured, they also received special treatment to 'cool the blood' and restrain the lust to kill. The King did not go to war. He was represented on the battlefield by a publicly appointed senior prince (*Mntfanenkosi*) who served as an essential complement to the commander or general (*ndvuna yemabutfo*), of non-Dlamini descent. Though the right to send out the army was reserved to the King, to do so required the support of officers and councillors.

The main non-military occasion requiring participation by senior and junior age-classes was the *Ncwala*, the annual ritual designed to fortify the King against rivals from within and enemies from without the country (Kuper 1947). Marriage, the entry into the fullness of manhood, was a status granted by the King to a regiment as a unit. A new regiment was usually considered essential when a senior regiment received permission to marry, for the roles of participants fell into two marked phases: premarital and postmarital. Membership of an age-class endured throughout life, and the organization constituted the major formal institution for education, in the broadest sense of that word.

The Swazi never fought the Whites and so were never defeated by them by force of arms. On the contrary, in 1879 King Mbandzeni, grandson of Mswati, had responded to the request by the British to help suppress a mutual enemy, the Pedi, in return for a guarantee of Swazi sovereignty and national independence. The help the Swazi regiments gave was verbally acknowledged, and the guarantee reaffirmed in two subsequent conventions (1891 and 1894). But these were not honoured. Instead, in the first period of Imperial expansion the Swazi, caught between rival Boer and British interests in their country, were victims of 'concessions' – a type of warfare outside the traditional techniques of open combat and familiar strategies of incorporation. Swazi talk of 'the papers that killed us'. A Land Concession Proclamation passed in 1907 was analogous to a treaty imposed by victors over the vanquished in that it deprived the Swazi people of two-thirds of their land, while associated Orders-in-Council subordinated Swazi leaders to a cadre of foreign administrators and police. Symbolically, only the British sovereign was empowered to the title King and the Ngwenyama was reduced to 'Paramount Chief'. But militarism itself was not attacked; on the contrary, Whites did not claim fighting was bad, bloodshed in war brutal, or nationalism dangerous. They fought amongst themselves, fought against Africans, and asked Africans to help them in their battles. They increased, rather than decreased, the importance of armed strength as a source of national identity and security. But they monopolized the right to the power of force. Before putting the Land Concession Proclamation into effect, the British, who had assumed control of Swaziland after defeating the Boers in the Anglo-Boer War, disarmed the Swazi of modern weapons and restricted the sale of arms.

No direct attack was made on the organization into age-classes *per se*. This might have been otherwise had the Swazi King been fully grown in the early years of British colonial rule and if the annual ritual of kingship necessitating the presence of all the regiments in battle dress had been performed.[1] But Sobhuza was only five months old when his father died (1899) and throughout a long

period of regency, which ended only in 1922, the full ritual was restricted by custom. By then, colonial rule appeared to be firmly established, and it seemed as though the *emabutfo* organization might
wither away as labour became a commodity in a market system,
and warriors became mine workers, farm hands, clerks and teachers
and new formal institutions took over the education of the young.
Moreover, in the first year of his rule, Sobhuza, acting on behalf of
the nation, had lost the law case challenging the validity of land
concessions before the British Court of Appeal. The British came to
regard the *Ncwala* as a custom that did not threaten their supremacy
nor challenge their legitimacy, and described it as 'a pageant',
which government officials attended for a short while on the main
day (Kuper 1973). But once Sobhuza was fully installed, though the
number of warriors in residence had drastically declined, the *Ncwala*
was performed with strict regard to tradition and the message of
Swazi identity was again carried throughout the country in the rich
media of ancient symbols, with the participation of *emabutfo*. Thus
structures from the pre-colonial model of monarchy were continued
in a changing historical context (Kuper 1973).

In an attempt to retain cultural identity and national unity Sobhuza, supported by a few White government officials, as well as most
of his own councillors, put forward in the early 1930s a suggestion for integrating the regimental system with the classroom. In
this way, he hoped to bridge a growing gap between the small but
increasing number of Western oriented pupils and their peers trained
in the values and discipline of the *libutfo*. Western oriented were distinct from western educated: Sobhuza and his closest councillors
were Western educated, and active in promoting better teaching in
schools but were oriented to Swazi culture. In 1934 Sobhuza formed
the Sikhonyane (Locust) regiment to bring together all boys between
the ages of 10 and 20, and a special curriculum was designed for
those in school. The scheme, though carefully planned, was largely
thwarted by missionary opposition and the experiment limited in
effect to non-sectarian, nationally financed schools. These proved to
be the training ground for many of the men active in later years in
the move towards cultural nationalism for independence.[2]

World War II precipitated the Swazi into a more active role in the
international arena. A military content was temporarily restored to
the *emabutfo*, when the British once again asked the Swazi for support. Sobhuza agreed on condition that his men be treated as true

soldiers and not relegated to non-combatant roles. In 1941, for the first time since the reign of Mbandzeni, the haunting clarion call to war rang through the country. Contingents of two age-classes between roughly 20 and 35 years were mobilized through local chiefs and Sobhuza sent them forth with traditional rites from the present ritual capital, Lobamba, to receive modern training in a Western military camp. As his personal representative he appointed a senior prince, and for the post of traditional *ndvuna yelibutfo* (commander) he selected Mfundza Sukati, son of Lomadokola Sukati, former governor of a royal village and brave warrior in the reign of Mbandzeni. Mfundza had proved his own mettle as head boy and *ndvuna* of the first regiment of pupils at the Swazi national high school. Addressing the men before they went up north, Sobhuza stated that it was not he who was sending them to danger but their forefathers reminding the British of earlier promises which they had not kept. The Swazi Pioneer Corps received special mention in dispatches for courage, cheerfulness and high morale. Letters from the men expressed their feelings of national identity and their loyalty to their own ruler. It had been agreed that they be demobilized as a unit; they were then 'ex-soldiers' of the British Army but were welcomed back as members of the Swazi *emabutfo*. In the meantime, Sobhuza had formed the next generation of youths between roughly 17 to 25 years into a regiment to which he gave the name *Malindane* – 'those who wait for the return' (of the regiments), or *Lindimpi* – 'those who wait for their turn as an army'.

Sobhuza-in-Council had pressed the British to help the soldiers benefit the nation by their new knowledge and not lose skills they had learned. A small proportion of the men (over 3 000) who had been up north received employment or help on their return: some were placed in the central government, including the police and local administration; a few hundred were allotted sites on settlement schemes on land acquired from the British during the war under pressure by Sobhuza-in-Council. Some 56 per cent of the country was still owned by Whites and the majority of soldiers went back to their families living on Swazi communal area or squatting on White-owned farms, and eked out a bare subsistence. Increasing public grants and investment, including irrigation and forestation schemes, did not resolve the inequalities rooted in the concession period. The general contrast between living conditions of Whites and Blacks became increasingly obvious, overriding the improvement in living

standards of a limited number of individual Africans (Fair *et al.*
1969).

Sobhuza put pressure on the political as well as on the economic
front. In the 1950s he had effectively negotiated the retention of
Swazi chieftainship and Swazi councils under conditions more favourable than the British had initially designed under their formula for
Indirect Rule (Hailey 1963). At the same time White settlers were
consolidating their representation through a formally recognized
Advisory Council, and discrimination in favour of Whites continued
to be legally sanctioned.

The situation was not unique to Swaziland; on the contrary, it was
the essence of the colonial situation, within which anti-colonial
movements were expressed, and dealt with, in different ways according to the ideology as well as the strength of competing power
groups. At one extreme the reaction was expressed in bloody combat,
at the other in strategy and compromise. In Swaziland, the British
attempted to adapt a model of their own twentieth century political
system; the Swazi had their own concept and model of a constitutional monarchy. But neither side wanted to use violence to achieve their
objectives.

Modern party politics can be said to have begun in the early 1960s
after Sobhuza had initiated a move for a government in which he
proposed that Swazi and Whites participate on a basis of equality.
His formulation was vague, the meaning of 'equality' controversial,
but the gist of his approach was fairly clear:[3] a 'traditional' dynamic
Swazi model, based on its own system of popular representation by
acclamation and nomination, under its own organization of authority, was to be created with Whites adequately represented and incorporated into a single government. Concurrently with this move,
and contrary to the Swazi model, the first Western-style political
party, the Swaziland Progressive Party, was formed. Its leaders –
J. J. Nquku, Dr Ambrose Zwane and Obed Mabuzo – advocated
open elections and competing parties. The sympathy of the British
was logically with the 'politicians' and their more Western model
of democracy. Obviously, the British were not in favour of abolishing
Kingship; nor indeed were most of the African politicians, but their
notion of an acceptable monarchy was essentially different from that
of their Swazi contemporaries. In Sobhuza's words: 'It is the tradition of all African Kingdoms that their Kings are leaders as well
as Kings. This is also true for Swaziland. Now, rightly or wrongly,

some people have mistaken this dual capacity as dictatorship. I would like to assure you here and now that the King both leads and is led by his people. I am my people's mouthpiece.'[4] The most vocal settlers felt their positions would be more secure under Sobhuza's formula of sharing than if they accepted a universal franchise in a society where Africans would be an unassailable majority.

Political leaders mushroomed and political parties proliferated. Sobhuza-in-Council (the so-called 'traditionalists') advanced cautiously and, at first, slowly, along the road to ultimate independence. The Western-oriented took a more aggressive stand. The former furthered their political policy with peaceful pressure from the top in their efforts to regain traditional economic control over land and mineral resources; the latter directed their efforts to acquire political control through organizing from the bottom. The majority of Swazi were village-rooted, dependent on chiefs for land and good will; more blatant inequalities and fewer solidarities confronted Africans in urban centres and company towns, where low wages and poor housing provided fertile ground for the new politicians. The complex and, at times, conflicting roles of British officials and White settlers (divided into their own factions) were crucial factors in the total framework of alliances. Discussions on Swaziland's first written constitution had reached a deadlock, and the British Secretary of State, finding it impossible, in spite of lengthy local discussions and a London conference, to resolve the conflicts between diverse interest groups and two models of monarchy, produced his own compromise. It was a complicated document that glossed over the contradictions in the models by inserting a short schedule: Matters Which Shall Continue to be Regulated by Swazi Law and Custom.

(a) the office of Ngwenyama
(b) the office of Ndlovukazi
(c) the appointment, revocation of appointment and suspension of chiefs
(d) the composition of the Swazi National Council, the appointment and revocation of appointment of members of the Council and the procedure of the Council
(e) the Ncwala Ceremony
(f) the Libutfo (regimental) system.

The rest of the White Paper included provisions for Western-style elections and elevated the position of Resident Commissioner to

that of 'Her Majesty's Commissioner' with executive power equal-
ling that of British governors and with the right to veto matters
passed by the Legislative Council. Certain privileges granted to the
Ngwenyama were more personal privileges accorded to a British
sovereign under the system where sovereignty itself was vested in
Parliament.

The cleavages between the Legislative Council and the Swazi
National Council were not eliminated by the fact that the representatives of the Swazi National Council, certified by the Ngwenyama,
were also on the Legislative Council. In short, the duality which the
new constitution was intended to overcome appeared in some ways
more acute.

The dilemma of Sobhuza was dramatically evident when acute
political disagreements converged with unprecedented economic
disturbances (Ballenden *et al.* 1963). On 20 May 1963, 1 400 Africans at the Havelock Asbestos Mine in the north of Swaziland
downed tools. On 9 June, domestic servants in the British administrative capital, Mbabane, did not go to work. That afternoon, the
Ngwane National Liberatory Congress Party called for a general
strike. The following day some 3 000 men and women demanded to
see the Resident Commissioner; he agreed to talk to 15 representatives but would not accept their demands. That night prisoners in the
Mbabane central gaol rioted; 10 escaped. The colonial police, some
300 men, was neither trained nor equipped for major crises. White
residents formed a special guard. The British still had the authority
of force. The Resident Commissioner requested Sobhuza to send
his regiments to assist the police. In Sobhuza's opinion, the British
had provoked the situation through their support of political parties
and of trade unions; they had then rushed in legislation allowing
them to arrest leaders they themselves had encouraged, thereby
provoking the masses to further violence. He refused 'to call up his
men to kill each other'. With some reluctance, the Resident Commissioner decided to call in a force from outside. Thirty-seven police
were flown in from Bechuanaland followed two days later by some
600 British soldiers from Kenya.

When the planes circled over Mbabane, people from the surrounding areas flocked to the Ngwenyama who had come to the ritual
capital of Lobamba. Political organizers of the strike, realizing the
danger of a possible clash between strikers and troops, then appealed
to him to call out his warriors, since, in their viewpoint, the con-

flict was no longer between Swazi politicians and traditionalists but between the Swazi and the colonial administration. Sobhuza refused. His warriors had no modern weapons and open confrontation would have led to a massacre of his own subjects and end any hope of national unity. Civil war had to be averted at all costs, and he had sufficient faith in the British to believe that if the strikers did not use force, force would not be used against them. Addressing the nation in the *sibaya* of the Lobamba, he sternly warned his people to return to work and urged everyone to keep the peace. Within a fortnight after the arrival of the soldiers, most of the men were back at work; later 15 leaders were charged with public violence.

For the first time in Sobhuza's reign a foreign army had been brought into the country. This was the act of the colonial power; Sobhuza's control had averted the bloodshed and bitterness of civil war. He had refused to call up his warriors to fight on the side of the police against the strikers as requested by the British, or against the police as requested by the party politicians. There was in his attitude the perception of Aristotle, who wrote: 'Kings are guarded by the arms of their subjects; tyrants by a foreign force. Ruling constitutionally, and with the consent of their subjects, kings have bodyguards drawn from their subjects; the tyrant, who rules contrary to the will of his subjects, has a (foreign) bodyguard to protect him against them' (Barker 1946: 138).

A deputation with a petition sent by Sobhuza-in-Council to ask the Secretary of State to reconsider the proposals, had met with a rebuff; the delegates were informed that Sobhuza had lost the support of his people to more modern and progressive politicians. To test this allegation, Sobhuza insisted, despite objections by the Resident Commissioner, on holding a national referendum with the simple direct question: Do you, or do you not, agree with the petition? Since over 75 per cent of Swazi adults were not able to read or write, opinion was expressed through symbols: a lion representing support for the petition, a reindeer (a foreign animal) rejection. The result was so overwhelmingly in favour of 'the lion' that even those who criticized the loaded symbols admitted that the British had underestimated the strength of Swazi attachment to their own system and to Sobhuza in particular. That year, 1963, the *Ncwala* was particularly well attended and among the *emabutfo* were many men who had previously taken no active part.

But the British went ahead and imposed the constitution. Initially

the Ngwenyama-in-Council as well as the leaders of the political
parties talked of boycotting the election. However, aware that to
be effective a boycott had to be total, the Ngwenyama, urged by his
advisors, agreed that representatives selected from the Swazi National Council should also enter the contest. He named the political arm
of the Swazi National Council the *imbokodvo*, explaining that the
*imbokodvo* (Grinding Stone), an essential utensil of every Swazi
home, ground separate grains together into a single paste. The
Imbokodvo was to be a national movement to bring unity; Sobhuza
urged his people to register their vote. Since voting was based on
racially defined electoral rolls, the Imbokodvo National Movement
(INM) formed an alliance with the majority group of White settlers
who had organized themselves into the United Swaziland Associations (USA). Together they won every seat.

At the opening meeting, Prince Makhosini, appointed by the
Ngwenyama as leader of the INM, asked for a committee to formu-
late a new constitution more in keeping with Swazi principles and
interests. This second constitutional committee was explicitly guided
by a 'model of the monarchy that had existed at the time of the original treaty relationship which Swaziland had with Britain in the
nineteenth century and the recognition of the kingdom of the
Ngwenyama' (Swaziland Constitutional Proposals Command 3119,
October 1966). Many of the specific objections to the constitution
imposed in 1963 had been removed: Sobhuza would be recognized
as King and Head of State; independence would be granted 'not
later than 1969' following a period of so-called responsible government; all Swazi-area land including former Crown lands would be
vested in the Ngwenyama on behalf of the nation. But a fundamental
incompatability between two models of kingship persisted: the
Swazi monarchy was still contained within an overriding Western
model, and there were, moreover, certain complex constraints on
the introduction of changes in the Constitution.

The difference in ideological assumptions was reflected at the time
in a disagreement over who should control the vital resources of
minerals and mineral oils. According to the British, control could
be vested in the monarch but he would be obliged to act on the
advice of the Cabinet representing the elected parliament; from the
Swazi perspective, the Ngwenyama had the right to appoint his own
committee independent of cabinet control and allocate the revenue
in ways which the Ngwenyama-in-Council considered to be in the

interest of the nation. The British were adamant and the Swazi, rather than delay independence, temporarily acquiesced.

The INM won every seat in the second election. Since voting under the new constitution was no longer by racial rolls, it had disassociated itself from its embarrassing bond with the more reactionary Whites and was able to incorporate into its programme many points of its former critics. Swaziland became in effect a one-party State led by a hereditary monarch, who, in addition to the 24 members of the INM, was granted authority to nominate six members to the House of Assembly and six to the Senate. These were to represent special interests and in his choice he included six Whites and one Eur-African.

On 25 April 1967, Sobhuza II took the oath as King of Swaziland and Head of State before a crowd estimated at 30 000 among whom the *emabutfo* and *emasotsha* of World War II were conspicuous. The place at which the ceremony was held was the same as that from which he had sent his men to fight in World War II. At the opening session of Parliament, Prince Makhosini, as leader of the INM, pressed for an earlier date for independence; and this was agreed to. By that time the clause relating to rights of minerals had been changed by a unanimous vote in Parliament itself. Other anomalies and contradictions in the elaborate constitution would emerge only later.

On 6 September 1968 the documents of independence were handed to Sobhuza in a spectacular celebration described by the British as 'granting independence' and by the Swazi as 'reacquiring independence'. Sobhuza, as Ngwenyama, together with his supporters, conveyed this message in the graphic language of costume, song and dance, as well as in more direct speech. The Ngwenyama, Ndlovukazi, queens, most Swazi notables and some 2 000 *emabutfo* appeared in full *Ncwala* costume; veterans of World War II were in their old army uniforms. After the main speeches, the *emabutfo* began a traditional dance song commemorating a major victory against prior enemies. The Ngwenyama and Prince Makhosini left their seats in the grandstand between representatives of the British to join their respective age groups. When the week of celebrations ended, the king dismissed the *emabutfo* and then went with a few trusted men to address the veterans. He stressed that whereas Whites called them ex-soldiers, no Swazi ever lost his position in the *emabutfo*. For the independent kingdom he created a new regiment, the *Gcina*

(The end of an Era) with a junior section, the *Tinkanyeti* (Stars [of the Dawn]).

Paradoxically, with nominal political independence, Swaziland became more vulnerable to actual physical force from its powerful neighbours, South Africa and Mozambique. The British had withdrawn the last of its series of troops in November 1966 and the Swazi were neither equipped, nor trained for modern warfare. A request to send young Swazi to Sandhurst had been refused, and the suggestion that the barracks left by the British be available for Swazi troops was turned down on the ground that a Swazi army was a political luxury which the country could not afford. Since the strikes, much attention had been given by the British to the development of the police force, which had been doubled in size and improved in efficiency, and included a paramilitary unit. The gulf between the police and *mabutfo* remained conspicuous. The lines of command were not yet identical. By reason of the training and system of promotion the King-in-Council was still less certain of the political allegiance of the police than of the *emabutfo*. At independence, the commissioner of police was an expatriate and only four out of 34 gazetted officers were Africans. Nor were all Africans necessarily Swazi and, hence, automatically part of the national age system. In short, the police entered the service by different modes of recruitment, were governed by different regulations and received remuneration from different sources than the *emabutfo*. In contrast to the older generation of *emabutfo* officers, the upper echelon of the police were all school educated (some had been sent to police colleges in England for further training) and were Western oriented. With responsible government the King-in-Council had taken a more direct interest in the police force (his personal bodyguard already included Swazi trained in the Police College, opened in 1965), and localization was pursued at all levels. In 1969, the force became the Royal Swaziland Police Force with the King as Commissioner-in-Chief. But this was nominal rather than an executive authority; the Commissioner of Police (who until 1972 was an expatriate) and senior officers were appointed by a Public Service Commission, a body inaugurated in the early 1960s.

With decolonization, the need for national unity was accelerated. The emphasis on colour, or 'race' changed to an emphasis on 'Swazi' not on 'White' or 'Black'; the concept of a Black 'Swazi' was itself to some degree redefined. To be accepted as 'Swazi' one did not have to know the language nor follow the rich body of Swazi custom, though a certain symbolic identification, especially through clothing, became desirable (Kuper 1973). More particularly the concept related to the political notion of service and loyalty to the state. The use of legal mechanisms, such as labelling persons 'prohibited immigrants' or controlling residents' permits, served the purpose in both the colonial period and independent period of limiting the need for force.[5] An investigation by a committee of the Swazi National Council appointed by the King to investigate the situation reported back that some 6 000 people were in Swaziland without any of the necessary evidence of traditional citizenship or documents entitling them to residence. The question of the definition of citizenship became crucial.

The King, the Prime Minister, and his advisors had continued to point to contradictions in the 'Independence Constitution'. Under it another general election, the third in nine years, was due to be held in 1972. In spite of objections, Sobhuza was prepared to go through with the procedure while working towards a re-formulation more in keeping with the Swazi model of government. In the Election Manifesto of 1972, the INM pledged that necessary changes would be made, and when Sobhuza dismissed the *emabutfo* at the end of the *Ncwala*, he hinted 'the time had come when young Swazi men should be well trained in modern methods and techniques to deal with trouble which may threaten the peace of the country' and he exhorted the warriors 'to live up to the great traditions of their past'.

The elections took place on 16 and 17 May 1972, with five parties contesting the 24 elective seats in eight three-member constituencies. The INM won all but one constituency, which went to three members of the NNLC. In view of the traditional Swazi attitude to party politics, this was seen as a threat to national unity and tantamount to having in one's midst a subversive and persistent enemy committed to opposition not by honest conviction but by organization. Moreover, the question of the eligibility of one of the winning candidates on grounds of citizenship had been raised prior to the election; after the election it was brought before the courts. A bitter and dramatic legal battle ensued in which two issues, the one related to the question of citizenship and rights of a particular individual, and the other to the broad interpretation of national sovereignty, became inextricably confused.

After a series of contradictory opinions and conflicting judgments by learned, Western-trained lawyers, an Immigration (Amendment)

Act, passed by the two Houses of Parliament, established a Special Tribunal to decide cases of doubtful citizenship. The Tribunal declared the candidate was *not* a citizen of Swaziland in terms of the 1968 Constitution; but his lawyer in the meantime had applied to the High Court challenging the validity of the Act itself. At a public meeting on 19 March at the ritual capital, the King posed the following specific questions: 'Ask yourselves: are we really like the British, the French, or the Germans; or are we nominally independent? Do we have a Parliament that is supreme like that of the British, the French and other independent nations? Or do we have a token Parliament?' A few days later, the President of the High Court declared the Immigration (Amendment) Act 'beyond the power of Parliament to enact save in accord with Section 134.[6] Hence the Act was void'.

On 12 April, a motion that the Constitution be repealed was passed unanimously in both houses of Parliament. The Prime Minister and Cabinet, together with other members of the Swazi National Council, fetched Sobhuza to the *sibaya* in the ritual capital. A special meeting of the Nation had been called in his name and between 7 000 and 8 000 were waiting. For the first time in addition to the police, Swazi soldiers (*emasotsha*) in army trucks and equipped with FN rifles appeared before the public. It was a modern army albeit small in number; the nucleus of it was the Gcina regiment inaugurated on the eve of independence.[7] The King, barefoot and in traditional dress, sat on the ground beside his counsellors. He listened attentively while the Prime Minister read the resolution passed by Parliament and supported by the Swazi National Council, then slowly and quietly responded with a historic prepared proclamation. He repealed the Constitution 'which had failed to provide the machinery necessary for peace and order'. He assumed 'supreme power' in the kingdom of Swaziland and declared that all legislative, executive and judicial power be vested in himself 'exercised in collaboration with a Council constituted by my Cabinet Members'[8]. He then called upon the Attorney General to read out the decrees designed 'to provide for the continuation of administration, essential services and normal life in the country'.

The King's announcement was received by many with warm and obvious approval and loud shouts of 'Bayethe'. But there were some who were silent, and the popular press outside of Swaziland reported the event in such terms as 'Swazi King scraps the Constitution',

'King Seizes Supreme Power', 'The Swazi Coup', 'Another African Dictatorship'. But inside Swaziland, there was a general feeling of 'wait-and-see', and those who knew Sobhuza well trusted that returning to him and his Council full constitutional authority would indeed solve the difficulties that had become increasingly acute. It was not a military coup but an effort to turn nominal political independence into full sovereignty, under a leader who had proved his wisdom and moral courage over the years, a man ready to listen to all sides before making a decision, a King who had demonstrated he was not a tyrant, a King inspired by ideals of the best in a traditional African monarchy in which there was an interplay of different levels of councils and the King was indeed 'the mouthpiece' of the majority of the people.

At the King's Birthday Celebrations in July 1973, the *emabutfo*, the Police and the Army, each with its own potential for destructive force, appeared together on a playing field in Mankayane to honour their King (Kuper 1974). The largest number was still the *emabutfo* in their traditional costume. Since then, the number of *emasotsha* (soldiers) has been increased by voluntary reserves who come for training over weekends.

The position of the King and the peace of his country became more difficult when Frelimo fighters gained independence for the people of Mozambique and at the same time pressure against the White supremacist regimes of South Africa and Rhodesia intensified. Much as Sobhuza desires peace, he has had to anticipate war. The Swazi Army – the Umbutfo Royal Defence Force – is, as its name implies, still tradition-rooted; it is designed primarily for protection, not aggression and is described as 'the dignity of the nation'. In November 1975 Sobhuza appointed as Commander-in-Chief Maphevu Dlamini, a man well-known for his experience and interest in rural development. He is not a career soldier, but was one of the first to join the Reserves. Some three months later, Sobhuza appointed Colonel Maphevu as the new Prime Minister, combining as in the earlier period of Swazi nationhood a military and civil authority in a single person.

According to some political theorists, 'the legitimacy crisis in the developing world rests on the inability of competing elites to sustain a political leadership long enough for its concept of public good to be supported by other elites and by the masses' (Horowitz 1968: 45). In Swaziland Sobhuza managed to secure the monarchy and protect its legitimacy by its own traditional constitutional defences. It remains to be seen whether it can survive a crisis of succession. But it provides a model different from that apparent in many other African territories, where violence and coups have disrupted the post-Colonial regime.

NOTES

[1]The situation was thus again different from that of the Zulu, who had resisted British rule by force and been defeated by force. Zulu chiefs in Natal had been prohibited by Theophilus Shepstone, British Agent, from holding the Zulu equivalent of the *Ncwala* and from summoning the regiments.

[2]For a full description of the experimental situation, see Beemer 1940: 195–204.

[3]Only a few salient features can be dealt with in this article; further details and, at times, different interpretations appear in Halpern 1965 and Potholm 1969.

[4]Speech by Sobhuza on taking the oath as King of Swaziland on 25 April 1967.

[5]The lines of who should be prohibited or who should get permits were of course differently drawn. Fanon argued that in the colonial situation, the colonizer created not only his own role and image, but that of 'the native' over whom he exercises control; in the post-colonial period the reverse image was created by colonization of 'the foreigner'.

[6]According to Section 134 of the Constitution, the amendment to entrenched clauses required a majority of two-thirds of all the members of a joint sitting of both Houses; if passed, the resolution had then to be submitted to a national referendum by secret ballot again requiring a two-thirds majority.

[7]A core of the Gcina were youths formerly quartered at a training camp started as a service by the Israeli government for the Swazi government after independence. The boys received two years instruction in community activities and agriculture and were expected to carry the knowledge back to benefit their home areas. A request by one of the Swazi ministers to include military training had been firmly refused by Israeli advisors. South Africa later supplied the Swazi army with equipment, but this was fully paid for from Swazi Nation funds and without any military alliances.

[8]For verbatim speeches, see Daniel *et al.* 1975: 205ff.

REFERENCES

BALLENDEN, P. ST. C. *et al.* 1963 – *The Report of the Committee of Enquiry into Unrest in Swaziland.* Mbabane: Government Printer.
BARKER, E. 1946 – *The Politics of Aristotle.* Oxford: Clarendon Press.
BEEMER, H. 1940 – The development of the military organisation in Swaziland. *Africa* 10, 55–74.

DANIEL, J., SIMELANE, G. N. & SIMELANE, V. M. (eds.) 1975 – *Politics and Society in Swaziland*. Readings, vol. 3 (mimeographed), Univ. of Botswana, Lesotho and Swaziland.

FAIR, T. J. D., MURDOCH, G., & JONES, H. M. 1969 – *Development in Swaziland*. Johannesburg: Univ. of Witwatersrand Press.

GLUCKMAN, M. 1960 – The rise of a Zulu empire. *Scient. Am.* **202**, 4, 157–68.

HAILEY, LORD. 1963 – *Native Administration in the British African Territories*. London: Oxford Univ. Press.

HALPERN, J. 1965 – *South Africa's Hostages: Basutoland, Bechuanaland and Swaziland*. London: Penguin.

HOROWITZ, I. L. 1968 – Political legitimacy and the institutional crisis in Latin America. *Compar. Polit. Stud.* **1.**

KENNEDY, G. 1974 – *The Military in the Third World*. London: Duckworth.

KRIGE, E. J. 1950 – *The Social System of the Zulus* (second edn.). Pietermaritzburg: Shuter and Shooter.

KUPER, H. 1947 – *An African Aristocracy*. London: Oxford Univ. Press.

–––––– 1972 – A royal ritual in a changing political context. *Cah. Étud. Afr.* **12**, 593–615.

–––––– 1973 – Costume and identity. *Comp. Stud. Soc. & Hist.* **15**, 348–67.

–––––– 1974 – The birthday celebrations of the King. *Swaziland Teachers' J.* (Mbabane), July.

–––––– 1977 – *Sobhuza II, King of Swaziland*. London: Duckworth.

MACIVER, R. M. 1926 – *The Modern State*. Oxford: Clarendon Press.

–––––– 1947 – *The Web of Government*. New York: Macmillan.

POTHOLM, C. P. 1972 – *Swaziland: The Dynamics of Political Modernisation*. Berkeley: Univ. of California Press.

WALTER, E. V. 1969 – *Terror and Resistance*. New York: Oxford Univ. Press.

# PROBLEMS IN
# AFRICAN RESEARCH AND SCHOLARSHIP

*Absolom Vilakazi*

Some serious problems of research and scholarship in studies of
African societies will be discussed in this paper. The first problem
concerns concepts and terminologies. Leonard Schapiro informs us
(1970:7) that 'Confucius regarded the "rectification of names" as
the first task of government [for] if names are not correct, language
will not be in accord with the truth of things'. We suggest that this
observation has particular relevance in the African situation to social
science research. Professor Njisane suggested[1] that the concepts and
terminologies used in research and teaching in African studies reflected the temper and mood of the colonial period; and conformed
to the images of African people and their cultures which the colonial
powers wished to create for purely political reasons. In that sense
these concepts and terminologies were ideological in that they were
tied to a particular form of domination and therefore biased. Professor Njisane went on to suggest that concepts like 'tribe', 'native',
'detribalization', 'tribal politics', etc., as used by anthropologists,
not only encompass the antithesis between civilized and savage,
Western and primitive; they also subsume norms of behaviour,
notions of proper and improper conduct, rights and duties, conformity and failure to conform. In this sense, the concepts are academically
dysfunctional, because they tempt many scholars to avoid explicit
definition of concepts and terms, to assume that they can be generalized and to assume their scientific validity. Further, these concepts
contribute to selective perception of reality, because the scholar
who uses them is rendered myopic by becoming interest-bound to
the implications of the concepts, so that he or she no longer sees
facts which are excluded from the subsumed behaviour patterns and
social characteristics. This myopia leads to serious distortion of
social reality.

Njisane pointed out that 'tribe' is an especially nostalgic concept
in Western society; and that as one forages through the writings of
anthropologists, it becomes clear that all non-Westerners, the out-
groups, are 'tribal'; and that the 'ethnos' is reserved for European
communities only. Professor Andreski also pursued this point.

Discussing the word 'tribalism', he remarked that it is used to define the solidarity or separatist tendencies of ethnic aggregates smaller than (or not co-extensive with) the population of the state, even if the aggregate in question is quite numerous.

> Why should 13 million Yorubas be called a tribe but the much less numerous Latvians a nation? Because the former are Africans and the latter Europeans? . . . Why should we call the opposition of the French Canadians to the English Canadian domination nationalism and the analogous attitude of the Ibo to the Hausa tribalism? Are the protagonists of the official view of African affairs not indulging in crypto-racialism when they call the same thing nationalism (which sounds good) when it occurs in Europe or America, but 'tribalism' (which sounds bad) when it occurs in Africa? (Andreski 1968:58)

Another area of difficulty is that the methods and practices of scholarship and research followed in Africa by both African and Western scholars blithely assume that the problems which face a Western scholar are the same as those which face an African researcher and scholar. We suggest that this is not so; and that an African field worker, for example, enters a hostile and an insecure intellectual environment when he decides to become an academic in his own right and not an assistant to a White researcher. It is a world full of unexpected dangers and disappointments. It is made insecure because, somehow, the African is assumed to need the tutelage of even the most junior of Western scholars, and his facts must be checked at every point by referring everything to White teachers or even to White government officials. There is also the problem that government circles in many African countries are more willing to extend facilities and courtesies to Whites than to Blacks. Difficulties arise also from the liability of the African researcher and his ethnic group to a negative definition. He is seen by the White world as someone with no ambition, irresponsible, lacking in the persistence which is supposed to characterize the White; and lacking in originality. He is also assumed to be incapable of learning or of practising knowledge and skills which are common to the White.

In South Africa, he is always painfully aware that as an academic he has been co-opted into a dominant and oppressive system in which he and his group are the dominated, and that, through his training, he has absorbed the ideologically-oriented values of his teachers.

This means that he accepts apartheid as 'a social given', and operates with values, definitions and vocabularies of an academic community which generally analyses social reality as reflected through the prism of apartheid. Indigenous social scientists in other parts of Africa share in the general intellectual dilemma of their South African counterpart, although less traumatically. They, too, are incorporated into a body of social science and social scientists from the West who must inevitably reflect the biases, ethnocentrisms and ideological orientation of Europe and Western civilization. Ruth Benedict spoke directly to this point:

> Western Civilization has spread itself . . . over most of the globe and we have been led . . . to accept the belief in the uniformity of human behavior . . . The psychological consequences of this spread of white culture have been out of all proportion to the materialistic . . . it has given to our culture a massive universality that we have long ceased to account for historically, and which we read off rather as necessary and inevitable. We interpret our dependence, in our civilization, upon economic competition, as proof that this is the prime motivation that human nature can rely upon, or we read off the behavior of small children as it is moulded in our civilization and recorded in child clinics as child psychology or the way in which the young human animal is bound to behave. It is the same whether it is a question of our ethics or of our family organization. It is the inevitability of each familiar motivation that we defend, attempting always to identify our own local ways of behaving with Behavior; our own socialized habits with Human Nature (Benedict 1934:3–4).

This predicament, then, raises the problems of ideology in social science which are much more far-reaching than is suggested by our discussion so far.[2] There are at least two questions here. The first relates to the socio-political context within which knowledge about society is produced; whether it is scientific (objectively true) or, in origin, is tied to particular forms of domination and, in effect, justifies such domination and is therefore biased, i.e. not objectively true. Second, there is the question relating to the socio-political context within which knowledge is, through policy decisions, utilized and the uses to which it is put.

Our contention is that our starting point in this inquiry should be the socio-political framework – the only factor which allows for 'social science' to be either emancipatory or imperialistic. In a world in which there is domination and imperialism, social science will be imperialistic; and in a world in which a socio-political struggle is waged by a significantly large section of the masses to free themselves from domination and imperialism, social science will be emancipatory. In a world such as ours, characterized by both domination and mass liberation struggles, there will be two major trends within social science: one tied, in effect, to the dominating classes, therefore obfuscating the liberation struggles; the other contributing towards liberation and therefore emancipatory.

We suggest that the two trends mentioned above are present in the social science of our time whether or not particular social scientists who create it are aware of them. This is simply because, as Jensen (1963:14) points out:

> Every scientific investigation formulates a very definite image of man; and the importance of this for the study of culture can hardly be exaggerated. Even the reporting of facts is usually unconsciously influenced by the 'image' which, uncontrolled, often subsumes interpretations not inherent in the situation itself. The effect of the 'image of man' becomes even more pronounced in the realm of the purely theoretical.

Works of social science give us a picture not only of 'what is', but also of 'what ought to be'. Thus social science and philosophy cannot be successfully separated. Social science is rooted in a certain form of practice and it justifies and encourages a particular form of practice – either the reproduction of the experience within which it is rooted or a departure from that particular experience. In other words, *all* social science is committed to a certain experience or pattern of experience. The implications of this commitment are significant, because many practising social scientists still believe in, and preach to their students the possibility of, an uncommitted, or ethically neutral social science.

The obvious implications are that as long as there is no major contest for positions and power in society, coming from a large group or class below, the existing intellectuals of that society rest attached to, or issue out of and draw nourishment from, the dominating classes. In such situations intellectuals are the allies and tools of the dominating classes. The dominant social science then formulates and articulates views and outlooks which favour and support the existing social order and power structure. That is, the fundamental underpinnings of the social structure are not questioned. They are simply taken as givens, as natural, as it were. We do not suggest that all social scientists take this position. Only the leading ones do; those who share official views and succeed, set the trend. This trend merely encourages the reproduction of social relations upon which a social science is based. It is not critical of the basis of such social relations. Works arguing a different case may appear, but they do not become successful or influential.

It is only when major changes take place, affecting the lives of the masses below and generating mass discontent and struggles, that a new trend in the social sciences arises, reflecting the critical nature of these liberation struggles, and, therefore, itself critical, not only of the existing society, but also of existing social theory. This new trend becomes tied to the liberation movements, in the sense that it boosts those individuals who, hitherto, may have been critical but, being isolated and lacking the basis of the power of a social movement, were overwhelmed by the trend that was tied to the ruling classes. It becomes tied to the liberation struggle also in the sense that new personalities now arise from below who articulate the aspirations of the movement and bring out a social theory which competes with, and seeks to replace, the existing theories.

As illustration of what we are talking about, one has only to think of the dominant trend in the social sciences of the 1950s in the U.S.A. and compare it with the situation in the late 1960s and today. In terms of personalities, one thinks readily of scholars like Parsons, Merton, Lipset, Herskovits, Murdock, Mead, Schlesinger, etc. From the middle 1960s to the present, mass social movements against the established system arose (Black Revolt, Student Revolt, Women's Lib, The New Left) and a new trend became noticeable in the social sciences – a leftist trend, and new names like Mills, Baran, Sweezy, Mandel, Marcuse, to name but a few, became the definers of it – a trend which is fertilized by the ideas of Marx.

We realize that we are stating unpopular views which will not find easy acceptance in the academic world. But this is to be expected because, as Birnbaum (1971:40) suggests, 'the primary ideological difficulty of many contemporary sociologists [he might have added anthropologists, as well] is that they are unwilling to face up to the implications of the problem of ideology for their work'. He goes on to point out that for many, the 'questions of ideological bias appear to be not wrong, but irrelevant – vestiges of a primitive stage of sociology now (happily) behind us'. In our view, this is perhaps one of the most offensive attitudes of Western social scientists towards Black social scientists, particularly in South Africa. It shows itself in quick and superior accusations of 'lack of scientific objectivity' and 'emotionalism' every time a Black scholar raises questions not only about the validity of their analyses but also of their perspectives. Scholarship thus becomes 'White' and White scholars arrogate to themselves the right to define what the standards of scholarship and objectivity are, or ought to be. This attitude has the effect of quickly muzzling intellectual dissent among the Blacks and smothers the emergence of different social analyses based on assumption which differ from those of the Whites who belong to the ruling elite.

There is another, equally serious, problem of scholarship and research which is particularly pertinent to the South African situation and which makes the emergence of mature Black scholarship very difficult. Leo Kuper first pointed this out (1965:143-66) when he drew attention to the inability of Black professionals to be really professional, because the system makes it difficult to participate in professional associations with their White peers. Even in their research they are limited, because their access to funds, libraries, museums and important research sites is restricted. They often encounter practical, if not legal, obstacles to joining professional bodies where they might read papers and discuss their academic interests with professional colleagues. Even visiting colleagues in South African universities requires special arrangements for accommodation. I have myself, since leaving South Africa, been invited to two academic conferences in South Africa where Blacks and their problems were discussed by predominantly White scholars with no South African Black scholars present; and where apartheid, even though the word was never mentioned, hung over the meetings like a brooding presence. All analysis assumed the rightness of the system. It is this social and intellectual climate which seems to me to be one of the biggest difficulties in South African research, but which is seldom, if ever, discussed in seminars on research.

There is another serious problem of social science and of anthropology in particular, in modern Africa. It arises essentially from the conservative nature of anthropological thought and especially its tendency to wish to preserve traditional societies and cultures and to regard change and modernization as intrinsically undesirable, if not altogether impious! Dr Batalla deals with this problem as it pertains to Latin America. He raises the serious question (1966:89–92) of whether social science, and particularly anthropology, possesses the theoretical equipment to understand the problems of developing countries, and to propose effective solutions to them. Clearly when the new societies of Africa, which are, like those of Latin America, demanding rapid change and 'complete satisfaction of their establish- ed needs, as well as of the new ones which arise from contact with forms of modern urban life' (Batalla 1966:89), are met with the anthropological temper which is for 'slow, gradual, evolutionary types of cultural change', then there is bound to be scepticism among African peoples about the usefulness of anthropology. Batalla points out that a 'basic postulate of the conservative trend of thought in applied anthropology is the almost axiomatic affirmation that the main function of the anthropologist is to avoid rapid changes, because of the resulting maladjustments and conflicts which fre- quently produce social and cultural "disorganization"' (1966:90). The consequence of this is that the universities train African anthropologists to accept a clearly Western perspective on change, and one oriented to what Roger Bastide (1973:56) identifies as be- longing to the capitalist mode of acculturation.

The moral judgement of the Western anthropologist about the evil consequences of change (protestation of cultural relativism notwithstanding) must be measured, in this case, against what the African societies see as the undesirable perpetuation of social systems which are both politically and morally unacceptable: politically, because they frustrate the political will of the societies which wish to develop rapidly; morally, because in the African view, slow development means the perpetuation of low economic productivity, slow sociocultural developments in education and health and the perpetuation of oppressive and unrepresentative rule by traditional authorities, beloved of anthropologists but en- joying little support from their own people.

An equally important point which Batalla makes has to do with the theoretical concepts of anthropology which are misused and transformed by Western anthropologists working in Africa into philosophical dogmas which masquerade as tested anthropological theory. He refers in particular to the concept of 'cultural relativism' which, in its genuine anthropological context, is a valid methodolo-

gical prescription. Dr Batalla quotes Edwin Smith (1934) who declared:

> As men and women we may have our opinions about the justice
> or injustice of certain acts and attitudes, but anthropology as
> such can pronounce no judgement, for to do so is to invade
> the province of philosophy and ethics. If anthropology is to
> judge and guide it must have a conception of what constitutes
> the perfect society; and since it is debarred from having ideals it
> cannot judge, cannot guide, and cannot talk about progress.

Batalla, in his comment (1966:90) on this statement, observes that
'when the meaning of cultural relativism is taken to such extremes,
one enters into a basic contradiction with the very claim of applying
anthropological science to the solution of human problems. That is,
the *raison d'être* of applied anthropology is denied'. He might have
gone on to show that cultural relativism itself, as a concept, is an
anthropological ideal and a value judgement on the part of the
anthropologists. And, he might have drawn our attention to Smith's
fallacy of reification of anthropology, evident in statements like
'anthropology cannot judge or guide', or 'anthropology cannot
talk about progress', which leads to sheer sophistry in his argument.
It is anthropologists, i.e. men and women who think, draw para-
meters for their social science; decree what shall or shall not be done.
And it is men and women in society who are informed by their
cultural prejudices and wear their society's ideological blinkers, who
make decisions about values, about progress, etc. Applied anthropology or any social science for that matter, is only 'a science of means'
(Bastide 1974) and does not or cannot decree ends.

   Margaret Mead (1956:99) refers to the same set of abuses of
anthropological theory when she refers to '. . . the frequent insistence
in anthropological theories that untouched primitive cultures were
not only "whole" but "whole" in a desirable way, so that head-
hunting, sorcery, cannibalism, could be represented as parts of an
optimally functioning system'. She continues: 'these beautifully
functioning primitive cultures have not, of course, been actually
witnessed by anthropologists, who arrive only after considerable
culture contact and cultural disintegration have taken place, and who,
in response to the state of disorganization which they find, conjure
up past functional felicities'. She ends her comments by referring
to the concept of cultural relativism: 'the nostalgic note which

creeps into our voices is undoubtedly partly responsible for the transmutation of the phrase "cultural relativism" from its strictly anthropological use, as "relative to a given culture", to its use by non-anthropologists as a label for an attributed belief that any practice that occurs as part of any culture is therefore ethically defensible, in an absolute rather than a relative sense'. Again, the dilemma for an African anthropologist who is trained by Westerners is obvious, because it is doubtful if any African, or for that matter, any non-Western social scientist can share the views of Westerners in these matters.

Closely associated with the problems of social change and the reluctance of the anthropologists to accept it is the development of the theory that loss of traditional culture means the loss of variety and the imposition of a deadening uniformity on natives. In this connection, it seems to us that the Wilsons, in their classic study *The Analysis of Social Change*, speak most pointedly and, to us, much more accurately to the problem of urbanization and modernization when they say: 'contemporary artists view with horror the "awful uniformity" which faces future generations. We deny that for the ordinary citizen variety diminishes with the increase in scale' (Wilson 1945:86). They proceed to analyse the situation in terms which, we suggest, are characteristic of different parts of Africa:

> for the member of a small-scale society, there is little variety in art. He enjoys only a limited range of manufactures and of songs and dances . . . It is not in a primitive village but in French menus and in the restaurants of the cosmopolitan Soho that variety of food is found. The disappearance of local styles in dress is often given as an example of increasing uniformity but again the appearance of uniformity is an illusion. The civilized woman, with her dance frocks and dinner frocks, street clothes and sports clothes, woollens and silks, cottons and linens, and with the rapid change of fashion, has a variety of clothes that surpasses the wildest dreams of her primitive sister. We do not suggest that local differences will vanish altogether, but rather that the size of differentiated groups increases, while art tends to be articulated more by class and profession and less on local grounds, as societies expand (1945:86–87).

But in the whole field of acculturation studies the biggest problem has been in the general theories and assumptions made about the nature of the process of change. The difficulties have arisen, as we have pointed out above, from the strongly held conservative anthropological view that change should be slow, if at all, disturbing the native cultures as little as possible. The implicit assumption was that the more rapid and complete the change, the more damage was done to the people and their ways of living. Anthropologists then developed all kinds of theoretical subterfuges to frustrate change, such as the postulate that if there is too big a gap between Western civilization and the native culture, it would be necessary for contact to take a long time, measured in many generations, before any transformation could take place at all.

The anthropologists' reluctance to see or accept change was soon to come into sharp conflict with the expressed wishes of the peoples of the non-industrialized and non-literate world who had come to know and to value what science and technology had to offer and were therefore clamouring for change at 'jet-propelled' speed, as Nkrumah phrased it. First, they clamoured for political freedom and political independence which immediately ran against the vested interests of the colonial world and the White power structure in South Africa. To counter these demands, theories of cultural resistance and cultural conservatism were developed; protest movements like the separatist churches and other nativistic cults seemed to confirm the anthropologists and their cultural conservatism, because they saw these movements as anti-White (e.g. Ethiopianism in South Africa) and anti-acculturative. But, as Mead points out (1956:103), these views obscured the fact that those movements were essentially progressive.

The postulates of cultural resistance and cultural conservatism were always viewed with suspicion by Africans in South Africa. The declarations by White anthropologists that 'the Bantu (often "our Bantu", as if they had proprietary rights over them) do not wish to give up their customs and cultures', were made in face of well-documented African enthusiasm for equal educational opportunities; for full and free participation in the economic system of the country which included private ownership of the land; their demand for equal justice and their complete acceptance of Western legal norms; their eager embrace of Christianity; their prolonged agitation for full participation in the democratic political institutions of the country. This readiness of the Africans to revamp their social and cultural institutions and to accept the dominant culture of the West on

the one hand and the postulated resistances on the other, should have
raised some suspicions about the validity of the assumptions behind
the theoretical formulations. But they did not, among some South
African anthropologists. We would have expected that, at least
after the doubts which were expressed by Linton (1943), by Herskovits
(1948) and by the Manus material produced by Mead and Fortune,
a re-evaluation of the ideas and theories might have been called for.
Their work suggested 'the possibility that we have over-rated the
factor of "cultural resistance" in people who have seemed to be unwilling to be assimilated, and under-rated the resistance factors in
the donor cultures' (Mead 1956:103). In South Africa, one does not
need to labour the point of White resistance; for there has been a
clearly stated view which has become public policy (and not just
Afrikaner policy) that Africans were not suited to participate on equal
terms in Western culture. The examples Mead has given (1956:105)
of the ways in which such participation may be denied, all apply to
South Africa. There, too, Africans have been encouraged to wear
traditional dress, have been compelled to travel in segregated and
inferior transport, have been unable to share Communion in church
with Whites, and have been prohibited from buying and selling land
in the reserves that were created supposedly to protect their economic
interests. And there, too, the denial of participation has been accompanied by the enthusiastic preaching of Christianity, by demonstrations of the superiority of Anglo-Saxon or Roman law, and by
induction into the money economy.

Mead further asks (1956:105) if it is not 'the degree of cultural
traumatization' experienced in the past, 'rather than the gap between
a given culture and the culture whose practices the people wish to
learn', which constitutes a most formidable barrier to cultural progress. She expresses the view that the ease with which local cultural
problems can be changed depends on 'our concept of how rapidly
this can take place, and, even more, upon the willingness of the
surrogates of the donor culture: government official, missionary,
trader, technical expert – to treat the members of the changing culture
as full human beings; as men who, having matured in the mastery
of one culture, are capable of mastering another' (Mead 1956:107).

Clearly, such a revolutionary view in the study of change in South
Africa would mean the concentration of attention, not on the
Africans, as hitherto, but on the Whites; and a direct confrontation,
by the anthropologists, with the accepted social ideology and the

role it plays in their theoretical formulations. It would yield, one suspects, totally different facts. It would raise the problem of the training of African anthropologists and their role in the scholarly enterprise and would bring to the fore what we asked earlier in this paper about social science: whether, in the South African situation, it is essentially imperialistic or emancipatory.

## NOTES

[1]In a paper delivered at the African Studies Association meeting, Montreal, Canada, 1970.
[2]We discussed this problem in a limited way in a paper on 'International Social Science Flows: Imperialism or Cultural Emancipation', written in collaboration with Herbert Vilakazi, who discusses the same problem much more extensively in an essay entitled 'Social Science as Ideology' (1973).

## REFERENCES

ANDRESKI, S. 1968. – *The African Predicament*. London: Michael Joseph.
BATALLA, G. B. 1966 – Conservative thought in applied anthropology: a critique. *Human Org.*, **25**, 89–92.
BASTIDE, R. 1974 – *Applied Anthropology*. New York: Harper and Row.
BENEDICT, R. 1934 –*Patterns of Culture*. Boston and New York: Houghton Mifflin.
BIRNBAUM, N. 1971 – *Toward a Critical Sociology*. New York: Oxford Univ. Press.
HERSKOVITS, M. J. 1948 – *Man and His Works*. New York: Alfred Knopf.
JENSEN, A.E. 1963 – *Myth and Cult among Primitive Peoples*. Chicago: Chicago Univ. Press.
KUPER, L. 1965 – *An African Bourgeoisie*. New Haven: Yale Univ. Press.
LINTON, R. 1943 – Nativistic movements. *Am. anthrop.*, **45**, 230–40.
MEAD, M. 1956 – Applied anthropology, 1955, in *Some Uses of Anthropology*. (eds. J. B. Casagrande and T. Gladwin). Washington, D.C.: The Anthropological Soc. of Washington.
NJISANE, M. n.d. – Toward a respecification and re-examination of ethno-racial concepts in anthropology. Unpublished.
SCHAPIRO, L. 1970 – Key concepts : an introductory note, in Plamenatz, J., *Ideology*. London: Pall Mall.
SMITH, E. 1934 – Anthropology and the practical man. *Jl R. anthrop. Inst.*, **64**, xiii–xxxvii.
VILAKAZI, H. W. 1973 – Social science as ideology. *Ninth International Congress of Anthropological and Ethnological Sciences*.
WILSON, G. & M. 1945 – *An Analysis of Social Change*. Cambridge: Cambridge Univ. Press.